THE SOPHISTS

This book offers a new way of looking at the fifth-century BCE Sophists, rejecting the bad reputation they have had since antiquity and presenting them as individuals rather than a "movement," each with his own specialty and personality as revealed through the scant surviving evidence.

It provides an account of the Sophists of this period that explains the historical and social developments that led to their prominence and popularity, demonstrating the reasons for their importance and for their seeming disappearance in the fourth century BCE. Restricted to discussion of the few Sophists for whom there are surviving quotations or other texts, *The Sophists* avoids generalizations often found in other books. It contains accurate translations of most of the surviving material, which forms the secure possible basis for understanding the Sophists as individuals in their various roles, not only as educators but also as ambassadors and pioneers in other fields. After a general introduction, the following chapters present each of the Sophists individually, followed by three chapters that present topics treated by more than one Sophist, such as Logos, Definition and the *Nomos-Phusis* contrast. The final three chapters reveal the way three important intellectuals of the fourth century (Plato, his rival Isocrates and Aristotle) dealt with the Sophists. An appendix contains several longer passages or works in their entirety in translation, allowing readers to have access to the original source materials and develop their own interpretations.

This thorough treatment of the fifth-century Sophists is of interest to scholars working on the subject and on ancient Greek philosophy more broadly, while also being accessible to undergraduate students and the general public interested in the topic.

Richard McKirahan is the Edwin Clarence Norton Professor of Classics and Professor of Philosophy at Pomona College, Claremont, California, United States of America and a Visiting Professor of Philosophy at the University of California, Santa Barbara.

Ancient Philosophies

This series provides fresh and engaging new introductions to the major schools of philosophy of antiquity. Designed for students of philosophy and classics, the books offer a clear and rigorous presentation of core ideas and lay the foundation for a thorough understanding of their subjects. Primary texts are handled in translation and the readers are provided with useful glossaries, chronologies and guides to the primary source material.

Epicureanism
Tim O'Keefe

Cynics
William Desmond

The Peripatetics
Aristotle's Heirs 322 BCE–200 BCE
Han Baltussen

The Philosophy of Early Christianity
Second edition
George Karamanolis

The Sophists
Richard McKirahan

For more information about this series, visit: https://www.routledge.com/Ancient-Philosophies/book-series/AP

THE SOPHISTS

Richard McKirahan

LONDON AND NEW YORK

Designed cover image: *Democritus and Protagoras*, by Salvatore Rosa.
Found in the Collection of State Hermitage, St. Petersburg. © Fine Art
Images/Heritage Images/Alamy Stock Photo

First published 2025
by Routledge
4 Park Square, Milton Park, Abingdon, Oxon OX14 4RN

and by Routledge
605 Third Avenue, New York, NY 10158

Routledge is an imprint of the Taylor & Francis Group, an informa business

© 2025 Richard McKirahan

The right of Richard McKirahan to be identified as the author of this work has been asserted in accordance with sections 77 and 78 of the Copyright, Designs and Patents Act 1988.

All rights reserved. No part of this book may be reprinted or reproduced or utilized in any form or by any electronic, mechanical, or other means, now known or hereafter invented, including photocopying and recording, or in any information storage or retrieval system, without permission in writing from the publishers.

Trademark notice: Product or corporate names may be trademarks or registered trademarks, and are used only for identification and explanation without intent to infringe.

British Library Cataloguing-in-Publication Data
A catalogue record for this book is available from the British Library

Library of Congress Cataloging-in-Publication Data
Names: McKirahan, Richard D., author.
Title: The Sophists / Richard McKirahan.
Description: 1. | Abington, Oxon : Routledge, 2025. | Series: Ancient philosophies | Includes bibliographical references and index.
Identifiers: LCCN 2024015709 (print) | LCCN 2024015710 (ebook) | ISBN 9781138902787 (hardback) | ISBN 9781138902794 (paperback) | ISBN 9781003493259 (ebook)
Subjects: LCSH: Sophists (Greek philosophy)
Classification: LCC B288 .M35 2025 (print) | LCC B288 (ebook) | DDC 183/.1--dc23/eng/20240605
LC record available at https://lccn.loc.gov/2024015709
LC ebook record available at https://lccn.loc.gov/2024015710

ISBN: 978-1-138-90278-7 (hbk)
ISBN: 978-1-138-90279-4 (pbk)
ISBN: 978-1-003-49325-9 (ebk)

DOI: 10.4324/9781003493259

Typeset in Times New Roman
by KnowledgeWorks Global Ltd.

CONTENTS

Preface vii
Acknowledgments xi
Abbreviations xii
Key Greek Terms xiii

1 Introduction 1

2 Protagoras of Abdera 17

3 Gorgias 38

4 Antiphon of Rhamnous 49

5 Hippias of Elis 58

6 Prodicus of Ceos 64

7 Thrasymachus of Chalcedon 74

8 Euthydemus and Dionysodorus of Chalcedon 77

9 *Logos* 86

10 Definition 96

11 Antilogic	105
12 *Nomos* and *phusis*	115
13 Isocrates	129
14 Plato's complicated relationship with the Sophists	135
15 Aristotle and the Sophists	147
Appendix: Texts relating to the Sophists	154

Bibliography	*190*
Index of Sophists and Presocratics and Accompanying Texts	*200*
Index of Names	*202*

PREFACE

More than a decade ago, I received a message from the editor of the *Ancient Philosophies* series inviting me to write this book. I was flattered, particularly since I had done little work on the Sophists at that time, but I was then engaged in other projects and felt that taking on yet another task was not possible. It took some time to decide, but in the end I wrote back, thanked the editor and declined. I did not expect the response I received, a masterpiece of persistence and persuasion. In the end, I agreed, provided that I would be left alone to find my way and there would be no deadlines.

This was a blessing because as I began to think seriously about the topic, I came to see that I needed to take stances on several difficult issues, among them the following:

What is a Sophist?

What is a defensible way to decide who are Sophists?

What chronological limits should be used?

Which Sophists should be discussed?

Some treatments of the Sophists begin by answering the first of these questions and go on to apply the answer to the individual Sophists. The answer will, in most cases, be based on features that are common to all or most of the Sophists discussed. This is useful as an expository tactic, but it begs the question of whether this is the best way to look at Sophists, as if there are some core practices that define you as a Sophist and if you do other things (such as mathematics), that does not strictly speaking count as a sophistic activity. To avoid this problem, I decided to find out who were actually called Sophists and find out what they did.

But first, it was necessary to decide on the question of chronology. It is agreed that Protagoras (born ca. 490) was the earliest Sophist and some of the best-known Sophists (including Gorgias, Prodicus and Hippias) lived into the fourth century. But in that century the word "sophist" became a term of abuse. (Isocrates called himself a philosopher and apparently labeled his cross-town rival and contemporary Plato a Sophist.[1]) It has been stated that "it is impossible to find in the fourth century an unequivocally neutral, let alone a positive, use of *sophistês*,"[2] and there seem to have been few, if any, who self-identified as Sophists after the deaths of the Sophists treated in this book.[3]

The next thing was to see what fifth-century figures were called Sophists by their contemporaries or by later ancient writers and to see who were counted as Sophists in standard modern treatments. The results of this work are given in the Appendix to the Introduction of this book.

What do we know about individual Sophists?

Disappointingly, next to nothing is known about many of these Sophists aside from their names and the fact that someone called them a Sophist. (In some cases even the names are not certain.) In fact, we have substantial amounts of information (by no means all of which is reliable) about only eight, including the brothers Euthydemus and Dionysodorus, who need to be treated together. We are told more about some Sophists than about others, but I found that if we look at them separately, we find that they are all different from one another.

Was there such a thing as the Sophistic movement?

The phrase "Sophistic movement" is often found. It is the title of an important book published in 1980 by George Kerferd, a pioneering scholar of the Sophists. But the study of the Sophists as individuals shows that their common points were few (although very important) and their individual differences were many. It is therefore unsafe, almost certainly incorrect and very misleading to say that any particular view (such as relativism) was a Sophistic view except in the very weak sense that one or more individual Sophists held it. Even in the case of the *nomos-phusis* debate,[4] which is usually and perhaps correctly supposed to be the hallmark of the Sophists, there is surprisingly little evidence linking it to them. We have original text relevant to this topic from only three of our Sophists, although since so little of their writing has been preserved I do not mean to deny that other Sophists wrote on this topic as well. But it is not clear who was (or who were) the first to broach this issue, and it is very clear that it was for quite some time a matter of great interest not only to (some) Sophists but to other writers as well, including playwrights and historians, orators, some Presocratic philosophers, Socrates, Plato and others. It is not surprising that some Sophists are known to have contributed to this discussion, but that does not make it a specifically sophistic topic.

Rather than seeing the Sophists as forming a cooperative movement, I have come to see them as professional rivals in competition with one another for students, money and fame (not necessarily in that order), each having his own special interests in addition to the features that they all shared, namely being teachers providing for the first time in Greece something that could be considered higher education, and, as far as the evidence goes, teaching the art of public speaking.

How are texts such as the *Twin Arguments* and the *Anonymus Iamblichi*, whose authors are unknown, to be treated?

Since we do not know who the authors of these texts were or when they were written or whether they were written by Sophists, they are not discussed in this book.[5]

What is a defensible way to deal with Plato?

This is the most basic question. Plato is by far the richest source of information about the Sophists, but it is clear that some of what he says about the Sophists is not historically accurate. On the other hand, if we exclude everything Plato tells us then there is too little information left to work with. This is a problem that everyone who works with the Sophists must face, and it took me several years to decide on criteria that I find defensible. Roughly speaking, they are the following:

1 Where Plato says that Protagoras was enough older than Hippias and Prodicus to be their father, or that Prodicus had a deep booming voice or where he indicates that Hippias was interested in mathematics, we should accept what he says without question. These are facts that would have been known to his contemporaries, who would have known of these Sophists as well as Plato did and in fact may have actually met them, and they would also have been among the first readers of Plato's writings. So he would have lost credibility and gained nothing by presenting an obviously false picture of the speakers in his dialogues. In some cases corroborating information from other sources than Plato (for example on Hippias' interest in mathematics) which tells us more than what Plato does, increases the likelihood that what Plato says is genuine.
2 The conversations in the dialogues are fictional, but the views, styles and even the personalities of the Sophists that appear in them will very likely have some relation to the views and styles of the Sophists themselves – allowing for some exaggeration and parody.
3 Since the conversations are fictional, even if the views attributed to an individual Sophist are somehow related to the views the Sophist actually held, we should not be confident that the arguments and discussion points are due to the Sophist in question.

4 We must remember that Plato was not a historian of philosophy and that the concept of the history of philosophy, in which we are concerned to discover as best we can what earlier philosophers' ideas were and why they held them, did not exist in Plato's time. Plato was a philosopher and most of his dialogues were written primarily with philosophical and educational (not historical) intent. A well-known case is his treatment of Heraclitus in the *Theaetetus*, where he misquotes a genuine fragment of Heraclitus and on that basis constructs the theory known as Heraclitean Flux. In the Platonic context, this theory challenges our beliefs about the world and Plato refutes it thoroughly – but what he refutes is not what Heraclitus said.[6] The moral of this for present purposes is that we should be cautious about philosophical views and arguments that Plato attributes to the Sophists, as well as to any generalizations he makes about them, and not accept them without good reason. This is a particularly important consideration in understanding Protagorean Relativism.[7]

Notes

1 See below, p. 132.
2 Gagarin, p. 12.
3 The members of the "Second Sophistic" are an exception, but they fall outside the scope of this and other books on the Greek Sophists.
4 See below, Chapter 12.
5 A translation of *Twin Arguments* is included in the Appendix of Translated Texts because it is so interesting an example of "antilogic," but no assertions are made about its authorship or even when it was written.
6 For discussion and references see my *Philosophy Before Socrates*, pp. 137–139.
7 See below, Chapter 2.

ACKNOWLEDGMENTS

One of the greatest pleasures I have had while thinking about the Sophists and writing this book is the excellent company in which I found myself and the generosity I was shown by scholars who know the Sophists better than I do. Some I knew already, some I sought out on purpose, and some I chanced across. I mention in particular (and in alphabetical order) James Allen, Chloe Balla, Rachel Barney, Mauro Bonazzi, Michael Gagarin, Stefania Giombini, Arnaut Macé, Christopher Moore, Edward Schiappa, David Wolfsdorf and Paul Woodruff. I owe special thanks to Chloe and Rachel for inviting me to speak at workshops devoted to the Sophists and to Paul for sharing with me a still-unpublished manuscript on Plato and Protagoras. My greatest debt is to Voula Tsouna, my wife of 35 years, who in this as in all my other endeavors has offered me her sage advice, her loyal support and her continuing love.

I am writing this preface a few weeks after Paul's untimely death and I dedicate this book to his memory. He was an outstanding professor, an outstanding scholar and an outstanding human being, and he will be missed by many.

ABBREVIATIONS

DK   Hermann Diels and Walther Kranz, *Die Fragmente der Vorsokratiker*, 3 vols. 6th edn. 1951.
L-M   Andre Laks and Glenn W. Most, *Early Greek Philosophy*. Vols. 8 and 9. *Sophists*. Loeb Classical Library: Harvard University Press, 2016.
LSJ   Liddell, Scott and Jones, *Greek-English Lexicon* 9th edition. Oxford, Oxford University Press, 1991.

KEY GREEK TERMS

agōn	a contest or debate
aidôs	respect for others, reverence, a sense of honor, moderation, concern about what others think about you
aiskhros	ugly, disgraceful, shameful
akosmia	discredit
alētheia	truth, reality
amphisbētētikos	able to engage in controversies
antidikoi	opponents in lawcourts
antilegein	to contradict, to speak on opposite sides, to speak against, to argue against, to dispute, to refute
antilogikē	antilogic, disputation, expertise in disputing, expertise in speaking against
aretē (pl. *aretai*)	virtue, excellence
dēmēgoria	demagogery
dialegesthai	to converse
dialektikē	dialectic
dikaiosunē	justice
dikē	a sense of fairness towards others
dunamis	power, capacity
eikos	likelihood
einai	to be, to exist
epideixis (pl. *epideixeis*)	performance speech
eris	quarrel, strife, wordy wrangling, disputation

xiv Key Greek Terms

eristikē	eristic
euboulia	excellence in deliberation, sound judgment, wise counsel
eudaimonia	happiness
euphrosunē	enjoyment
eusebeia	reverence
exetastikos	that works by examination
grammē	the mathematical term for "line"
gumnastikē	fitness training
hēdonē	pleasure
historiē	inquiry
hosiotēs	piety
iatrikē	medicine
kalos	beautiful, good, fine, morally good
kanōn	straight-edge
khara	enjoyment
kommōtikē	beauticians' work
kosmos	credit
kuklos	wheel, circle
legein	say, mean
logos (pl. *logoi*)	For the many meanings of this word see the first page of chapter 9
muthos	tale
nomos (pl. *nomoi*) and *phusis*	For the meanings of these words see the first pages of Chapter 12.
opsopoiïkē	gourmet cooking
philosophia	philosophy (literally "love of wisdom")
philosophos (pl. *philosophoi*)	(as a noun) philosopher, sage-wannabe, pretender to wisdom; (as an adjective) pretending to be wise
phusis	nature
polis (pl. *poleis*)	city
politika	statesmanship
politikē tekhnē	(the craft of) citizenship, expertise in being a citizen
politikos	having to do with the city
polymathia	much learning, learning or knowing many things
pragma	matter
psukhē	soul
rhētōr (pl. *rhētores*)	orator, public speaker, teacher of oratory
rhētorikē	rhetoric, oratory, the art of speaking

sophia	wisdom, skill
sophistēs (pl. *sophisteis*)	sophist
sophistikē	sophistry, the skill of sophistry
sophos	wise
sōphrosunē	self-control
tekhnē (pl. *tekhnai*)	expertise, skill, craft, art
terpsis	delight
tribē (pl. *tribai*)	knack, practice, routine based on experience
turannos	monarch, tyrant

1
INTRODUCTION

People do not call themselves sophists. They call other people sophists and it is not a compliment. It is not a general term of abuse but refers specifically to their manner of speaking (or writing), which is called sophistry. Sophistry is a matter of misleading people through flawed and unscrupulous reasoning and deliberately deploying verbal tricks and dishonest arguments ("sophisms") to persuade others and get your way.

The word "sophist" (*sophistēs*, pl. *sophisteis*), however, comes from the Greek word *sophos* ("wise"), which was a term of unreserved praise. Why, then were *sophisteis* – literally, wise people, or specialists in wisdom – regarded as disreputable and untrustworthy? What makes this puzzle even more acute is that originally *sophistēs*, like *sophos*, was a word of praise. This held true up to the first half of the fifth century BCE, and the word continued to be used occasionally afterward in this positive sense,[1] but by the end of the fifth century it was commonly used to designate a new kind of wise men – figures who were judged by many to be dangerous, subversive and a threat to the traditional fabric of society in the Greek city-states. Plato subsequently ruined their reputation forever by comparing the individual Sophists unfavorably with his philosophical hero Socrates and presenting them as his intellectual inferiors, and by drawing a contrast between the sophistry they taught and practiced, and philosophy, which Socrates and Plato himself pursued. Plato's hostility to Sophists (although not to individual Sophists[2]) was adopted by his student Aristotle[3] and the combined influence of these two philosophers[4] and their influential schools, which continued in existence long after their deaths, succeeded in creating the unflattering and negative image of these fifth- and fourth-century individuals that persists today in the negative connotations of "sophist" and related words in many modern languages (including Modern Greek) in which such derivatives are found.

This simple story is only part of the truth. In the first place, it does not account for the fact that the Sophists were popular in their time. They gave public performances attended by large crowds who paid to attend them. They set themselves up as teachers of young men whose families paid fees for their education. To judge by the opening of Plato's dialogue *Protagoras*, the arrival of a famous Sophist in Athens caused a great deal of excitement in ambitious young men who were eager to attend their classes, and it appears that at least some of them received hospitality at the homes of wealthy people who evidently had no fear of what the Sophists represented.[5]

The bad reputation that was attached to Sophists in the fourth century came from two different directions. Most influential in the long run was Plato, who appears to have both invented the word "sophistic" (*sophistikē*, the skill of sophistry) and defined it by unfavorably contrasting it with philosophy (*philosophia*, which for Plato meant literally "love of wisdom"[6]), another word that may have originated with Plato.[7] According to Plato, philosophy is concerned with knowledge – discovering and knowing the truth – while sophistry does not care about truth but instead aims at persuasion – persuading others to believe things that may or may not be true.

Plato's contemporary Isocrates had a different conception of *philosphia*. Like Plato, Isocrates, who taught oratory, claimed to deal with wisdom (*sophia*) and taught his students to aim for wisdom and to love it and so called them *philosophoi* (the singular is *philosophos*). Oratory, as the fifth-century Sophists had taught it, was regarded as an important skill for ambitious young men to acquire because of the practical nature of their teaching, and Isocrates, who actually founded a school in Athens, continued this tradition. Some think that Isocrates' school was more popular than Plato's. It is possible, then, that Isocrates may have initially been more influential than Plato in giving sophists and sophistry a bad name.[8]

This unfavorable reputation prevailed for over two millennia. The earliest writer to defend them was George Grote in the mid-nineteenth century, who "saw them as the champions of intellectual progress and rejected crucial features of the traditional assessment of their work. In particular he argued first of all that they were not a sect or school but a profession, and that there was no community of doctrine." Grote also denied that they taught immorality, as had often been alleged. "Not even Plato brought this as a charge against the principal sophists." Further, even if one or more sophists taught anti-social theories of justice, as many had alleged, "it would be wrong to infer from this anything as to the other sophists."[9]

The tendency to generalize about what "the Sophists" believed is still strong. Guthrie's still-valuable book on the Sophists is a case in point.[10] But a very different picture emerges when we look more closely at the individual Sophists, their cultural and intellectual setting and the varied kinds of information we possess about them from antiquity. Even Plato proves not to be the implacable enemy he is usually represented as being. This book aims to present a more complete and nuanced account of the fifth-century Sophists that emphasizes their differences and presents them not as pseudo-philosophers but as multifaceted individuals, not as members of a united movement but as professional competitors, and (for the most part) not as suspect characters and unscrupulous debaters, but as respected citizens who made important contributions to their society and to Greek intellectual culture.

We begin with *sophia*, the word that means "wisdom" in the Classical period (roughly the fifth and fourth centuries BCE), but in its earliest recorded use[11] it refers to the practical skill of an expert carpenter. In this sense a *sophistēs* was a person whose wisdom was judged important for the community, a person who declared and sustained the community's traditional values and offered sage counsel on important matters. Among those called *sophisteis* were Solon and the other fabled wise men collectively known as the Seven Sages, and also Presocratic philosophers such as Pythagoras and Anaxagoras, diviners and seers, poets, musicians and rhapsodes.[12] However, as far as we know none of these people called himself a *sophistēs*.

The changes in society that took place most notably in Athens in the early fifth century, particularly after the Persian Wars (which ended in 478), for numerous reasons demanded a new kind of wisdom in order to conduct the affairs of a democracy instead of a traditional aristocracy, monarchy[13] or oligarchy (the principal forms of government found in Greek city-states until then). In Athens, the city whose history is best known, a series of reforms broadly extended political power and access to holding public offices. For example, democratic laws required that most political offices be held for only one year and prohibited re-election to the same office in successive years. In addition proposals for new laws and for political decisions were brought to the Assembly (which consisted of all adult male citizens) to be discussed and put to a vote only after the Council of 500 citizens, who were chosen by lot and served for just one year, had decided that they were worth considering. This meant that the success or failure of a proposal would depend not only on who proposed it but also on how well it was presented, first in the Council and afterward in the Assembly, and this in turn depended to some extent on the cases made for and against it in the discussion. The influence of the aristocratic families nevertheless remained considerable.

Membership in the aristocracy traditionally depended largely on the family you were born into and admission of outsiders was not easily achieved. But with the changes in the constitution and Athens' increased wealth and international importance, the balance of power had shifted. Political decisions were now made by bodies of men that were too large to manipulate easily by bribes and favors and the old boys' network. Reasons needed to be given in favor of proposals or against them. The changes in the polity made it possible for any (adult male) citizen to speak, and effective speaking became a valuable asset which was not restricted to the elite. The presence of non-elite citizens who doubtlessly made up the majority in meetings of the Council and Assembly had a further implication. The discourse could no longer be the same as before – privileged people speaking to privileged people. Speech had to be directed to a wider range of citizens, not all of them sharing the same views or equally able to understand what was said. A similar situation occurred in judicial trials too, where juries could be quite large (over 500 in Socrates' trial).

Teaching people to speak effectively in these settings became a new profession. Protagoras, usually held to be the first of these teachers of whom we know anything substantial, called himself a Sophist, claimed to be "a teacher of education and *aretē*,[14] and was the first to think it right to take pay for this,"[15] and in doing so he gave a new meaning to an old word, or rather an application of an old word to a new practice called into being by this change of circumstances, a practice beneficial to society if used for good purposes. The application of rhetorical techniques to political speech and their availability to anyone who could afford the fees that Sophists charged challenged the traditional power structure – which became an important and lasting source of opposition to the Sophists since in effect Protagoras was promising a new way of teaching success in these fields and one that constituted a threat to the aristocracy.

Some people are just naturally better than others at public speaking and a few, like Pericles and Themistocles, were superb, but inexplicably so, and their success appeared to be a fluke or a gift from the gods rather than something learned, since in certain notable cases they were unable to teach it to their own children, even though, it was supposed, this would be the skill that a successful public speaker would want his sons to master. The mediocrity of the two sons of Pericles was taken to be evidence of this. However, as became apparent, speaking effectively is an expertise (*tekhnē*) that can be taught. The first such teachers mentioned are Corax and his pupil Tisias (460s BCE), citizens of Syracuse in Sicily. Little is known of them – so little that it is not even certain that they were two different people, or what exactly they did. The general opinion, for which there is but little evidence, is that they helped prepare people to represent themselves in court trials.

Education in Greek cities had previously been minimal: hearing and learning by heart a great deal of poetry (Homer's *Iliad* and *Odyssey* in particular), learning to play a musical instrument, perhaps learning to read and write and do some elementary arithmetic as well as exercise and athletics. This education stopped at about 14 years old. During this time the children were preparing for their future life: the boys by watching and helping their father at his craft and the girls by participating in household activities with their mother. Afterward there was nothing that could be called higher education. During adolescence the young men of aristocratic families would learn from their father and his acquaintances how to manage their households and play a role in their cities. Part of this training took place in symposia (literally "drinking parties") – the equivalent of men's clubs where they were brought by their fathers and were introduced to others of their own age and, importantly for their future, they were introduced to the ways of society by older men of high social standing who had "learned from those who had been gentlemen before them."[16] Under an aristocracy, these practices reinforced and virtually guaranteed the perpetuation of the status quo. But the eventual result of the democratic reforms in Athens was a decline in the power of the traditional elite and a corresponding increase in the power of (some of) the formerly powerless.

Literacy is another relevant factor. The Greek alphabet was invented in the eighth century, but the great bulk of the population remained illiterate. Not coincidentally, poetry was far more prevalent than prose as a medium of writing until the mid-fifth century. Some sixth-century figures, such as the Presocratic philosophers Anaximander and Heraclitus, wrote down their ideas and some fragments of their writings have been preserved. Written texts have advantages over orally transmitted compositions because they do not depend on memorization. Oral transmission is uncertain and fragile. Uncertain because memory is uncertain. Tell a joke to several friends and ask each of them separately a week later to repeat it and their versions (if they remember it at all) will probably not be word-for-word identical. And fragile because it could be that at some point everyone has forgotten – a fate that was almost inevitable.

In Greece Homer's *Iliad* and *Odyssey* were the earliest material[17] to be transmitted orally. These epic poems were easy to remember because of the rhythm and verse forms, the formulaic expressions, the relatively simple syntax and the fact that the stories they contained were so well known and so often told. This is not to say that everyone knew them by heart, but any mistakes made in a quotation or a performance would have been noticed immediately. Learning a poem is a matter of familiarization, which leads to memorization and does not usually go further. We know the poem when we can recite it, even if we do not know what it means or how to go about interpreting it.[18]

By contrast prose is harder to remember and so invites us to revisit the written text, a practice that encourages study, reflection and analysis. Written works can exist for centuries without anyone's knowing them. (Think of newly discovered papyri that have been buried in the Egyptian sand since antiquity, or manuscripts and very old books in very old libraries that no one has looked at for centuries.) This may have been what Thucydides had in mind when, writing at the end of the fifth or beginning of the fourth century he called his *History of the Peloponnesian War* a "possession for always." Almost nothing in prose has survived that was composed prior to the fifth century. It may not be a coincidence that the first prose works of which we know are philosophical,[19] historical and oratorical. As we shall see, Sophists too dealt in prose.

Protagoras introduced several practices that aroused suspicion and became hallmarks of a Sophist: traveling from city to city for his work, promoting himself through public performances, charging fees for his teaching, claiming to teach *aretē* (a word that can be translated either "virtue" or "excellence") and calling himself a Sophist. Not all of these practices were new. Xenophanes, a poet who is regarded as a Presocratic philosopher, claims to have traveled from city to city, presumably giving recitals of his poetry and probably of Homer and other poets as well, from the age of 25 and to still have been doing so 67 years later.[20] As an exile he must have been dependent on people's hospitality and generosity to have lived this life, apparently without abuse, for so long. Whether his performances were public or private and whether people paid to hear him is not recorded. The idea that someone would ask to be paid for teaching may not sound strange to us, but it was held against the Sophists. Why? It may have been sheer elitism[21] – Plato and other aristocrats, such as Anytus[22] sneering at the idea that people would demand payment for something that a good person would naturally give freely. Finally, the claim to teach *aretē* must have raised hackles. In that the word means virtue in the sense in which honesty, courage and the like are virtues, surely these would be inculcated in young people from a young age, beginning at home. In that it means excellence more generally, in effect the claim amounted to the promise to make students outstanding human beings (without specifying what qualities make someone outstanding) – a vague claim that could easily be thought to undermine whatever values the students had been brought up in and to aim to replace those values with whatever values the Sophist in question might prefer. Protagoras, when pushed by Socrates to explain what he means by his impressive boast that each day his students will get better,[23] says that he teaches "sound deliberation, both in domestic matters (how to manage one's household) and in public affairs (how to realize one's maximum potential for success in political debate and action").[24] In other words, he promised to teach his students how to persuade, since he believed persuasiveness to be the key to success in life, and therefore to the best life, which only the best people can live.

The Sophists

Two questions must be faced at the beginning: (1) what makes a person a Sophist and (2) of all the people called Sophists by contemporary or near-contemporary authors, which ones to discuss? It is necessary to give answers to these questions in order to determine the scope of this book. If it is to include everyone we know who lived in or about the time of the known Sophists (mid-fifth century to early fourth century BCE) who is known to have discussed or written on topics treated by known Sophists, we will include in addition to the Sophists themselves, the tragedians Sophocles and Euripides, the writers of comedy including Aristophanes, the historians Herodotus and Thucydides, the rhetorician Isocrates and most of the ten "Attic orators" – far too much to include in a book of this scope. But how can we choose from among the candidates without being arbitrary? Without an answer to this second question any answer, we give to the first will inevitably be equally arbitrary because it will be based on our arbitrary answer to the second.

Authors of books on the Sophists have taken a variety of approaches to this problem and have arrived at different solutions. Some figures are always or almost always identified as Sophists: Protagoras, Gorgias, Hippias, Prodicus, Antiphon, Thrasymachus, Critias, the brothers Euthydemus and Dionysodorus and the Anonymus Iamblichi are the ones most commonly listed, but many others are called Sophists in ancient texts. The number of Sophists discussed in these books varies from fewer than 10 to about 30. This book treats eight of the Sophists named above, a selection that is explained in the Appendix to this chapter, where reasons are given for omitting the other figures identified as Sophists. The eight are:

Protagoras of Abdera (a city on the north shore of the Aegean Sea)
Gorgias of Leontini (a city in Sicily)
Antiphon of Rhamnous (a city in Attica)
Hippias of Elis (a district in the Peloponnese)
Prodicus of Ceos (an island near Attica in the Aegean)
Thrasymachus of Chalcedon (a city on the Bosporus)
Euthydemus and Dionysodorus of Chios (an Aegean Island)

Chapters 2–8 will treat these Sophists individually. Rightly so, I will argue, because they were distinct individuals,[25] with different (but overlapping) interests and specialties. They were all teachers but they did not have a common teaching method and they were professional rivals, which encouraged individuality. Chapters 9 through 12 are devoted to particular topics of philosophical interest that were discussed by more than one Sophist. The final section consists of chapters on Isocrates, Plato and Aristotle, all figures of the fourth century, who illustrate different ways of viewing the Sophists and in particular the relation between sophistry and philosophy. The intention of this organization is to present a picture of the Sophists that is historically plausible, and one that turns out to be significantly different from what is found in previous treatments of the subject.

Philosophy, rhetoric and sophistic

The fifth-century Sophists figure prominently in histories of philosophy and histories of rhetoric. Reasonably so, for they taught people how to speak effectively and many if not all of them engaged in discussion of topics widely considered to be philosophical in nature. This section should properly be called *philosophia*, *rhētorikē* and *sophistikē* but I begin with the English derivatives of these Greek words in order to illustrate what is at stake.

What do we take philosophy to be? A short answer might be "what they teach in Philosophy departments" – in other words, a branch of learning. This leaves open the question "What do they teach in Philosophy departments?" and there is no simple answer, since the people known as philosophers do not agree. Some hold that philosophy is necessarily characterized by arguments that establish the truth of its claims, while others do not, and consider wise sayings asserted without justification to be philosophical. Where there are different traditions and schools of philosophy (as there have been since its beginnings) the members of one tradition may not recognize the questions answers, theories, world views and reasoning (if any) of the followers of another tradition as being at all philosophical. And if someone declares "My philosophy is to leave well enough alone," is it or is it not philosophy? People who engage in the study of the history of philosophy, then, are employing (perhaps without sufficient forethought) some notion or another of what counts as philosophy to guide their choice of which thinkers and texts to include. This point has been forcefully made in a recently published book.[26]

The same holds for rhetoric, albeit to a lesser degree. One definition of rhetoric is "the art of persuasion," and I believe that the word is most commonly employed to mean this or something like this. However, this is not the focus of Rhetoric departments in universities, which focus on questions of interpretation and criticism. For example, the Department of Rhetoric of the University of California at Berkeley defines itself in terms of "the study of rhetorical traditions from the classical to the contemporary eras. Linked by a common interest in the functions of discourse in all its forms, faculty and students engage the theoretical, historical and cultural dimensions of interpretation and criticism, in fields as diverse as political theory, gender, law, media studies, philosophy, arts, and literature."[27] So at Berkeley and in many other universities rhetoric is the study (not the practice) of discourse, focusing on interpretation and criticism.[28]

What, then, did the corresponding Greek words mean in the period during which the Sophists were active (the latter half of the fifth century)? The surprising answer is that they meant nothing at all, simply because they did not exist. The nouns *rhētōr* (orator) and *sophistēs* (originally "wise person," and only later "sophist") existed as did *philosophos* (but as far as we know it was then used only as an adjective, not as a noun). In fact *philosophia*, *rhētorikē* and *sophistikē* do not occur in extant texts until the fourth century. All three words are found, perhaps for the first time, in Plato's dialogue *Gorgias*, which is thought to have been composed in the 380s, by which time the known Sophists were dead or very old.

There is general agreement that Plato actually coined the last two of these words, perhaps in that very dialogue, and it is likely that the same holds for *philosophia*.[29] He did so for a purpose – in order to talk about the nature of the profession of the Sophists and to contrast it with the nature of the profession of philosophers, preeminently Socrates and himself. By categorizing philosophers, orators and sophists in this way he was for the first time in a position to explain what he and Socrates were trying to achieve in their work and to show how different their goals were from the ambitions of the Sophists.[30] Significantly, in the dialogue named after him, Gorgias declares not that he is a Sophist, but a *rhētōr*, a word that was current in his lifetime. As the dialogue goes on, Socrates draws a distinction between *sophistikē* and *rhētorikē*, but he twice declares that they are practically the same.[31]

One consequence of this is that the word *sophistikē* was born with a stain upon it, even though its cognate *sophistēs* had originally had positive overtones and even though Protagoras may actually have called himself a *sophistēs* and did so surely not with the intention of advertising that he taught sophistry (as we now use this term).

The reverse may have occurred in the case of *philosophos* and *philosophia*. On the traditional account, Heraclitus' assertion

> Men who are *philosophoi* must be inquirers into many things indeed.
> (Heraclitus B35 DK)

encourages people to practice inquiry like the Ionian philosophers, to cast their net wide and form their understanding from a broad acquaintance with varied phenomena. This interpretation has recently been challenged with another. It is indisputable that in other fragments Heraclitus condemns much learning and repeatedly holds up Pythagoras as a prime instance of a person who took this wrong approach.

> *Polymathia* does not teach insight. Otherwise it would have taught Hesiod and Pythagoras and also Xenophanes and Hecataeus,
> (Heraclitus B40 DK)

> Pythagoras the son of Mnesarchus practices inquiry (*historiē*) more than all other men, and making a selection of these writings constructed his own wisdom — *polumathia* [literally "learning or knowing many things"], evil trickery.
> (Heraclitus B129DK)

By contrast, in several surviving fragments Heraclitus asserts that *merely* seeing and hearing many things is not enough to make a person wise.[32] Instead he prefers gaining insight (obtaining a deep understanding of things, which is not simply a matter of collecting facts, but finding the ultimate explanation of them, which Heraclitus calls the *logos*) to *polumathia*.

On Moore's recent well-argued account,[33] the earliest surviving occurrences of *philosophos* mock the Pythagoreans and perhaps Pythagoras himself for taking an entirely mistaken path toward wisdom. Since Heraclitus disparages polymathy (*polumathia*) and shows his low opinion of Pythagoras in other fragments,[34] Moore concludes that in calling these people *philosophoi* he did not mean to compliment them, and suggests "sage-wannabees" as an appropriately nuanced translation.[35]

Heraclitus probably wrote this in the first decades of the fifth century. The word *philosophos* recurs in Gorgias' *Encomium of Helen*.[36] Its next appearance in surviving texts occurs a century after Heraclitus – once again in Plato,[37] who gave it the positive sense it has retained ever since. It is also worth mentioning that in Heraclitus and Gorgias, the word is an adjective describing the nouns "men" and "arguments," respectively;[38] again, the earliest use of it as a self-standing noun is found in Plato, where the correct translation is "philosopher" in the literal sense of "lover of wisdom" (*philo-* + *sophia*). Further, just as with *sophistikē* and *rhētorikē* the first known occurrences of the word *philosophia* are found in Plato's *Gorgias*.[39]

Appendix

I begin by giving a catalogue of people who were identified and labeled Sophists by their contemporaries and near-contemporaries, and for good measure looking at some others who are considered Sophists in some twentieth and twenty-first-century books. Next I will eliminate from consideration figures for which too little information survives to help us, and others for whom there are good reasons for thinking that they were not Sophists. This will leave a small and manageable number of Sophists who will be considered individually in the following chapters. The picture that emerges is that they had less in common than is usually believed and consequently that it is mistaken to suppose that there is a litmus test for deciding who was a Sophist and who was not.

Die Fragmente der Vorsokratiker,[40] compiled by Hermann Diels and Walther Kranz and still a point of reference for work on early Greek philosophers including the Sophists, has eight entries under the heading "Early Sophistic."

> Protagoras of Abdera
> Gorgias of Leontini
> Lycophron
> Prodicus of Ceos
> Thrasymachus of Chalcedon
> Hippias of Elis
> Antiphon of Rhamnous
> Critias of Athens
> plus two texts whose authors are unknown
> the Anonymus Iamblichi,[41]
> and the *Twin Arguments*.[42]

Dillon and Gergel in their extensive collection (in English translation) of Sophist-related material[43] give material on nine Sophists plus the two additional texts, largely following DK, omitting Lycophron and adding Alcidamas of Elaea and the brothers Euthydemus and Dionysodorus of Chios.

> Protagoras
> Gorgias
> Prodicus
> Hippias
> Antiphon
> Thrasymachus
> Critias
> Euthydemus and Dionysodorus
> Alcidamas
> the Anonymus Iamblichi
> "Double Arguments"[44]

Laks and Most in their two Loeb Classical Library volumes devoted to the Sophists[45] treat eight people and two texts:

Protagoras
Gorgias
Socrates[46]
Prodicus
Thrasymachus
Hippias
Antiphon
Xeniades of Corinth
the Anonymus Iamblichi
and the *Twin Arguments*

Plato sometimes gives the impression that there was a large number of Sophists – enough to be a serious threat to society, but in fact he names only eight of them without identifying them as Sophists:

Protagoras
Gorgias[47]
Hippias
Prodicus
Euthydemus
Dionysodorus
Evenus of Paros
Miccus

Aristotle mentions

Protagoras
Gorgias
Antiphon
Hippias
Prodicus
Euthydemus
Thrasymachus
Polus of Akragas

In fact he calls only four individuals Sophists

Lycophron
Bryson of Heracleia Pontica
Aristippus of Cyrene
Polyidus

Some modern works on the Sophists include treatments of

Callicles
pseudo-Demosthenes

12 Introduction

Xeniades of Corinth
Isocrates of Athens
Eudoxus of Cnidus
Theodorus of Byzantium
Aristippus of Cyrene
Polus
Licymnius of Chios

So far we have 27 candidates for consideration:[48]

Alcidamas of Elaea
Antiphon of Athens
Antisthenes of Athens
Aristippus of Cyrene
Bryson of Heraclea Pontica
Callicles
Critias of Athens
Dionysodorus of Chios
Eudoxus of Cnidus
Euthydemus of Chios
Evenus of Paros
Gorgias of Leontini
Hippias of Elis
Isocrates of Athens
Licymnius of Chios
Lycophron
Miccus
Polus of Akragas
Polyidus
Prodicus of Ceos
Protagoras of Abdera
pseudo-Demosthenes
Theodorus of Byzantium
Thrasymachus of Chalcedon
Xeniades of Corinth
Anonymus Iamblichi
the author of the *Twin Arguments*
Pseudo-Demosthenes

The Anonymus Iamblichi and the unknown author of the *Twin Arguments* must be omitted because we have no knowledge of who these people were – when they lived, where they were from or whether they engaged in activities (such as teaching) that were regarded as typical of Sophists. In the total absence of information about their authors, the extant texts, even though they contain material related to views expressed by some Sophists, give no help toward determining what a Sophist is.

Theodorus of Byzantium and Licymnius are reported to have written books on rhetoric but too little is known about them to form any impression of their activities. Tisias and Corax[49] are said to have written the first books on their subject, but they are not standardly called Sophists in the ancient sources. (Their books no longer survive.) And in any case being the author of books on the subject of rhetoric does not entail that you are a Sophist: Plato and Aristotle, who were certainly not Sophists, wrote on rhetoric – Plato in the *Gorgias* and *Phaedrus* and Aristotle in the *Rhetoric* – as did many others who are not regarded as Sophists.

Aristippus, the founder of the Cyrenaic school of philosophy, is normally considered a philosopher, not a Sophist. He was a student of Socrates and unlike Socrates charged money for teaching, but aside from that there is no information about his "sophistic" activities.

Bryson is known as a mathematician; we know nothing about his being a Sophist aside from the fact that Aristotle called him one. Eudoxus was another mathematician, and he is referred to as a Sophist on the insufficient evidence of his eloquence and prose style.

Critias was a wealthy Athenian who associated with Sophists and other intellectuals. He has been regarded as the author of a satyr play, the *Sisyphus*, from which a fragment has survived that gives an account of the origin of religious belief, and principally for this inadequate reason some have considered him to be a Sophist, or have declared that he "shared the intellectual outlook" of the Sophists and on these clearly inadequate grounds have included him in treatments of the Sophists. Nowadays most scholars think that the play was written not by him but by Euripides.

Antisthenes was a pupil of Gorgias and afterward of Socrates. He is standardly viewed as a "Socratic" – that is, as one of Socrates' associates who developed Socrates' ideas in various distinctive ways. Like Protagoras he held that virtue can be taught, but it is not known that he claimed to teach it. No ancient source refers to him as a Sophist.

Isocrates and Alcidamas were students of Gorgias who set up rival schools of rhetoric in Athens in the fourth century. Isocrates did not consider himself a Sophist, as indicated by the fact that he wrote a work with the title *Against the Sophists*. He associated himself, rather, with philosophy.[50] Later authors regarded him and Alcidamas as rhetoricians rather than Sophists.

Polus is presented as Gorgias's eager but not very bright student in Plato's *Gorgias*. He was also a student of Licymnius. He became a Sophist, attracted students and wrote a book on rhetoric. Little else is known of him.

Callicles, who is present in Plato's *Gorgias* but nowhere else, may well be a literary creation of Plato's. In any case, even though in the *Gorgias* he represents an extreme position in the conversation about the relative merits of *nomos* and *phusis*, he is not presented as a Sophist; in fact he calls Sophists "entirely worthless" (Plato, *Gorgias* 520a).

Finally, other candidates must be eliminated from our discussion for want of further information: Lycophron (another student of Gorgias), Evenus, Miccus, Polyidus and Xeniades.

There remain only the following eight.

Protagoras of Abdera
Gorgias of Leontini
Antiphon of Rhamnous
Hippias of Elis
Prodicus of Ceos
Thrasymachus of Chalcedon
Euthydemus and Dionysodorus of Chios

These are the only fifth-century Sophists about whom there survives sufficient information to form an idea of their interests and contributions. The following chapters will show that they present not a uniform picture but a wide variety of interests and views.

Notes

1 Compare the positive connotations of the English word "sophisticated," whose original meaning was "altered," "not genuine."
2 See below, Chapter 14.
3 See below, Chapter 15.
4 Xenophon, a less well-known follower of Socrates, expresses his opinion of Sophists as follows: "Sophists speak in order to deceive, they write for their own profit and they do no good to anybody. None of them is or has become wise, but each of them is content to be called a Sophist, which right-thinking people regard as a slander." (*On Hunting* 13.8)
5 Plato, *Protagoras* 310b–316b. Part of this is translated below in the Appendix of Translated Texts, pp. 154–6.
6 This is how it was taken by Plato, but the history of the adjective *philosophos*, which was in use long before Plato, suggests that this was a novel twist on its original meaning. See below, pp. 138–9.
7 The earliest occurrences of *philosophia* and *philosophos* (as a noun rather than an adjective) are found in Plato and Isocrates, and since the dates at which their works were written are not known it is not sure which of them used the words first. I follow the majority of scholars in attributing them to Plato. See below, pp. 231–2 for further discussion.
8 Isocrates is the subject of Chapter 13 below.
9 Quotations are taken from the chapter "Towards a History of Interpretations" in Kerferd 1980, p. 3. Kerferd provides an excellent overview of the varying fortunes of the Sophists prior to his own book, which seeks to establish them as making serious contributions to philosophy.
10 Guthrie (1991) devotes his 28-page Chapter 3 to the question "What is a Sophist?" and does not discuss the individual sophists until the last chapter in the book, where he discusses six of the eight sophists treated in this book in just 38 pages. The intervening chapters are devoted to topics which Guthrie treats by presenting and discussing the

Introduction **15**

views of (some) Sophists together with relevant passages from other fifth- and fourth-century authors. (This practice is especially evident in "Nomos-Phusis" which is far the longest chapter in the book.)
11 Homer, *Iliad* 15.412.
12 Kerferd 1950, p. 8.
13 The Greek word *turannos* is the source of our word "tyrant" but applied equally to good monarchs as well as evil ones.
14 For the meanings of this term see below, p. 5.
15 Plato, *Protagoras* 349e.
16 Plato, *Meno* 92e.
17 More precisely, the earliest surviving material.
18 Much of what is said in this paragraph does not apply to the rhapsodes, who in effect re-composed poetry as they performed it. See A. Lord, *The Singer of Tales,* 1960, rep. 1978, chapter 2. Cambridge MA: Harvard University Press.
19 I use this term broadly. For the difficulties associated with this word see below, pp. 228–31.
20 Xenophanes, fragment 8 DK.
21 This is the view of Gagarin 2002, p. 10.
22 Anytus, one of the men who brought the charges against Socrates that led to his trial and execution, was a member of family that had possessed great wealth for generations. He is the one who expresses the traditional aristocratic opinion about how to become a success in Plato's *Meno* (quoted above, p. 4).
23 Plato, *Protagoras* 318a-b.
24 Plato, *Protagoras* 319a.
25 With the exception of the brothers Euthydemus and Dionysodorus, who worked together.
26 Moore 2019.
27 Quotation taken from the department's website.
28 Since the word "sophistic" is not commonly used in English I have said nothing about it in this paragraph.
29 The word occurs in an essay of Isocrates that was written probably around the same time as the *Gorgias*. See below, p. 130.
30 This matter is treated more fully in Chapter 14.
31 Plato, *Gorgias* 465a, 520c.
32 Heraclitus B19, B34, B107 DK.
33 Moore (2019) chapters 1–2, following the lead of Lloyd (2009).
34 Heraclitus B40, B129 (cf. B81).
35 Another possibility is "pretenders to wisdom."
36 This work is included in the Appendix of Translated Texts, pp. 171–4. I believe that here too it has the same negative overtone that it does in Heraclitus. Unfortunately, the date and even the century when Gorgias is likely to have written the *Encomium* is unknown; he is said to have lived over a hundred years, which would put his death well into the fourth century. *Philosophos* (translated "pretending to be wise") is found in section 13.
37 The word is also found in the writings of Isocrates, a contemporary and rival of Plato; most scholars believe that Plato invented the word. Isocrates' quite different conception of *philosophia* is discussed below, pp. 132–3.
38 A more literal but less attractive translation of B35 would begin "*Philosophoi* men."
39 For further discussion see below pp. 13.6–7.
40 5th edn. 1935. This work is referred to as "DK."
41 The work is referred to (in Latin) as "anonymous" because the identity of its author is unknown. The text is preserved in a work of Iamblichus, who lived in the second century CE.
42 *Dissoi Logoi*, frequently translated "Twofold Arguments."
43 Dillon, J. and T. Gergel, *The Greek Sophists*, 2003. (This work is referred to as DG.)
44 Another translation of *Dissoi Logoi*.
45 These volumes are referred to as L-M.

46 The appearance of Socrates in this catalogue may come as a surprise in view of the strict distinction that Plato drew between Socrates and the Sophists, but Laks and Most give reasons for their choice to include him in their sourcebook. (L-M vol. 8, 4–5). While I agree that Socrates is like Sophists in important ways, I have not followed the example of L-M in including him on the grounds that it would skew the discussion and distract attention from the people who are normally considered Sophists and who are the focus of this book.
47 In Plato's *Gorgias* (455c3) Gorgias calls himself a *rhētōr* (orator and teacher of oratory) not a Sophist, but in the *Greater Hippias* he is referred to as "the well-known Sophist" and he is clearly considered a Sophist at *Meno* 95b-c.
48 The chapter "Minor Sophists" in O'Grady (ed.) *The Sophists. An Introduction* (2008) identifies dozens more about whom too little is known, many of whom lived after the fifth century and many of whom are not called Sophists.
49 Some scholars believe that Corax ("crow") was not a separate person, but a somewhat insulting nickname for Tisias.
50 See below, p. 130, below, 13.3.

2
PROTAGORAS OF ABDERA

Protagoras, the earliest Sophist of whom we have substantial information, was famed as a teacher and a public speaker. He also engaged in literary criticism and the study of language. His reputation was such that he was invited by the great Athenian statesman Pericles to write a constitution for the newly founded city of Thurii, a joint venture of numerous Greek cities, in southern Italy. He claimed to teach his students virtue (*aretē*, otherwise translated "excellence") and became notorious for his alleged doubts about the gods and for his claim to teach his students to make a weaker argument[1] stronger. He is best known for his statement "a human being is the measure of all things," which was associated with the philosophical thesis known as Protagorean relativism, a doctrine that is still a matter of keen philosophical interest.

Protagoras was born ca. 490 BCE in Abdera, a city in northern Greece which a generation later would be the birthplace of Democritus, the most important proponent of the original atomic theory. As is the case for most of the Sophists we know few details of his life and much of what we are told is dubious or almost certainly false, in particular the spectacular story, preserved and elaborated in several ancient sources, that his books were rounded up and burned in public, that he was charged with atheism and that in order to avoid the trial he fled Athens and died when the ship carrying him sank.[2] This story, various versions of which are found in sources written over a century after his death, is belied by Plato's assertion that he practiced his profession as a Sophist for forty years with great success, and always enjoyed an excellent reputation until he died at about the age of 70.[3]

Plato, our earliest major source for Protagoras and other Sophists, presents a cameo picture of him as well as of Prodicus and Hippias in a memorable scene in his dialogue *Protagoras*[4] where he offers a unique picture of the personalities and special interests of the three rival Sophists which (although perhaps involving some exaggeration and parody) I believe is generally reliable – not only because Plato lived close in time to the Sophists, but because there is every reason to suppose that, unlike later sources, Plato (born in 427) actually had seen Prodicus and Hippias on occasions when they came to Athens. It is less certain that he encountered Protagoras too, since would have still been a boy when Protagoras died. But in any case, he will have had no difficulty obtaining information about him. Further since not only he but also his contemporaries, who were the readers for whom this dialogue and his other writings were intended in the first instance, would have had access to the same information, it would have made no sense for him to grossly misdescribe Protagoras or the other well-known Sophists that appear in his works.

In the dialogue named after him, most of which is devoted to a fictional conversation between Socrates and Protagoras, the latter is presented as a senior statesman, old enough to be Prodicus' and Hippias's father. All three are guests in the home of Callias, the wealthiest man in Athens, and each has his coterie of followers, Athenians and foreigners (non-Athenian Greeks), one of whom intends to become a professional Sophist himself. Many of the Athenians come from leading families of the city. Asked what a student will get from studying with him, Protagoras begins by saying that he makes people better:

> The very day you start you will go home a better man, and the same thing will happen the day after. Every day, day after day, you will get better and better.

When Socrates points out that this answer does not make it clear what his students actually learn, Protagoras declares that he teaches *euboulia*, which can be translated as "excellence in deliberation," "sound judgment," and "wise counsel."[5] Success depends on these traits, or rather the single trait *euboulia*, which includes the ability to deliberate well about public and private affairs, to form sound judgments on the basis of this deliberation, and to plan well and offer good advice on the basis of those judgments. This is what Protagoras claimed to teach. We don't know how he taught this art but some of his statements are suggestive.

> Learning must begin at an early age.
> (Protagoras, Fragment 3 DK)

> Teaching requires nature (*phusis*) and attention.
> (Protagoras, Fragment 3 DK)

> Expertise (*tekhnē*) without practice and practice without expertise are nothing.
> (Protagoras, Fragment 10 DK)

> Education is not implanted in the soul unless one reaches a greater depth.
> (Protagoras, Fragment 11 DK)

These assertions give us good reason to suppose that Protagoras' instruction involved three things. First ("nature"): he selected his students for their suitability to become successful.[6] Second, his instruction required his students to be attentive, and involved not mere memorization but practice in the techniques he taught them. Third, it involved *tekhnē*, which suggests that his teaching may have included a range of activities both practical and intellectual, including studying purpose-written speeches (which was reputed to be the practice of Antiphon),[7] and mastering different turns of speech and argumentative strategies. "Reaching a greater depth" may indicate that Protagoras recognized that rote memorization was not enough to guarantee success, nor was spontaneity. The *tekhnē* he taught had methods that could be studied, learned, assimilated and understood so that they could be applied when appropriate.[8]

Socrates takes him to be "talking about the craft of citizenship (*politikē tekhnē*) and to be promising to make men good citizens,"[9] and Protagoras agrees. Socrates takes this to be a promise to teach virtue (*aretē*) – something that Socrates doubts can be taught. His doubts are due to the fact that in the past men famous for their political success had sons who lacked this virtue even though they had received the finest education then available. And so he asks Protagoras to explain how *aretē* can be taught. Protagoras accepts this rephrasing of his promise in terms of *aretē*, later using the word himself. Since the *Protagoras* and many other Platonic dialogues focus on *aretē* or individual *aretai*, the word needs some discussion.

Aretē originally meant "excellence" in general and it never entirely lost this meaning, but when applied to humans it eventually came to mean something like "virtue" more or less in the sense that we use the word. It is easy to specify the excellence of a chair – what makes a chair an excellent chair: it is comfortable, it is well made out of appropriate materials, etc. It is also easy to roughly identify the excellence of a carpenter – it is whatever makes the carpenter an excellent carpenter: the ability to do well what a carpenter does – making furniture, etc. But when it comes to specifying the excellence of a human being, it is not so simple. What are the relevant considerations? Wealth? Beauty? Health? Intelligence? Physical strength? Courage? Kindness? What others think of you? What you think of yourself? Or, loyalty, endurance, self-control, cleverness, and *aidôs* (a word with meanings that range from respect for others to reverence, a sense of honor, and moderation) to mention some features considered *aretai* in earlier Greek literature, All of these? Or none?

This issue is at the heart of the earliest work of Greek literature, Homer's *Iliad*, composed centuries before the time of the Sophists, Plato and Aristotle were born. The basic question raised in the *Iliad* is who is "the best of the Acheans"? The two candidates for this title are Achilles and Agamemnon. Each claims to be the best, for different reasons. Achilles led one contingent of troops while Agamemnon's contingent was the largest and he was the commander of the entire army and was also the powerful king of Mycenae, while Achilles was a prince (not yet king) of a less important region. Achilles and Agamemnon both had divine ancestry, but Achilles, whose mother was the daughter of Zeus, had better divine connections than Agamemnon with the divine powers that controlled the fates of humans.

Agamemnon was older than Achilles but not as strong. He was also a poor tactician and leader. Both were hot-headed and marked by pride, such great pride in fact that if slighted they would go to extraordinary and even self-destructive lengths. Neither possessed or showed any thought of mercy. Turning the other cheek was unthinkable to both as was taking advice from anyone of a lower station. Both lacked wisdom although they valued it, particularly when advice came from an older and more experienced person, such as the aged Nestor, once a great warrior but still valued as a counselor even though he was no longer able to fight in the front ranks.

These values were perhaps appropriate for conditions in the legendary world of the Trojan War, where each region was a warrior society governed by a hereditary king who claimed to be a descendant of the gods, where peace was the exception and strife the normal condition, even if it was simply a matter of stealing livestock from the subjects of neighboring chiefs, and where success meant everything because loss meant total extirpation, as happened to Troy. Power was uncertain and needed to be guarded at all costs.

But even in Homeric times there was more to life than war, and appropriately different virtues. In Homer's *Odyssey*, which tells of Odysseus' journey from Troy back to his native island of Ithaca, the qualities that make his return possible include patience, endurance, self-control, cleverness, adaptability and *aidōs* (another virtue that has no single English equivalent, but includes respect for others, knowing your place and not over-reaching).

Aside from Homer, the earliest author is Hesiod, who in his poem *Works and Days* describes the life of an ordinary member of a poor farming community on Mount Helicon, and tells his lazy brother Perses how to improve his character, which may make the difference between life and death. For Hesiod the key to survival and, depending on the whims of the gods, was hard work. "Work work upon work!" he exhorts Perses. Do not sit idly around the fire during the cold winter, but prepare your tools for planting when spring comes. Be thrifty because if you run out of food you cannot count on your neighbors to feed you. Be generous when you can because this will incline your neighbors to be generous to you when you need it. Respect the gods. Be honest in your dealings with others. These are the specific values of a poor farmer but they were applicable to the life of many others in Hesiod's day and later on in fifth-century Athens, and to our own lives as well. Why should anyone follow this advice? First, because not doing so will make you disliked and invite bad treatment from others; second, because the gods will surely punish you – and if not you, then one of your descendants. Likewise, it provides an explanation for cases where you are a good person and suffer undeserved misfortunes. The explanation will be that one or more of your ancestors did something bad and for whatever inscrutable reason, the gods decided to punish not them but you. The idea that the sins of the fathers shall be visited upon their children is not found only in the Bible.

The common thread among these three different sets of recommended values and characters is survival and success. But even if the heroic values we see in the

Iliad were appropriate in the mythical Homeric world, they were far from applicable to the realities of life in small city-states governed by aristocracies (which was the norm in Greece during the times of the Sophists) or in some cases by monarchs who had seized power, and much less so under the democracies that were established in Athens and in many of Athens' subject cities. Here there was need for cooperation, in both war and peace. Unlike Homeric battles in which the fighting was mainly man-to-man (which made heroic behavior possible), in battles of the fifth-century phalanxes of hundreds or even thousands of citizen-soldiers who had been trained together from a young age fought together, typically in tight formation where individual exploits played but a small role. Likewise, as mentioned earlier[10] in the Assembly that governed the city, all adult male citizens had a voice and a vote, and in the law courts cases were decided by the majority vote of large juries chosen from the adult male citizenry.

The term *politikē tekhnē* also requires some explanation. *Tekhnē* (pl. *tekhnai*), means "skill," "craft," "expertise" or "art" (including the fine arts but by no means restricted to them). Carpentry was as much a *tekhnē* as sculpture. In general *tekhnai* could be taught and typically the skill that earned the family income was taught by father to son. *Tekhnai* were typically manual arts, but intellectual skills such as arithmetic were also called *tekhnai*. *Politikē* does not mean "political" in the sense familiar to us. Its basic meaning is "having to do with the city" (*polis*, pl. *poleis*), and since in ancient Greece each *polis* was in effect an independent country (although sometimes cooperating with other *poleis* in a league or being controlled by another, more powerful *polis*) it is reasonable to translate the phrase as "citizenship" or "expertise in being a citizen," including one's domestic and civic behavior.

In describing *aretē* as *politikē tekhnē* Protagoras is already suggesting that people can be taught to be successful in both the public and the private spheres of their lives. Setting himself up as a teacher – indeed the senior teacher – of this subject amounted to claiming to give (or, rather, to sell) them the ticket to success. Since *aretē* means "excellence" in general, Protagoras' promise to make people better makes sense. We now have the answer to Socrates' initial question: Protagoras claims to make his students better *people*, to give them the equipment to succeed in life.

In view of Socrates' rebuttal that this cannot be taught since the best men have failed to make their sons good, Protagoras offers a long two-stage reply[11], first (320d–322d) a tale (*muthos*) establishing that humans have the capacity to acquire *aretē* even if not everyone achieves that distinction, and second (323d–328d) an account (*logos*) that shows how humans are actually taught *aretē*, ending with his boast to be a better teacher of it than others.

In what follows I treat both parts of the speech as genuinely Protagorean. This is an important interpretive decision since it is disputed how to treat this long account. If it is quoted or paraphrased from a work of Protagoras it has great value; if it is simply Plato's invention, then it is no more than a guess at how Protagoras might have dealt with Socrates' objection. The two stages of Protagoras' reply make the matter more complicated: one part might be due to Protagoras and the other to Plato. Most scholars now think that the first part, the tale, originated with Protagoras but there is no consensus on the second part. The chief argument against its authenticity is that its style is so different from the tale that it is unlikely to be by the same author. I find this argument unpersuasive because in the dialogue Protagoras himself calls attention to the difference in style by labeling it an account as opposed to a tale, and I find no reason to suppose that he could not have written in different styles. Indeed we can be sure that the kind of speeches he trained his students to make were certainly not all mythological tales.

The first part of the speech offers a tale, a mythological account of human nature framed in terms of survival. Humans were not endowed by their Creator like other animals with equipment for survival such as fur to protect them from cold, speed to escape attack from predators, or claws to kill prey, but instead were given the knowledge of crafts (*tekhnai*) and of how to use fire (needed for some crafts and most importantly for cooking), which set them apart from the other animals. By these means they were able to build shelters from the cold, to make clothing, to grow and cook food. Even so, as individuals they were unable to withstand attacks from savage beasts, but when they tried to live in communities they quarreled and failed to organize themselves effectively. Returning to their solitary lives they became the prey of animals again and were in danger of extinction until the gods took pity on them and gave them the two things they needed in order to live together in harmony: *aidōs* and *dikē*, which respectively mean something like concern about what others think about you and a sense of fairness. If properly developed they make a person just and temperate (323a), and also pious (324a). In order to form a community people must recognize that it cannot be a matter of everyone being out for his or her own good and the devil take the hindmost. On Protagoras' account human survival requires both traits. *Aidōs* makes us recognize that others have rights and deserve respect, and how much they are due, while *dikē* makes us respect their rights and give them their due. Unlike skills like medicine or farming, which are sparsely distributed among the population, everyone has a share in these. This is why in a democracy everyone has a right to an opinion about political affairs whereas in technical matters only experts are allowed to give advice.

It is disputed whether or not the tale is intended as an account of human development.[12] It is certainly presented that way: first humans had no social skills, with disastrous results; over time they acquired the qualities of *aidōs* and *dikē* that enabled them to cooperate and thrive. On an alternative interpretation, the tale is an account of human nature, which includes both the capacity to learn useful crafts and also to acquire social skills, both of which are needed to flourish in communities. On this latter view, the point is that human nature in its entirety was a gift of the gods, just as sheep and snakes were provided with the wherewithal to survive, so were humans; the tale simply shows that technical skills are not enough; that social skills or at least the capacity to acquire them are part of our nature. I favor the second interpretation because on the first, in terms of the tale itself it is unclear how humans gained their social abilities and were not destroyed either by wild animals or by one another.

The question of whether the craft of citizenship (like other *tekhnai*) can be taught is the subject of the second part of Protagoras' speech. Here he argues that it is taught to everyone from infancy, first by parents, later by other relatives, teachers, and finally by the laws of the community. This means that *aidōs* and *dikē* are not moral states but potentialities that can be developed to different degrees and in different ways, and this explains why some people are more effective members of their community than others – they have a greater share of the two potentialities and/or they have received better training. Protagoras' account also accounts for other features of human society. It explains why the sons of excellent men do not always have the same success as their fathers: they lack the shares and/or the proper training that made their fathers excellent. Clearly, the training one receives from one's parents is only a small part of one's socialization. It also explains why everyone is allowed to give advice on political matters (recall that Athens, where Protagoras is presenting this tale was a city with a democratic constitution): everyone has a share of political virtue. In addition it leads to the view that the purpose of punishment is not to exact revenge but to deter others from committing the offense at all and to correct the wrong-doers so that they will not repeat the offense (323d–324c).

Protagoras concludes his speech, which is simultaneously a justification of his profession as a Sophist and a piece of self-advertising, by declaring that although everyone contributes to training children to be effective members of a community, some contribute more effectively than others. In fact he himself is the most effective teacher of this craft, as his students evidently agree.

Subversive or Conservative?

In that the Sophists promoted democracy there was resistance from the wealthy Athenians who had formerly held a virtual monopoly on political power and who alone gave their own sons the social connections and knowledge of the ways of the city that readied them for leadership. Some perceived the Sophists as a serious threat to the status quo because they were foreigners who claimed to train young men to be leaders in the state and did this work for pay. There is no reason to dispute this, but we should not forget that the number of young men who had enough free time and the wealth to learn from Sophists could not have been large. It doubtless included the sons of most of the traditionally leading families, and it will have excluded the sons of the farmers, craftsmen and other workers who constituted the great majority of the citizens that could speak in the Assembly and vote. Apart from the aristocracy the more prosperous families in the commercial class will have provided the bulk of the potential students. This was indeed a threat to the traditional power base, but not as radical a threat as it is sometimes made out to be and doubtlessly was made out to be by some of the aristocrats.

24 Protagoras of Abdera

Aside from this, there is little reason to think that the best-known Sophists promoted radical political or social views either as a group or individually. Evidence on either side of the question is simply lacking for most of them, but what we are told of Protagoras suggests that he was anything but radical in his views. Most of the following discussion should be treated with caution since much of it is drawn from Plato's *Protagoras*, but the generally respectful and favorable presentation he receives there as well as the fact that the dialogue takes place in the home of the wealthiest citizen of Athens, where Protagoras is staying as an honored guest, is evidence that he was by no means a hated figure among the rich and powerful.

For reasons given earlier[13] I take the portrayal of Protagoras as fairly accurate. It reveals him to be reasonable and by no means extreme in his claims for his field and for himself. The craft of citizenship, which he professes to teach and which he equates with virtue/excellence (*aretē*), is not just the ticket to more power or money, but is intimately linked to the ethical virtues of justice (*dikaiosunē*), self-control (*sōphrosunē*) and reverence (*eusebeia*). These are different from *aidōs* and *dikē*, the traits or sensibilities shared by all humans that enable them to live in communities. Rather I take the first two to be those traits as developed in particular communities. The rules, standards and expectations varied from community to community: justice and self-control in Sparta were different from justice and self-control in Athens. *Eusebeia* has to do primarily, although not exclusively, with religious worship; we can also have *eusebeia* towards our parents. In Protagoras' myth, humans worshiped the gods even before they were given *aidōs* and *dikē*. But again, beliefs and practices related to the divine were different in different places. Protagoras, then, was teaching moral virtue, and in particular the moral virtue appropriate to the cities where he taught: there was no point in teaching Athenians to be good Spartans. Before he could do this, he would have to learn a good deal about the expectations and preferences of people in cities he planned to visit and he would have had no incentive to advocate reform.[14] For these reasons it would seem that suspicion against Sophists on the grounds that they were foreigners and might teach foreign ways to the future leaders of one's city is easy to understand even if not always justified.

When Socrates inquires about the relations among the various virtues (329d ff.) Protagoras gives answers that accord with ordinary intuitions. When Socrates first asks "Is virtue a single thing, with justice and self-control and piety (*hosiotēs*, standing in for *eusebeia*) its parts, or are the things I have just listed all names for a single entity?" Protagoras' reply, "This is an easy question to answer, Socrates: the things you are asking about are parts of virtue, which is a single entity," is what we expect, given his stated view that the single virtue he teaches includes these three qualities and the generally acceptable view that the qualities justice, self-control and piety are different.

To Socrates' next question, "Are they parts like the parts of a face – mouth, nose, eyes and ears – or like the parts of gold do they differ not at all from one another and from the whole except in size?" Protagoras replies, predictably and equally reasonably, "In the first way, as the parts of a face are related to the whole face."

If virtue is agreed to be a single thing, a whole consisting of the particular virtues (justice, etc.), which are different from one another since, for example, they lead us to do different kinds of actions, then, faced with a choice between one model in which "the parts are no different from the whole except in size" and another in which the parts are different from one another and enable us to do different things (as eyes enable us to see, and ears to hear, etc.), then Protagoras' choice is the obvious one.

To Socrates' third question, "Do some people have one of these parts of virtue and others have another, or is it necessary that if you have one you have them all?" Protagoras again replies reasonably: "Not at all – since many are brave but unjust and just but not wise." Socrates then asks whether Protagoras has introduced two more parts of virtue (courage and wisdom) and Protagoras (again reasonably) agrees, declaring that wisdom is the most important part, and insisting that each of them is different from the others.

Socrates then asks whether each of these parts has its own proper power or capacity (*dunamis*), like the different parts of a face. Protagoras agrees, presumably because he interprets Socrates' question as asking whether the difference between, say, justice and wisdom amounts to the fact that possessing justice leads you to do just actions, while possessing wisdom leads you to do wise actions, and people who have either of these qualities but lack the other will be inclined to do actions of the one sort and will not be inclined to do actions of the other.

The following discussion (330c–334a) contains three arguments in which Socrates attempts to show that contrary to what Protagoras has said, justice is the same thing as piety, wisdom is the same thing as self-control, and self-control is the same thing as justice. If these arguments succeed, then four of the five qualities Protagoras has named are proved to be not different from one another but identical. How these arguments go and how successful they are matters of dispute. I believe that they show that Socrates and Protagoras have different understandings of what it is to be virtuous. But in any case, one of the things that emerge from this discussion is that it is Socrates and not Protagoras who holds views that would strike an ordinary Athenian (and an ordinary twenty-first-century person as well) as doubtful.

This section of the *Protagoras* breaks off abruptly shortly afterward. Socrates asks Protagoras whether there are things that are good and whether these good things are what is advantageous to people, and Protagoras replies (again reasonably) that there are good things that are not advantageous to people, and then goes on to say the following.

> I know of many things that are disadvantageous to humans: foods and drinks and drugs and many other things, and some that are advantageous; some that are neither to humans but one or the other to horses; some that are advantageous

only to cattle; some only to dogs; some that are advantageous to none of these but are so to trees; some that are good for the roots of a tree but bad for its tendrils, such as manure, which is good when spread on the roots of any plant but absolutely ruinous if applied to the new stems and branches. Or take olive oil, which is extremely bad for all plants and is the worst enemy of the hair of all animals except humans, for whose hair it is beneficial, as it is for the rest of their bodies. But the good is such a multifaceted and variable thing that, in the case of oil, it is good for the external parts of the human body but very bad for the internal parts, which is why doctors universally forbid their sick patients to use oil in their diets except for the least bit, just enough to dispel a prepared meal's unappetizing aroma.

(*Protagoras* 334a–c, Hackett tr.)

As part of a cameo performance this speech is very likely to represent Protagoras' views and interests.[15] It is enthusiastically received by everyone in the audience except Socrates, who complains that the answer was too long and requests Protagoras to answer more briefly, which he surely can do since he is able to speak at great length or with extreme brevity. (I take it that this refers to a claim that Protagoras made for himself and for what he could teach his students to do.[16]) When Protagoras protests, Socrates, for the only time in Plato's dialogues, abruptly declares that he cannot continue the discussion and gets up to leave (335b–c). For present purposes, what matters is that everything Protagoras says in the speech and that Socrates found inappropriate would be considered by ordinary people to be both obvious and plausible.

The Myth of Protagorean Relativism

A human being is the measure of all things – of things that are, that they are and of things that are not, that they are not.

(Protagoras, Fragment 1 DK)

These are the most famous words to survive from any Sophist. They are the grounds of the theory known as Protagorean relativism. Statements like the following are commonly found.

There are virtually no relativists among significant figures in the history of philosophy. The principal exception to this last claim is Protagoras of Abdera, who apparently put forward a version of relativism in a treatise entitled *Truth*. None of Protagoras' writings have come down to us, but his views are reported by others, chiefly by Plato in the dialogues *Protagoras* and *Theaetetus*. By [Fragment 1] Protagoras apparently meant that each individual person is the measure of how things are to that person: things are or are not (to me) according as they appear to me to be or not be. Protagoras was thinking of cases like this: to me the wind feels cold, while to you the wind feels warm. About this case Protagoras wants to say the following: The wind isn't (absolutely or in itself) either cold or warm; "cold" and "warm" are merely subjective states or feelings. To me the wind feels (or is) cold, and to you it feels (or is) warm, and beyond this there is no fact of the matter concerning the temperature of the wind."[17]

In the absence of independent evidence the authority of Plato has determined the virtually unanimous acceptance of this interpretation of Protagoras, which it is my purpose in the present section to dispute. The example of the wind that is both hot and cold comes from Plato's *Theaetetus*, which introduces this interpretation. There is nothing in the *Protagoras* that suggests that Protagoras proposed a theory in any way connected with this kind of relativism.

The topic addressed in the *Theaetetus* is the nature of knowledge. Theaetetus, introduced as a brilliant young man with great philosophical promise, makes a tentative stab: knowledge is nothing other than perception (151e). Socrates replies: "This was the view that Protagoras maintained, but he expressed this very theory in a different way" (152a) and then quotes Fragment 1. The next exchange is significant:

[Socrates] Of course you have read it?

[Theaetetus] I have indeed, many times in fact.

[Soc]: He means something like this, doesn't he – that things are for me as they appear to me and things are for you as they appear to you, where you are a human and so am I?

[The] That's what he means.

(Plato, *Theaetetus* 152a)

The word translated "means" (*legei*) can also be translated as "says" and that is how it is usually translated. But in the present context that makes little sense. We have already been told what Protagoras said, namely Fragment 1. And in this context the way the fragment is presented assures us that it is a literal quotation, not a paraphrase or interpretation. It follows that what Socrates and Theaetetus assert in the final two speeches quoted above is not a quotation but something else – a paraphrase or an interpretation, and "means" (or "is saying") is an appropriate way to express this. The question that immediately arises is what Plato's grounds were for this assertion, which he put in the mouths of two people he admired. One possibility is that Protagoras actually asserted it in *Truth* or elsewhere, another is that Plato thought it is implied by Fragment 1. On the first of these possibilities, it is genuinely Protagorean, on the second it is Plato's interpretation. The first is implausible for the following reasons. If Protagoras stated it elsewhere, there would be no reason to quote Fragment 1 as authority for it, since that fragment does not say anything that resembles what Socrates and Theaetetus agree that it means. It would be simpler and clearer to quote or paraphrase Protagoras' actual statement of the doctrine. Second, Plato quotes the "human being is the measure" fragment ten times in the *Theaetetus* and "each time the wording is identical or very nearly so," and "in five of these he refers it specifically to Protagoras' writings, twice noting that the saying stood at the beginning of Protagoras' *Truth*." But the alleged quotation in 152a "is cited twelve times, but with no mention of writing and with varying wording. Evidently Plato had no text for the relativistic interpretation that he claims followed"[18] the human-measure saying. Further, Protagorean relativism as developed in the *Theaetetus* is a very implausible theory, which is destroyed effectively and at length in the following pages of the *Theaetetus* – which sits badly with the presentation of Protagoras in Plato's *Protagoras* as a person who avoids uncontroversial claims (except, of course, in the defense of his work as a Sophist). The second possibility needs to be taken seriously.

Unlike the *Protagoras*, the *Theaetetus* is not concerned to show Protagoras the person; he does not appear as a character in the dialogue. The topic of the *Theaetetus* is the nature of knowledge, and Protagoras and other earlier figures, Heraclitus in particular, appear simply in association with theories that Plato finds relevant to this purpose. The treatment of Heraclitus provides an illuminating parallel. Later in the same section of the *Theaetetus* Socrates attributes to Heraclitus the doctrine that all things flow like streams (160d). This interpretation of Heraclitus is spelled out at greater length elsewhere:

> Heraclitus says somewhere that all things move and nothing remains, and likening existing things to the flow of a river, he says that "you could not step twice into the same river."
>
> (Plato, *Cratylus* 402a)

This doctrine is known as Heraclitean flux and it is the most widely known idea attributed to Heraclitus. But the words in quotation marks in the *Cratylus* passage are now widely agreed to be not direct quotations from Heraclitus, and the same holds for the fragment "all things are in flux" (*panta rhei*, found at *Cratylus* 439d). Current scholarship favors an interpretation securely based in Heraclitus' genuine fragments, a translation that places equal weight on stability and change, on unity and plurality, on identity and difference; Heraclitean flux is simply a misinterpretation or at best a one-sided elaboration of the genuine river fragment which says not that it is impossible to step into the same river twice, but that

> Upon those who step into the same rivers, different and again different waters flow.
>
> (Heraclitus, Fragment 12 DK)

in which the possibility of stepping into the same river twice is not disputed but presupposed.

Regardless of whether or not Plato is responsible for these misinterpretations, the point remains that Plato is not a reliable source for understanding his predecessors. This is not surprising, for two principal reasons. In the first place, in Plato's time the study of the history of philosophy had not properly begun. The Sophist Hippias had made a collection of passages from the works of poets and philosophers and grouped them under various headings,[19] but collecting information is not the same as the study of the history of philosophy. This latter study involves seriously engaging with what earlier thinkers wrote, attempting to understand what questions they were trying to answer, how they understood those questions, what they meant by the answers they gave, and how those answers were related to the views of their predecessors and successors. This enterprise was not inaugurated until much later.[20] In the absence of a tradition of historical work on the earlier thinkers, Plato had no precedent for doing otherwise than he did – using material from earlier authors as the source of ideas for his own work – and there is no reason to suppose that he was particularly interested in accurately reconstructing their theories for their own sake.

In the second place, Plato's concern in the *Theaetetus* is above all philosophical. How accurate he is in ascribing to others views he wants to take into account makes no difference to his philosophical enterprise – investigating the nature of knowledge. Similarly we speak of people doing Marxist philosophy or Kantian ethics who are not engaged in interpreting Marx or Kant but are working on later developments of ideas in the Marxist or Kantian tradition. So it should come as no surprise that we find Plato drawing on his predecessors for ideas without troubling about how accurately he is representing the views they actually held.

What holds for the presentation of Heraclitus in the *Theaetetus* holds equally well for the presentation of Protagoras. The only ancient sources that attribute Protagorean relativism to Protagoras are Plato and authors dependent on him, and our remaining information (much from Plato himself) makes it unlikely that he held this view. Thanks to Plato Protagorean relativism has an important place in the history of philosophy, but there is no good reason to hold that Protagoras himself proposed it.

Why, then, did Plato associate him with this theory? The most likely explanation is the passage previously at 334a–c,[21] which correctly and uncontroversially points to a characteristic of the words "advantageous" and "disadvantageous," and "good" and "bad": nothing is simply advantageous or disadvantageous, etc.; what is advantageous or good for someone or something may be disadvantageous or bad for someone or something else. Whether or not terms like these apply to something is relative to, or depends on, what that thing is. This is an important point both linguistically and philosophically, but it in no way implies that all terms are relative in this way and there is no reason to suppose that Protagoras thought so. Still, this passage might have been what made Plato, drawing on Protagoras' own ideas for his own purposes, generalize the claim in a way he found philosophically useful.

If Fragment 1 is not about Protagorean relativism, then, what is its meaning? A good sense can be given to it on the basis of the picture already formed of Protagoras as primarily a teacher of how to make the strongest possible case for one's position in public settings, primarily the Assembly and the lawcourts. On matters debated in the Assembly knowledge is generally unattainable, since no one can know exactly what will result if a proposed law or policy is passed or defeated. Likewise in jury trials the jurors typically have no first-hand knowledge of what actually happened. One's purpose as a speaker (in a courtroom either as the accuser or as the accused, or in a political assembly either as the proponent or opponent of a measure) is to convince others rather than to establish the truth. What counts is not what you know to be true but what you can get the audience (the jurors or the members of the Assembly) to believe. The measure of your success is the proportion of votes for the side you are advocating, which in turn is the aggregate of the votes of the individual members of the jury or Assembly. Fragment 1 will then mean that what counts above all in these venues is the individuals in your audience: they are the ones you need to convince as best you can.[22]

Protagoras on the Gods

> Concerning the gods I am unable to know either that they are[23] or that they are not or what their appearance is like. For many are the things that hinder knowledge: the obscurity of the matter and the shortness of human life.
>
> (Protagoras, Fragment 4 DK)

This pronouncement was reputed to have led to Protagoras' books being burned in public and to his being charged with being an atheist. As noted earlier,[24] this colorful story is false, but the quotation is genuine and its proper understanding requires careful treatment.

In the first place, it does not declare that the gods do not exist (which would be atheism) but that Protagoras cannot (which implies that he does not) know whether or not they do (which is agnosticism). This in itself is not enough to refute the legend of the trial for atheism – the distinction between agnosticism and atheism is a relatively fine one which may well not have been recognized in the time of Protagoras, and even if it were well known, the person who brought the charge may not have been aware of it.[25]

Fragment 4 needs to be understood in its intellectual setting, since Protagoras was by no means the first Greek thinker to question the existence and nature of the gods. His most important predecessor in this regard is Xenophanes (ca. 570– ca. 475), who was born almost a century before Protagoras and who critiqued the anthropomorphic Olympian gods and the myths around them in the following statements, among others.

Praise the man who does not relate battles of Titans or Giants or Centaurs – the fictions of our fathers.
(Xenophanes, Fragment 1 DK)

Both Homer and Hesiod have ascribed to the gods all deeds which among men are matters of reproach and blame: thieving, adultery, and deceiving one another.
(Xenophanes, Fragment 11 DK)

Ethiopians say that their gods are snub-nosed and black, Thracians that theirs are blue eyed and red haired.
(Xenophanes, Fragment 16 DK)

But if oxen or horses or lions had hands or were able to draw with their hands and accomplish the same works as humans, horses would draw the figures of gods as resembling horses and oxen as resembling oxen, and each would make thegods' bodies have the same bodily form as they themselves had.
(Xenophanes, Fragment 15 DK)

Apparently Xenophanes thought there was no good reason to believe (as the Greeks traditionally did) that gods look like Greeks or even that they look like humans, let alone that they behave in ways that humans consider immoral. But this does not imply that he was an atheist. In fact he was not, as the following fragments show.

God is one, greatest among gods and humans, not at all like mortals in bodily form or thought.
(Xenophanes, Fragment 23 DK)

All of him sees, all of him thinks, all of him hears.
(Xenophanes, Fragment 24 DK)

Without effort he shakes all things by the thought of his mind.
(Xenophanes, Fragment 25 DK)

He always remains in the same place, moving not at all, nor is it fitting for him to come and go to different places at different times.
(Xenophanes, Fragment 26 DK)

Xenophanes rejected the traditional Greek gods but asserted that there is a single all-powerful god which by its mental, not physical, powers is the cause of everything that occurs ("shakes all things"). The characteristics he attributes to this god are what he believes "it is fitting" for a divinity to be like. In this way Xenophanes abandoned religious tradition and replaced it with rational criteria. How shocking this was to his contemporaries we do not know, but there is some evidence in other fragments that he left his homeland at the age of 25 and traveled through the Greek lands for the next 67 years giving performances of his poetry (and presumably the works of Homer, Hesiod and others) – something he could hardly have done if his novel ideas were found unacceptable. Other Presocratics agreed with Xenophanes to some extent. The traditional gods of Greece make little appearance in their surviving works, but none of them were reputed to be atheists or appear to have got into trouble for holding that other entities or powers were divine: Anaximenes considered air, which for him is the basic substance of which all things are made, to be divine, Heraclitus criticized many religious practices of the Greeks, Empedocles held fire, air, water, earth, and love and strife to be divine and sometimes calls them by names of Olympian gods. So Protagoras was hardly doing anything new in saying that he did not know whether or not there are gods and in fact that it is impossible to have knowledge on this topic.

The second half of Fragment 4 echoes another fragment of Xenophanes:

> No man has seen nor will there be anyone who knows the clear truth about the gods and about all the things I speak of. For even if a person should in fact say what has come to pass, nevertheless he himself does not know, but in all cases it is opinion that has been wrought.
>
> (Xenophanes, Fragment 34 DK)

Like Protagoras, Xenophanes remarks on the difficulty of attaining knowledge about the gods. Protagoras says that he (and presumably everyone else) cannot know even whether the gods exist, let alone what they look like, and presumably their other attributes and activities; Xenophanes points out that no one has certain knowledge about them, but only fallible opinion. The two fragments contain similar ideas but their emphasis differs. Unlike Xenophanes Protagoras offers an explanation, or rather two explanations, for the difficulty: the subject matter is too obscure and human life is too short. The explanations do not sit well together. If the subject matter is too obscure for humans to learn, then it is irrelevant how long they live. On the other hand he might mean that although the subject matter is too obscure to be mastered in a single human life it might be mastered if we had a longer life-span or by the collective effort of humans over several generations. Xenophanes at least believed that progress can be made towards knowledge if not about the gods at least about other matters, as the following fragment indicates:

> By no means did the gods intimate all things to mortals from the beginning, but in time, by searching, they discover better.
>
> (Xenophanes, Fragment 18 DK)

It seems likely that Protagoras, the teacher who held that teaching must begin at an early age and requires training (Protagoras, Fragment 3 DK[26]) and practice

(Protagoras, Fragment 10 DK), will have agreed with Xenophanes on the matter of intellectual progress in general, but it is unlikely that he would have extended this view to include knowledge of the gods.

In conclusion, it appears best to regard the reports that Protagoras was an atheist due to an incorrect interpretation of Fragment 4 and to hold that the views Fragment 4 expresses about the gods were by no means exceptional among intellectuals in fifth-century Greece. What Protagoras added to theological speculation remains unknown, but Fragment 4's identification of factors that place limits on human knowledge was a useful contribution to epistemology and scientific method.

Repudiation of Geometry

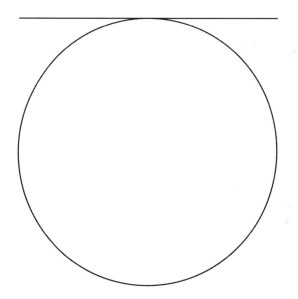

A circle does not touch a straight-edge at a point, as Protagoras used to say in refuting the geometers.[27]

Anyone who has studied geometry knows that the geometers are right and Protagoras is wrong. But geometry deals with lines (both straight and curved) that have no thickness, unlike physical objects (straight edges, for instance) which do.[28] And so do physical drawings like the diagram above, which perfectly illustrates Protagoras' assertion. In addition, "circle" has a precisely defined technical sense in geometry ("a plane figure surrounded by a line such that all the straight lines drawn to it from a point inside the figure [the center] are equal"[29]) but the Greek word *kuklos* existed long before geometry did. In the *Iliad*, which is the earliest Greek literary text, a wheel is called a *kuklos*. Perhaps Protagoras thought that geometry was useless because it failed to describe the real world; but instead he may have meant to point out that the relation between geometry and the physical world needed to be clarified. In the latter case it would not be unreasonable for him to challenge the mathematicians as he did. In fact, the complex relationship between geometry and the physical world had not yet been explored. This important topic was first taken up in the fourth century by Plato and then by his student Aristotle, and in fact the topic is philosophical rather than mathematical.

Two More Alleged Fragments

"It is impossible to contradict"

Some scholars have interpreted the brief statement "it is impossible to contradict"[30] as a fragment related to Protagoras' alleged relativism, although most editors[31] do not recognize this as a genuine fragment. It occurs in the following passage from Plato's *Euthydemus*.

> I am always surprised that in fact I have heard this statement, that contradiction is impossible, from many people at many times. For the Protagoreans used to make use of it a great deal and others still before them. It always seems to me to have a wonderful way of upsetting not just other arguments, but itself as well.... The argument amounts to claiming that there is no such thing as false speaking, doesn't it? And the person speaking must either speak the truth or else not speak.[32]

There has been disagreement about the value of this testimony and at present there is no consensus. In the context of Protagorean relativism the statement makes some sense. If you say the wind is hot and I say that it is cold, we are not contradicting one another: it does feel hot to you and cold to me. But once Protagorean relativism is rejected there is less reason to consider the statement genuinely Protagorean. I suggest that it is due to Plato himself, and that the *Euthydemus* passage itself reveals how Plato reached this conclusion. Having come to believe that Protagoras believed in Protagorean relativism, and supposing that we mean what we say, then the wind is both hot and cold, and extending this to all statements as Protagorean relativism does, Plato concluded that Protagoras was committed to the view that all statements are true, so that contradiction is impossible. I am not contradicting you, I am just saying something different. But then, it turns out, as Plato points out in the final sentence quoted above, it is impossible to say (and mean) anything false, so either we speak the truth or we do not speak at all – which is absurd. We might be inclined to doubt that Protagoras would have failed to notice this problem, but in any case, if Protagorean relativism was the invention not of Protagoras but of Plato, then this Platonic interpretation of his invention has nothing to do with Protagoras.

The Didymus Fragment

> It is manifest to you who are present that I am sitting; but to a person who is absent it is not manifest that I am sitting; whether or not I am sitting is non-evident.[33]

The text from which this extract is taken from a fragment of a commentary on the Biblical book of Psalms that has been attributed with some likelihood but without certainty, to Didymus the Blind, a Christian who taught and wrote in Alexandria (Egypt) in the fourth century CE. Protagoras is not mentioned in the fragment but is discussed in the fragment's immediate context:

> Protagoras' followers come to a different opinion – Protagoras was a Sophist. He says that (1) for things that are, being is in being manifest. He says that (2) [here the alleged fragment is quoted] ... (3) They [the Protagoreans] say that all things that are, are in being manifest. (4) For example, I see the moon, but another does not see it. Whether it is or is not is non-evident. (5) To me when I am healthy there comes an apprehension of honey that it is sweet; to another, that it is bitter, if he should have a fever. Therefore whether it is bitter or sweet is non-evident. (6) And in this way they mean to assert dogmatically the absence of self-verifying apprehension.

As Woodruff shows, the text is full of terminology characteristic of Skepticism, which was not in existence until well after Protagoras' lifetime, which indicates that Didymus did not have a text of Protagoras in front of him, but relied on intermediate sources that reworded and interpreted what they thought were Protagoras' ideas in their own philosophical vocabulary, including the words "manifest" and "evident." In fact at most only sections (1) and (2) of the passage are attributed to Protagoras, and at best Didymus gives us only a distorted paraphrase of something Protagoras might have said.

What we have here is interesting and is not found in other surviving Protagorean material. Section (1) implies that there is nothing that is not perceived, alternatively that for every fact there is someone to perceive it, and section (2) by implication warns us not to claim knowledge of things that we do not perceive.[34] As noted earlier, it is quite uncertain that this material goes back to Protagoras, but it is not derived from Plato's interpretation of Protagoras and it is hard to understand why anyone would have made it up.

Protagoras of Abdera

Two further contributions of Protagoras that are equally important as the topics treated in the present chapter will be taken up later. These are (1) his interest in the Greek language and in literature as an object of critical study and his (2) practice of what came to be called antilogic, which was part of his teaching method and became an essential tool of critical thought and philosophy. These topics are discussed below, in Chapters 9 and 11, respectively.

Notes

1 *Logos*, which has a wide range of meanings. See Chapter 9.
2 For discussion see Schiappa (2003) 143 f.
3 Plato, *Meno* 91e.
4 Plato, *Protagoras* 314e–316a, translated in the Appendix of Translated Texts, pp. 154–6.
5 Plato, *Protagoras* 318e.
6 See Socrates' recommendation of Hippocrates to Protagoras at Plato, *Protagoras* 316c.
7 See pp. 51–2.
8 See below, Chapter 11 for a discussion of "antilogic," a practice closely associated with Protagoras which formed part of his teaching.
9 Plato, *Protagoras* 319a.
10 P. 3.
11 A translation of his entire reply is in the Appendix of Translated Texts, pp. 258–264.
12 For discussion see Beresford and Manuwald in van Ophuijsen et al., 2013.
13 Pp. 17–18.
14 In Plato's *Greater Hippias* (285b–e), Hippias says that the Spartans had no interest in hearing him talk about astronomy, geometry, arithmetic, language or musical theory (subjects in which Hippias specialized), but cared to hear him speak only about their history, with the result that Hippias had to memorize "the genealogies of heroes and men" in order to please them.
15 The same holds for the brief and irrelevant interventions of Hippias and Prodicus shortly afterwards (337a–338b). See below, pp. 61 and 65.
16 Gorgias and Thrasymachus too could speak both briefly and at length, and Gorgias boasted that no one could speak more briefly than he could (Plato, *Gorgias* 449c). For Thrasymachus see p. 75).
17 https://www.csus.edu/indiv/e/eppersonm/phil002/documents/relativism_readings.pdf
18 Gagarin (2003) p.32 n.69.
19 See below p.60.
20 Plato's student Aristotle made much use of earlier thinkers, but again, he used them for his own philosophical purposes and did not attempt to study them for their own sake in their historical context.
21 Pp. 25–6.
22 This view favors interpreting "are" and "are not" in Fragment 1 as meaning "are the case" and "are not the case," which is a common use of the Greek word.
23 This may be the earliest known occurrence of the verb *einai* (to be) to mean "exist." See Schiappa (2003) 141.
24 P.17.
25 I once had a conversation with someone (an elderly Christian lady) who referred to someone as an atheist. When I asked her whether the person actually said that he was an atheist I was told "Well, he belongs to a different Christian denomination than I do. It's the same thing."
26 This is a fragment of his *Great Speech*.
27 Aristotle, *Metaphysics* 998a2–4.

28 The word translated "straight-edge" is *kanōn*, which was originally used to refer to straight rods, not *grammē*, which came to be the mathematical term for line.
29 Euclid, *Elements*, book 1, definition 15.
30 Other possible translations are "contradiction is impossible" and "there is no such thing as contradiction."
31 Including DK, Graham (2010) L-M (2016).
32 Plato, *Euthydemus* 286c. Part of this translation is taken from *Plato Complete Works*, Hackett, p.723. The statement is also associated with Protagoras elsewhere, including Isocrates, *Helen* 1–2, which was written at about the same time as the *Euthydemus*.
33 This and the following extract are taken from Woodruff (1985).
34 Woodruff (1985) 496.

3
GORGIAS

Gorgias was somewhat younger than Protagoras. Born in Leontini, Sicily in the 480s, he lived over 100 years and died in Thessaly, in retirement as a guest of the ruling family at Pherae. He traveled widely and had an excellent reputation. In 427 he visited Athens on a crucial diplomatic mission for his native city during which he made a great impression, astonishing everyone by his remarkable style of public speaking which had a lasting influence on other speakers. He gained fame through his spectacular performance speeches (*epideixeis*), which he performed (and for which he charged admission fees) wherever he went and notably at Olympia and Delphi during the great festivals held there every four years. He is said to have made a vast amount of money from his teaching as well as from his performances, during which he invited his audiences to ask him any questions they wished. He dedicated a golden statue of himself at the sanctuary of Apollo at Delphi which was still seen there 500 years later. Another statue of him was dedicated at Olympia by a member of his family. He made important contributions to the relatively new medium of Greek prose writing.[1]

As with Protagoras a Platonic dialogue is named after him, in which his conversation with Socrates introduces the dialogue. He is one of only two Sophists some of whom whose works have survived in their entirety.[2] We have the entire *Encomium of Helen* and *Defense of Palamedes* and a sizeable passage from a *Funeral Oration*. In addition we have two different summaries of a third work which had the odd title *On What is Not or On Nature*, although the original text has not survived. These writings are designed to surprise by both their content and their style, which gives us some sense of Gorgias the well-known showman, a role that complemented and promoted his roles as teacher, statesman and ambassador. Each of his surviving works is written in a style appropriate to its purpose. The brilliantly playful expressions of the *Helen*, the closely reasoned judicial defense presented in the *Palamedes*, the solemnity of the *Funeral Oration* and the carefully constructed systematic deductive arguments of the *On What is Not* display a mastery of a wider variety of prose genres than anyone up to Gorgias' time is known to have attempted.[3] It is noteworthy that Gorgias' surviving writings were composed not in Ionian Greek, which was spoken in his native city, but in Attic (the dialect spoken in Athens). The reason for this choice may have been the greatly increased political, military and cultural importance of Athens after the end of the Persian wars in 478 BCE. It was during this time that Attic became the primary dialect for Greek literature and it remained so for centuries afterwards.

In Plato's dialogue *Gorgias*, Gorgias denies that he is a Sophist, insisting that he is a *rhētōr* (public speaker or orator), a master of persuasion through speech who teaches others to be *rhētores* too (449a–b). Shortly before this, at 448d, we find what may be the earliest known occurrence of the word *rhētorikē* ("rhetoric," or perhaps better "oratory"[4]). This, he holds, is the most powerful craft, the best way to gain personal and political clout. With it you can get your own way, you can become a political leader, you can persuade people even on subjects of which you know nothing – in fact being more persuasive than experts. In Plato's *Meno* (95c), Meno, a former student of Gorgias, says that unlike Sophists, Gorgias taught people to be clever speakers but ridiculed those who claimed to teach *aretē* (virtue/excellence). This would distinguish him from Protagoras,[5] but it is by no means certain that all Sophists promised to teach *aretē*, so whatever he may have said, this assertion of his not a sufficient reason to exclude him from being a Sophist.

In fact, he was standardly considered a Sophist by later ancient authors and implicitly by Plato,[6] and modern scholars are unanimous in treating him as a Sophist. Since *aretē* is closely connected with success, a person who has it is an excellent and therefore a successful person. And in promising to teach the skill of persuasion, which enables people to succeed in political life and to get their own way with others (*Gorgias* 452d–e), Gorgias was in effect promising to teach *aretē*, and his claim not to do so may seem disingenuous. It is quite possible that he made this claim in order to distinguish himself from his rivals in competing for students as not just one Sophist among others (who taught a variety of subjects, as Plato's *Protagoras* shows), but as a teacher who specialized in exactly what was perceived as the key to a successful life. In any case, like the other Sophists he travelled, taught and accepted pay for his teaching. And even though the *Gorgias* draws a distinction between rhetoric and sophistic (463b–465c), both there and at the end of the dialogue (520a) they are said to be "one and the same or nearly so, and pretty similar."[7] Ironically, and perhaps as a dig against Gorgias,[8] Plato even suggests that rhetoric (which he compares to pastry-baking) is inferior to sophistic (which he compares with gymnastics): gymnastics keeps healthy bodies fit, whereas pastry is meant to give pleasure without regard to health.

Plato's *Gorgias* depicts him as promoting oratory as the greatest good for humankind.

(452d) [Socrates] What is this thing that you claim is the greatest good for humankind, a thing you claim to be a producer of?

[Gorgias] The thing that is in actual fact the greatest good, Socrates. It is the source of freedom for humankind itself and at the same time it is for each person the source of rule over others in one's own city.

[Soc.] And what is this thing you're referring to?

(452e) [Gorg.] I'm referring to the ability to persuade by speeches judges in a law court, councillors in a council meeting, and assemblymen in an Assembly or in any other political gathering that might take place. In point of fact, with this ability you'll have the doctor for your slave, and the physical trainer, too. As for this financial expert of yours, he'll turn out to be making more money for somebody else instead of himself – for you, in fact, if you've got the ability to speak and to persuade the crowds.

(453a) [Soc.] *Now* I think you've come closest to making clear what craft you take oratory to be, Gorgias. If I follow you at all, you're saying that oratory is a producer of persuasion. Its whole business comes to that, and that's the long and short of it. Or can you mention anything else oratory can do besides instilling persuasion in the souls of an audience?

[Gorg.] None at all, Socrates. I think you're defining it quite adequately. That is indeed the long and short of it.
(Plato, *Gorgias* 452d3–453a4, Hackett tr.)

The persuasion Gorgias teaches does not require the speaker to have relevant expert knowledge and what it produces in the audience is not knowledge, but merely conviction (454e). His boast to be able to answer any question on any subject is evidence of this. Gorgias provides an example of how this is possible: when his brother, a physician, failed with all his knowledge of medicine to persuade a patient to undergo surgery or cauterization, Gorgias with no medical knowledge would succeed through his skill at oratory (456b).[9] It is not difficult to imagine that this actually took place and that Gorgias did not simply repeat the medical advice his brother had already given. Rather, Gorgias was able to persuade the (understandably reluctant) patient by saying things his brother had not said – perhaps pointing out what would happen to the patient if he did not follow his brother's advice, or saying that without surgical intervention the patient's condition would surely lead to his death which would be catastrophic for his family, or by telling him (whether truly or falsely) that his brother had done dozens of these procedures before and the patients had all been completely cured, or convincing him that it only makes sense to undergo severe pain for a brief time in order to have a long pain-free life afterward. No matter if what he said was not true – his aim was simply to persuade, to obtain the desired result. Even so, Gorgias' boast to be able to answer any and all questions put to him in a public setting, and, we may imagine, the questions that he was asked, must have demanded a quick mind and the gift of the gab. But since this was a stunt, he did in public performances with many people present expecting to be entertained, there would have been no need to give a correct answer. He only needed to say things the audience would enjoy hearing and then move quickly on to the next question. It seems fair to say that at least in some contexts Gorgias thought style more important than substance.

This is the antithesis of Socrates' manner of discussion, but Socrates[10] was interested in exploring difficult topics through one-on-one discussion, not in entertaining the masses. If Socrates was a deep thinker, Gorgias (at least in his public performances) may have shown himself as the opposite. As the conversation in the *Gorgias* shows, Socrates' goal was to gain knowledge of the truth while Gorgias' goals were to entertain the audiences of his public performances, to make others believe whatever he wanted them to believe and likewise to teach others how to make people believe whatever they wanted them to believe. This he took to be "the source of rule over others in one's own city"[11] and he boasted that a successful orator is more persuasive in matters requiring technical expertise than the experts themselves.[12] Socrates engaged in a cooperative search for the truth while Gorgias engaged (and taught others to engage) in competitive situations where there were winners and losers. Socrates investigated his topics slowly and thoroughly (like a philosopher) while Gorgias avoided the tedium of close considerations. Socrates was never content with an answer but kept returning to it for further examination while Gorgias aimed only to persuade the present audience.

Performance speeches in general may not be the best place to look for the serious discussion of ideas, but in different ways Gorgias' surviving works introduce and explore important and interesting topics over and above displaying his virtuosity.

The *Encomium of Helen*[13] treats a seemingly lost cause. The adulterous elopement of Helen of Troy with Paris was the cause of the Trojan War, which led to the death of thousands of Greeks not to mention the complete destruction of the Trojan city and civilization. But in the *Encomium* Gorgias sets out to prove that she was not to blame for what she did. It seems impossible that any argument could persuade anyone of this. But there were alternative narratives about Helen. The best-known one is presented in Euripides' play *Helen* (produced in 412 BCE), which presents her – doubtless to the audience's great surprise – as far from being a woman of strong passion and loose morals, but as a faithful wife who spent the duration of the Trojan War in Egypt waiting patiently for her husband to come and bring her home. Gorgias' Herculean task is to prove her innocence even though she did abandon her husband for another man. This rhetorical masterstroke may well not convince us (and at the end Gorgias calls it a "plaything") but it is certainly an excellent advertisement for Gorgias' skills in argument as well as displaying his remarkable stylistic tricks (which can be fully appreciated only by those who can read the original Greek).[14] It also stands as an advertisement for his profession.

It has the form of argument by elimination. Gorgias accepts that Helen behaved as she behaved and then asks why. He identifies four possible reasons for her behavior, declares that they are the only possibilities, and then proceeds to discuss each of the four one by one, systematically proving that no matter which of these was the cause of her behavior she was not to blame for her actions.

The four possible reasons for Helen's elopement are that her action was done (1) through the will of Fate and the designs of the gods and the decrees of Necessity, or (2) because she was taken by force, or (3) because she was persuaded by words, or (4) because she was conquered by Love. The arguments for all but the third are similar. (1) Fate, the gods and Necessity cannot be resisted. (These explanations probably have to do with the mythological background of the event, which includes the beauty contest among the goddesses in which Paris awarded the prize to Aphrodite, who rewarded him with Helen, the most beautiful of mortal women, and also includes the series of catastrophes that beset the family of Agamemnon over several generations and were ascribed to divine punishment.) Likewise, (2) if she was kidnapped and raped, the blame resides with Paris and not with her, and (4) if Love conquered her, well, Love is a god, so the fourth case falls under the first, which has already been taken care of.

The remaining possibility, (3) that Paris persuaded her to elope, receives a more extended treatment. Gorgias maintains that speech (*logos*) "is a powerful master" and presents evidence: mere words can have powerful effects – they can frighten us, make us happy or sad, and so forth even though they have "the smallest and most invisible body." Simply listening to poetry can strongly affect our emotions. Magical incantations and spells have power too although they are mere words: "conversing with the soul's opinion, the power of incantation charms, persuades, and changes it by witchcraft." So if Paris persuaded Helen to elope, he was to blame, not Helen since she was overcome as if by magic.

Gorgias then goes on to say something that is surprising and philosophically challenging: "All who have persuaded and do persuade anyone of anything do so by fashioning a false *logos*." To support this claim, he points out that we know very little about the past, the future and even the present, and "on most matters most people make opinion an adviser to the soul. But opinion is fallible and uncertain and involves those who make use of it in fallible and uncertain successes." If we know something then we cannot be persuaded otherwise, but *logos* can change our opinions. When it comes to deciding what to do, we are talking about the future, about which we have opinions, hopes, desires and fears, but only rarely do we have knowledge. In this case, *logos*, if it is successful, compels us to believe. He goes on to mention three kinds of situations where *logos* changes the opinions of a person who hears it: (1) "the accounts (*logoi*) of the astronomers, who replace one opinion with another and so make things incredible and unclear seem apparent to the eyes of opinion, (2) compulsory competitions which use speeches (*logoi*) in which a single *logos* written with art (*tekhnē*) but not spoken with truth delights and persuades a large crowd, and (3) contests of philosophical accounts/arguments (*logoi*), in which is revealed how easily the swiftness of thought makes our confidence in our opinion change."

This list gives insight into some of the public entertainment available in Gorgias' time. (1) "Things in the air and things beneath the ground" were considered unknowable, but that did not prevent people from having beliefs about them. This is evident in the earliest Greek literature, but attempts to understand the nature of the heavenly bodies and their movements became a major topic of conjecture and theorizing in the sixth and fifth centuries BCE among the thinkers known as Presocratic philosophers, who made progress by proposing accounts they believed were superior to accounts that had been proposed earlier. (2) refers among other things to the public performances of such works as the *Helen* before large audiences, but possibly also to public debates on set subjects and even, perhaps, to speeches in the Assembly or in court. What Gorgias has in mind in (3) is less certain in part since the adjective *philosophos*, here translated "that pretend to be wise,"[15] could apply to any number of situations and the noun *philosophia* (and the concept of philosophy) had not yet been invented.[16] The third category may be meant to include such works as Gorgias' own *On What is Not, or On Nature*,[17] which in its own way could claim victory over Melissus' *On Nature, or On What Is*. It may also be a reference to debates on such topics as *nomos* and *phusis*[18] in public or private settings, such as the conversations presented in many of Plato's dialogues. The surprising statement that all persuasion is the product of false *logos* is not explained or defended in the *Helen*, but Gorgias' justification for it can be found in *On What is Not, or On Nature*.[19]

The *Defense of Palamedes* presents another lost cause. Like Helen, Palamedes is a figure of mythology, a Greek warrior at Troy whom Odysseus falsely accused of accepting a bribe to commit treason, and who in consequence was put to death. This time Gorgias' task is easier: to prove him innocent, or rather to make a plausible case for his innocence. The structure of the speech is a multi-phased layered argument of the form: For A to have happened (for Palamedes to have betrayed the Greek army) B must have happened. But it is difficult, improbable or impossible for B to have happened, therefore A could not have happened. But even supposing that B happened, even so A could not have happened since in addition to B, C must have happened. But it is difficult, improbable or impossible for C to have happened; therefore once again A could not have happened. And so on. Sometimes something can happen in more than one way: for example, for B to happen it would have had to happen in one of three ways, but the first of these ways is difficult, improbable or impossible, and so is the second, and so is the third; therefore B could not have happened. And even if we are not convinced that all or even *any* of the sub-arguments establish that something is impossible, the cumulative effect is designed to be overwhelming. Anyone hearing or reading this speech would certainly want to have Gorgias represent him in court, or at least to take lessons from him to learn how to compose equally effective speeches. For example, consider the arguments that proceed by eliminating one by one all the possible cases. When was the bribe delivered to Palamedes? Not by day (because the transaction would have been seen) and not by night (because the guards posted in the army camp would surely have noticed). He would have needed others to bring off his treason, but where would he go for help? Not to Greeks (they would want to kill him as a traitor) and not to foreigners (they would not trust him).

The two works just discussed have a strong similarity: each depends on the assertion that if something happened it could have happened only for one or more of a short list of stated reasons, and it proceeds by showing that none of the reasons holds. Gorgias expects his audience to accept that there are no more possible explanations. This means that the arguments can be defeated simply by producing yet another reason that does not fall under the ones listed. For example, if Helen left her husband in order to get revenge on him for something he had done or just because she was bored with him, then Gorgias' argument does not prove that she is not to blame. And even if he were to supply a further explanation to show that in these cases too she would not be blameworthy, it might be possible to propose yet another reason, and so on. Unless he can *prove* that he has covered all possible explanations, he does not have an ironclad case for her innocence – but even so, the arguments as presented, particularly those in the defense of Palamedes, might well be able to convince all but the most skeptical audience.

On What is Not, or On Nature is a curious work. It consists of a series of arguments for outrageous claims that no one believes: (I) nothing is, (II) even if something is it cannot be known or conceived by humans, (III) even if something is and is known, it cannot be communicated to anyone else. There is an obvious parallel with the overall structure of the *Palamedes*, but the argumentation is tighter and more precise. The text raises several questions: Did this kind of argumentation originate with Gorgias or was it already known? How successful are the arguments – do they stand up to close examination? Why did Gorgias write in such a way on such an odd topic (which seems to have little to do with his specialty in public speaking)? Did he really believe the three claims that this work purports to prove?

The title of Gorgias' work is a parody of Melissus' work *On Nature, or On What Is*, in which Melissus argued that "what-is is one" – in other words, that there exists only one thing – and that this one thing is eternal, unlimited, uniform, and has several other properties. This kind of arguing for totally implausible views stems from Parmenides, who according to the unanimous view of antiquity maintained that there is only one thing and it exists eternally, is unchanging, motionless and has no properties that the senses can perceive.

Since no one would accept this as true simply because someone said so, how did Parmenides set out to convince them? By reasoning. Parmenides was the earliest figure in the Greek philosophical tradition to back up his views by deductive arguments rather than simply asserting them. Parmenides argued obscurely and his arguments were not much discussed in antiquity, but his conclusions were notorious and provoked important philosophers, notably Plato and Aristotle, to engage with them. It is not surprising that argument rather than assertion was first used in philosophy to support Parmenides' apparently outlandish claims. After all there certainly appear to be many things. Since all our experience suggests and reinforces this idea and since everything we do relies on this fundamental belief, Parmenides cannot appeal to experience, to the evidence of our senses, to *show* people that there is only one thing. So he claims to establish it by a proof. He reasonably asserts that our senses are fallible, so they are not reliable guides to reality. He proceeds to argue from a principle that he holds to be unquestionably true, something approximating the principle of non-contradiction, that it is impossible for the same thing to be and not to be.[20] It is self-contradictory to say of something that is that it is not, because what is not is nothing. It does not exist, and since it is nothing it cannot be known, comprehended or thought of, and neither can it be expressed in language. Since a conclusion that follows deductively from true premises must itself be true, Parmenides holds that the conclusions he draws are incontrovertibly true. Since the senses can and sometimes do deceive us, they should be disregarded when they disagree with Parmenides' reasoned conclusions.

According to the standard interpretation Parmenides was supported by Zeno, who used clearer deductive arguments to refute ordinary views that conflict with Parmenides, such as that there are many things and that motion exists. Melissus, also following the Parmenidean tradition, argued for theses largely similar to those of Parmenides, but his arguments were clearer and their errors easier to identify. Gorgias was a contemporary of Melissus and the arguments he presents for the thesis that nothing is mimic Melissus' style and argue for claims even more outrageous than Melissus', beginning with the thesis that nothing is.

On What is Not, or On Nature employs some of the same techniques used in the *Helen* and the *Palamedes*. It is divided into three clearly articulated parts. The first (I) (sections 66-76), which concludes that nothing is, proceeds by stating that there are only three conceivable situations and then proving that each of the three is impossible, as he lucidly states at the beginning.

> If something is, either (I.A) what-is is or (I.B) what-is-not is, or (I.C) both what-is and what-is-not are. But it is the case neither that (I.A) what-is is, as he will show, nor that (I.B) what-is-not is, as he will justify, nor that (I.C) both what-is and what-is-not are, as he will teach this too. Therefore, it is not the case that anything is.

His argument against (I.B) is as follows.

> And in fact, what-is-not is not. For if what-is-not is, it will be and not be at the same time. For in that it is considered as not being, it will not be, but in that it *is* not being, on the other hand, it will be. But it is completely absurd for something

to be and not be at the same time. Therefore, it is not the case that what-is-not is. And differently: if what-is-not is, what-is will not be, since they are opposites, and if being is an attribute of what-is-not, not-being will be an attribute of what-is. But it is certainly not the case that what-is is not, and so neither will what-is-not be.

This is immediately followed by his argument against (I.A), which in turn presents three possible situations and argues that each of the three is impossible:

Further, neither is it the case that what-is is. For if what-is is, it is either (I.A1) eternal or (I.A2) generated or (I.A3) eternal and generated at the same time. But it is neither (I.A1) eternal nor (I.A2) generated nor (I.A3) both, as we will show. Therefore it is not the case that what-is is.

The argument disproving case (I.A1) goes as follows:

For everything that comes to be has some beginning, but what is eternal, being ungenerated, did not have a beginning. But if it does not have a beginning it is unlimited, and if it is unlimited it is nowhere. For if it is anywhere, that in which it is different from it, and so what-is will no longer be unlimited, since it is enclosed in something. For what encloses is larger than what is enclosed, but nothing is larger than what is unlimited, and so what is unlimited is not anywhere. Further, it is not enclosed in itself, either. For "that in which" and "that in it" will be the same, and what-is will become two, place and body (for "that in which" is place, and "that in it" is body). But this is absurd, so what-is is not in itself, either. And so, if what-is is eternal it is unlimited, but if it is unlimited it is nowhere, and if it is nowhere it is not. So if what-is is eternal, it is not at all.

And so on for cases (I.A2) and (I.A3). He then takes a different tack, arguing that if something is, it is either one or many, but it is neither one nor many, and therefore it is not the case that what-is is.

Gorgias goes on to give several arguments to prove that (II) even if something is it cannot be known or even thought of (sections 77–82). The first is typical:

If things that are thought of are not things-that-are, what-is is not thought of. And reasonably so. For just as if things that are thought of have the attribute of being white, being thought of would be an attribute of white things, so if things that are thought of have the attribute of not being things-that-are, not to be thought of will necessarily be an attribute of things-that-are. This is why the claim that if things that are thought of are not things-that-are, then what-is is not thought of is sound and preserves the sequence of argument.

Again, the arguments are unsound but some of the claims made *en route* cry out for further analysis and clarification of a philosophical nature.

The final part (sections 83–86) argues (III) that even if something is and can be known, it cannot be communicated to another. It consists of a single extended argument. The basic idea is that we communicate about things by means of speech, but speech consists of words, which are not at all like the things we use them to communicate about. So just as hearing reveals different things from what sight does, so speech reveals different things from what the senses do, and so cannot communicate about things that are visible, etc. This reasoning has close connections with the assertion in the *Encomium of Helen* that all persuasion is the product of false *logos*. The persuasion in question has to do with things and events that are apprehended by the senses, but the words that persuade are not the same as the things and events in question and so they are false.

We are not convinced by Gorgias' reasoning in section III, but it is not as straightforward to diagnose the errors as it is for the arguments in the previous sections of the work. To do so requires us to investigate the relations among language, thought, concepts, perception and other types of comprehension, and between all these and the external world. Gorgias' work provokes thought about these subjects. This comprehensive philosophical project was soon taken up by Plato and remains one of the central areas of philosophy. There is of course no reason to suppose that Gorgias understood the problems he raised, much less that he had worked out solutions or any idea of how to approach them. On the other hand there is no reason to suppose the contrary either.

I cannot believe that Gorgias accepted the conclusions of the arguments in *On Nature*. However it is unclear whether or not he was aware that there were errors in his reasoning and if he was aware of them, whether the errors were deliberate and Gorgias knew precisely where they were or how to diagnose them. Perhaps it made no difference to him. If, as I think, the principal purpose of this work was to show that he could go further than the most extreme philosopher – that in using Melissus-style reasoning he could out-do even Melissus – it fits in well with the interpretation of the *Helen* as a performance piece whose purpose was not to so much to convince anyone that Helen was blameless but rather to display Gorgias' inventiveness and to provoke attention. It also fits well with the fact that the *Helen*'s praise of the power of speech in producing persuasion and in other ways (for example its ability to produce strong emotional effects in people) was an advertisement for himself. Moreover it introduces some philosophical ideas that are worth taking seriously in their own right. Like the *Helen*, the *On What is Not or On Nature* can be read as an advertisement for Gorgias' ingenuity and for his supremacy in yet one other area of discourse, not only the genres of encomium and defense speech but also the genre of technical, abstract, deductive philosophical argument.

On What is Not or On Nature leaves us wondering how seriously Gorgias intended it to be taken. Was its *only* purpose to achieve the effects described in the previous paragraph? Was Gorgias content to impress and confuse? Or did he not only raise and argue for these challenging theses but actually puzzle about them? Did he realize that some of his arguments were fallacious or did think that they

48 Gorgias

were sound? The available information does not permit a decisive answer to any of these questions.

The important point here is that the philosophical interest of the work is independent of Gorgias' intentions in composing it. It is also independent of whether or not he actually believed that what he argued for in this work is true or that it would persuade anyone, and of whether he was or was not aware of the mistakes in his reasoning or, supposing that he was aware of them, whether he could diagnose them.[21]

I defer discussion of Gorgias' contribution to the study of definitions, to Chapter 10.

Notes

1. See above, p. 5.
2. Antiphon is the other.
3. The history of Greek prose style is outside the scope of this book. I recommend J.D. Denniston, *Greek Prose Style* (Oxford University Press 1952).
4. See above, p. 8 for the meaning of this word and the importance of this distinction.
5. See above, pp. 19–21.
6. See above, p. 8.
7. "Because they are so close, sophists and orators tend to be mixed together as people who work in the same area and concern themselves with the same things." (Gorgias 465d).
8. Isocrates, Plato's cross-town rival, is another possible target.
9. The passage in which this occurs is translated in the Appendix of Translated Texts, pp. 162–70.
10. By "Socrates" I am referring to Plato's Socrates as we find him in the *Gorgias* and some other dialogues, as opposed to Xenophon's quite different Socrates.
11. Plato, *Gorgias* 452d. This sentiment is attributed to Gorgias also in the *Philebus*: "The art of persuasion is superior to all others because it enslaves all the rest with their own consent, not by force, and is therefore by far the best of all the arts." (Plato, *Philebus* 58a)
12. Plato, *Gorgias* 459c.
13. The entire work is translated in the Appendix of Translated Texts, pp. 171–4.
14. For an excellent attempt to imitate Gorgias' style, I recommend the translation in DG and for a discussion and sympathetic evaluation, Schiappa 1991, chapter 6.
15. For this fifth-century interpretation of the adjective *philosophos* see p. 9.
16. For the significance of the invention of this word, see below, pp. 132, 138.
17. See Appendix of Translated Texts, pp. 174–7.
18. This important topic of debate is treated below in Chapter 12.
19. Discussed below, pp. 44–47.
20. Aristotle was the first to explicitly state and discuss this principle (*Metaphysics* 4.3–6), which he regards as the most certain principle of all things. He formulates it in several ways; the one quoted here is given at *Metaphysics* 4.4 1006a1.
21. A particularly useful discussion of these issues is presented in Bonazzi 2020, 33–36.

4
ANTIPHON OF RHAMNOUS

The central question about Antiphon is raised by the fact that we have texts attributed not only to "Antiphon the Sophist," the author of *On Truth* and *On Concord*, but also to "Antiphon of Rhamnous" otherwise known as "Antiphon the Orator," the author of oratorical study-pieces called tetralogies and three forensic speeches. Some ancient sources argue that these were two different men with the same (not uncommon) name, and this was the prevalent view until it was argued in 1961[1] that these two Antiphons and another Antiphon who interpreted dreams were the same person – a view that has since gained ground and which now prevails.[2] If the two (or three) Antiphons are the same, then students of the Sophists have much more material to work with than if they are restricted to basing their discussions on only the material attributed to Antiphon the Sophist. In assessing Antiphon the Sophist it is impossible not to take sides on this issue. This chapter is based on the prevalent "unitarian" view, which I find most likely to be true, even though this matter cannot be settled with certainty.

Our single Antiphon, then, was born in Rhamnous, a *deme* (district) of Attica, located on the seacoast some 20 miles from the city of Athens. For this reason he was known also as Antiphon the Athenian. He was born ca. 480, which makes him somewhat younger than Protagoras and a contemporary of Gorgias, and he appears to have spent most of his time in Rhamnous, teaching oratory and giving advice on court cases. He was a logographer (literally "speech writer"), which means that he composed speeches for others to use in court, being perhaps the first to practice this profession, which became a major enterprise in fourth-century Athens. Several of his written works have survived, quite different from one another. The best known of these, called *Tetralogies* consists of speeches in three imaginary murder trials. Each tetralogy consists of four speeches (as the word means in Greek): opening speeches in which the prosecutor and the defendant make their cases, followed

DOI: 10.4324/9781003493259-4

by a rebuttal speech for each side. These are the only examples of this genre that we have. In addition we are fortunate to possess important fragments of a work named *Alētheia* (a word that is standardly translated "Truth" but which can also be rendered "Reality") that contained discussions of a wide variety of topics, some of them scientific. Also surviving are fragments of another work, *Concord*. Finally we have three speeches which Antiphon wrote for actual murder trials, two for the defense and one for the prosecution.[3] This is a far greater amount of original material than we have for any other Sophist.

We have no information about when he devoted himself to these different genres of writing, but on a plausible account[4] he was a teacher (as his father is reputed to have been). Like Protagoras and Gorgias he taught his students how to speak effectively in public settings. His first writings were the *Tetralogies*, composed in the period 450–430, perhaps in part for his students. After 430, he may have continued to teach, but the increased importance of jury trials in Athens combined with the fact that knowledge of reading and writing was becoming widespread during this period led him to become a legal adviser and also to write speeches for litigants to present in court, and these occupations were his chief activities until late in his life he got involved with politics and in 411 took part in a coup that temporarily replaced the Athenian democracy with an oligarchy. After the democracy was restored, Antiphon was put on trial for treason. He spoke on his own behalf in court with a speech (which unfortunately has not survived) in which he defended not only his actions in the particular case but also his career as a whole and which was considered a masterpiece both in his time and afterwards, but despite his eloquence he was found guilty and executed.

Antiphon is normally considered an outlier among the Sophists: he was an Athenian, he did not make it a standard practice to travel to other cities,[5] he was not a showman and did not give public displays of his virtuosity, he was involved in Athenian politics (at least at the end of his life), and many of the fragments of book 2 of *On Truth* are on scientific subjects, which are less characteristic of Sophists than of the thinkers known as Presocratic philosophers. In my opinion none of these considerations carries much weight. Other Sophists had individual interests and specialties which they pursued and taught, and which enabled each to stake out his own special place in the competitive professional world of sophistic endeavor. If Antiphon focused his efforts on teaching oratory and if his nature led him to do so in comparative isolation in distant Rhamnous, that need not exclude him from being considered a Sophist. Likewise, if he was able to find enough pupils without having to travel throughout Greece – and if many of these same pupils were willing to spend the best part of a day traveling from the city to Rhamnous and back, so much the better. His practice (unique, as far as we know, among the known Sophists) of writing speeches to be delivered by others in court, can be viewed as a specialty of his just as geometry and astronomy were specialties of Hippias – and one for which we may assume he was well paid. In effect he may have been the first professional legal consultant or solicitor. Further, since laws and legal practice varied considerably from city to city, Antiphon's intimate knowledge of Athenian law would not have been easily transferable to other locations – another reason for staying at home. Further, he was not the only Sophist interested in scientific subjects or who made contributions to mathematics. Although the other Sophists of whom we know very much were not Athenians and therefore could play no role in Athenian political life, we know that Gorgias, Prodicus, Hippias and Thrasymachus were highly regarded in their own cities, which they represented as ambassadors in negotiating with other cities, and there is no convincing reason to suppose that they did not participate in the political life of their cities in other ways as well.

Antiphon's multifaceted career can usefully be explored by considering him first and foremost a teacher. The purpose of the *Tetralogies* is a matter of dispute, but it is implausible to think that they could be intended as models for speeches in actual trials, since they omit features that are essential in presenting a case, such as a narrative of the events concerned and the use of the testimony of witnesses. Instead, they focus on arguments and rebuttals and have the effect of prompting thought about complex issues.[6] For example, the second *Tetralogy* concerns a case of accidental death at a gymnasium where during javelin practice a boy (being defended in court by his father) following the instructions of his coach threw his javelin which then struck and killed another boy who had been told by another coach to pick up some javelins that had already been thrown.[7] It is agreed that the death was unintended, but still the boy was dead. The prosecution alleges that the defendant killed the victim and therefore should be found guilty, while the defense argues that the defendant is not guilty because he cast the javelin in the place where other boys were doing the same thing, that he did so on the orders of the instructor, and that if anyone is guilty it is the boy who ran into the path of the javelin. The case is complicated by the belief that killing, even if involuntary, brings pollution on the killer, and that unless the killer goes into exile the pollution could infect the entire city. This case raises interesting questions concerning legal responsibility, how to interpret existing laws, and how to balance legal requirements against religious beliefs. Importantly, neither side is declared the winner. Antiphon does not take sides, but, as happens in real trials, both sides have points in their favor but unlike in real trials there is no need to make a decision.

Antiphon presumably wrote the *Tetralogies* to present some of the relevant considerations in each case and to encourage his readers to think about them. He may have written them for the purpose of intellectual exercise and entertainment, or to get his readers (and/or students) to think about and discuss with others potential fault lines in the legal and social fabric of Athens, or to reflect on the arguments they contain as part of their rhetorical training. In any case, they are outstanding examples of antilogic, the practice based on Protagoras's dictum that there are two mutually opposed *logoi* on any subject. Antilogic has obvious applications in judicial trials, where the prosecution and the defense are by definition arguing on opposite sides, presenting considerations that favor their side and considerations that rebut arguments made in support of the opposing side. And unlike a real case where a verdict (whether correct or incorrect) is reached after the speeches have been heard, in the *Tetralogies* where we have only the speeches, we are left to ponder the relative strength of each side and perhaps to decide that neither side is clearly in the right. This is a conclusion that could not have been the verdict in an Athenian trial; the fact that the number of jurors was always odd and that each juror had to vote one way or the other guaranteed that hung juries did not occur. But reflecting on imaginary situations such as these may have led students and other thoughtful readers to think about how best to support one side of an unclear case against another and to accept that it sometimes happens that neither side is clearly right or wrong.

Antilogic can also be found in Antiphon's *On Truth*, whose surviving fragments have given rise to conflicting interpretations. *On Truth* consisted of two books. We have many bits of information about the views expressed in the second book, which appears to have contained an account of the natural world. It is impossible to form a picture of Antiphon's purpose or methodology since much of this information focuses on unusual words that Antiphon used. Here is an example.

> 'Extension' (*diatasis*): Antiphon, in the second book of *On Truth*: 'concerning the extension that now prevails,' referring to the orderly nature of the universe.[8]

This suggests that Antiphon had views about how the universe is ordered, but tells us nothing about what his views were. Even so, the fact that he wrote on what we consider scientific subjects is noteworthy. The following fragments contain much of the surviving information about his theories on matters which we would classify as belonging to meteorology, astronomy, medicine and biology.

> [The sun] is fire which approaches the moist air that surrounds the earth, causing sunrises and sunsets because it continually leaves behind the air that it scorches, and draws close again when the air has recovered its moisture.
>
> (Antiphon, fragment 26 DK)

> The moon shines by its own light and the hidden part of it becomes dim because of the sun's approach, since a stronger fire naturally dims a weaker one. In fact this is also the case with the other stars.
>
> (Antiphon, fragment 27 DK)

> Alcmeon, Heraclitus and Antiphon [held that eclipses of the moon] are due to the turning of its bowl-shaped body and its declination.
>
> (Antiphon, fragment 28 DK)

These three fragments are interesting particularly because they seem outdated. Parmenides, born some 60 years before Antiphon, had discovered the true cause of the phases of the moon[9] and his explanation had been adopted by others. Also, eclipses of both the sun and the moon had been correctly explained by Anaxagoras, Antiphon's older contemporary (born ca. 500).

The following fragments give Antiphon's explanations of the formation of hail or possibly snow and of the origin of the saltiness of the sea.

> Whenever rain showers and winds in contrary directions occur in the air, the water is condensed and becomes thick in many places. Whichever of the colliding ingredients prevails becomes thick and is condensed as it is blasted by the force of the wind.
>
> (Antiphon, fragment 29 DK)

> [How the sea came to be and why it is bitter] Antiphon [says] that it is the sweat caused by heat. From this the moisture that was enclosed was separated off by boiling, which occurs in all cases of sweat.
>
> (Antiphon, fragment 32 DK, using Pendrick's text)

The following fragment is remarkable not only for its unexpected content but also for the detail and the large number of examples it gives as evidence for its claims about the effects of bile on the human body. It suggests that Antiphon's intellectual interests were wide-ranging and that this otherwise unattested knowledge of (or perhaps his contribution to) physiology, was only one among many areas of his studies.

> If you ask me for evidence from the utterances of the rhetors to serve as proof, so that you may know that these too meant by the word "fever" fiery unnatural heat, then listen to the utterance of Antiphon, where he says: "These, as I told you, are things that were caused by bile, because it was present in the hands and feet; whereas the bile which advanced to the flesh produced chronic fevers, when its mass was great. For when it advances to the flesh, there arises through it a corruption in the flesh's very substance and it swells up. The unnatural warmth therefore will come from this place; and if it lasts and becomes ingrained, that will be a result of the bile when it is present in abundance in the flesh and does not quickly disperse and subside, but remains, persisting alongside the unnatural warmth." ... Again in the second book of his discourse *On Truth* he makes another remark in which he traces the cause of the genesis of fever to varieties of gall, by saying: "every bit of it (any one of them) which advances to the flesh produces strong, long-lasting fevers." ... And you can see that they also used to call it fever from the following remark, which I reproduce for you from the text of Antiphon: "thus when more gets into the vessels than they can bear, they open up, and because of this there arises through them a boil and when a boil arises through them

and starts to cause pain for the one afflicted by it and it takes root, then one calls this disease gout."[10]

Book 1 of *On Truth* contained an attempt to square the circle – that is, to construct a square equal in area to a given circle. This, along with the problems of trisecting an angle and duplicating the cube,[11] was one of three difficult problems that received a great deal of attention from ancient mathematicians. Aristotle reports that his proof was incorrect and not even geometrical, so that geometers need not trouble to refute it.[12]

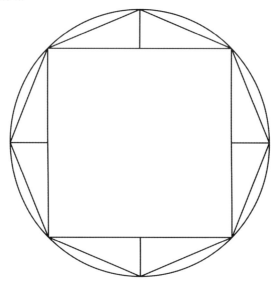

Fortunately we have two (slightly differing) accounts of his proof. (1) Inside the given circle, construct a square all of whose corners touch the circle. Between each pair of successive points there is an arc which is one-quarter of the circle. (2) From the center of each side of the square construct a straight line perpendicular to the side of the square and extending to the circle. 3) Draw straight lines from the point where the line meets the circle to the nearest corners of the square. We now have an octagon inscribed in the circle. Repeat the procedure in steps (2) and (3) to get a figure of 16 sides inscribed in the circle. Each time we do this we get a polygon with twice as many sides as the previous one and each time we do so the resulting polygon is closer to filling the square. There is also a theorem in geometry that shows how to construct a square equal in area to any polygon,[13] so if we ever reach the point where we have a polygon that coincides with the circle, we can apply the theorem to determine the size of the square equal in area to the circle.

Now it is a fact that if we carry out this procedure enough times we can get as close as we like to a polygon that has the same area as the circle, but we can never, using this procedure, reach the point where a polygon (which has straight sides) coincides with the circle (which is everywhere curved). Clearly Aristotle was correct to criticize Antiphon from a mathematical point of view.

But it is worth recalling that Protagoras said that a circle does not touch a straight line at a point (as geometry would have it) but in a (short) line.[14] And although this is not true for the perfectly straight lines and perfectly round circles that are the subjects of geometry, which have no thickness and so do not exist in the physical world, it is true for the (approximately) straight lines and circles with which we actually work. And so Antiphon's method works well enough for practical purposes, just as Protagoras was correct in what he said. Whether Antiphon had this response ready or actually believed that it was geometrically possible to construct a polygon equal in area to the circle is unknown, but one thing that is safe to say is that geometry had progressed considerably between the time Antiphon made this suggestion (i.e., sometime before his death in 411) and when Aristotle composed his *Physics*, presumably at least 60 years later. This makes it possible that Aristotle's (correct) complaint about Antiphon's method was a matter of blaming him for not knowing something that was unknown in his time.

Other testimonials have to do with a discarded bed. In commenting on the unusual word *embios* (a compound of the preposition *en* ("in") and the noun *bios* ("life") that means "having life") Harpocration quotes Antiphon as follows: "the rotting of wood might become *embios*." Fortunately Aristotle gives some context for Antiphon's statement.

> Antiphon states that if someone were to bury a bed and the rot that remained acquired the capacity to send up a shoot, it would become wood, not a bed.[15]

> Also a human is born from a human but not a bed from a bed. This is why they say that not the shape but the wood is its nature, because if it were to sprout it would become wood, not a bed.[16]

This is a typical example of Aristotle's use of the ideas of earlier thinkers in developing his own philosophical views. (Here he is making the distinction between form and matter.) The Aristotelian commentators elaborated this statement further, as in this representative passage.

> As Aristotle stated in the first book of the *Physics* using the example of a bed, if it is buried and acquires the power to send up a shoot, wood (which was its substrate) is sprouted from it, not a bed (which was its form).[17]

Here Alexander (second to third centuries CE) uses the same example as Aristotle and goes on to explain it in Aristotelian terminology (here "substrate" – i.e., its matter – and "form"). Others went farther, thus Proclus (fifth century CE) –

> Some of the ancients like Antiphon called matter "nature."[18]

– as if he had the conceptions of matter and nature that were first employed by Aristotle. These testimonia reveal some of the problems that must be faced in attempting to recover the views and theories of thinkers (including all the Sophists) whose ideas have been transmitted and in many cases distorted by later interpreters over the course of centuries.

More clear are the fragments in which Antiphon reflects on human life.

> In my opinion, education is the most important element in human life, since when one starts anything correctly – no matter what – it is likely that the end will turn out right too. Just as whatever kind of seed one plants in the ground, this is what we must expect the fruit to be. And when one plants a noble education in a young body, this lives and flourishes throughout the whole of life and neither rain nor drought can take it away.
>
> (Antiphon B60 DK)

> Living is like service on a day-watch and a lifetime is like a single day, during which, after gazing upwards at the light we entrust it to others who come next. (Antiphon B50 DK).

> The whole of life is amazingly easy to complain about, my friend, since it contains nothing that is special, important or serious, but only things that are unimportant, feeble, short-lived and involve great suffering.
>
> (Antiphon B51 DK)

> You can't take back your life like a move in a game.
>
> (Antiphon B52 DK)

> People enjoy working and saving, struggling and adding to what they have, as you would expect them to, but when they subtract from it and use it, they suffer as if they were losing their own flesh.
>
> (Antiphon B53 DK)[19]

By contrast, book 1 of *On Truth*, contains provocative and difficult to interpret ideas about human matters. The three surviving fragments were found by chance in Egypt, the remains of papyrus scrolls that had been buried in the desert sand for over two millennia. The relevant parts of the scrolls contain many lines with missing letters and words, making interpretation difficult, and certainty about the place of the content of these fragments in the overall strategy of *On Truth* impossible. Antiphon's well-known interest in antilogic compounds is the impossibility. Even so, what survives is fascinating and deeply involved in central issues in late fifth-century Athens, in particular the discussion concerning the concepts of *nomos* and *phusis*. These texts are translated in the Appendix of Translated Texts and discussed below in Chapter 12.

Notes

1. Morrison 1961.
2. The case for a single Antiphon is made by Gagarin (2002, 37–38), and adopted by Laks-Most (2016, 2) Pendrick (2002, 1–26)) argues for the alternative view.
3. These speeches are translated in DG.
4. See Gagarin (2002), 178–181.
5. There is a report that our Antiphon (or, as I think very likely, someone else with the same name) set up a kind of counselling clinic in Corinth where he treated distressed people by talking, asking what caused their unhappiness and consoling them. (pseudo-Plutarch, *Lives of the Ten Orators* 883C–D)
6. Gagarin 2002 convincingly argues for this view.
7. See above p.111 for a similar story told about Protagoras and Pericles. It seems that this story was well known, at least in outline, and it is likely that Antiphon utilised it because it was well known and he explored some of the issues it raises more fully than had previously been done.
8. This and similar information are found in the second century CE *Lexicon* of Harpocration.
9. Parmenides, fragment 15 DK.
10. Galen, *On Medical Names* 34.9–38. This test is preserved only in an Arabic text. The present translation is slightly modified from Pendrick 2002.
11. See above, p.54.
12. Aristotle, *Physics* 184a14–17.
13. Euclid, *Elements* book 2, proposition 14.
14. See above, p.34.
15. Aristotle, *Physics* 193a12–14.
16. Aristotle, *Physics* 193b8–11.
17. Alexander, *Commentary on Aristotle's Metaphysics* 357.16–21. Similar accounts are found in other ancient commentaries on Aristotle's *Physics*.
18. Proclus, *Commentary on Plato's Timaeus* 1.10.5–6.
19. A longer and equally downbeat fragment on the nature of married life is included in the Appendix of Translated Texts, pp. 177–8.

5
HIPPIAS OF ELIS

Hippias was a member of the second generation of Sophists, probably born between 460 and 440. As is the case with Prodicus, we have no information about how long he lived but a remark in Plato's *Apology*[1] indicates that both Sophists were still alive in 399. He was born in Elis, the district of the Peloponnese in which the Olympic festival took place, and he represented Elis on official diplomatic missions to other cities, most frequently Sparta, but visited Athens comparatively rarely. Very little of his work is left and we are more dependent on Plato for information about him than we are for other Sophists. He appears in three Platonic dialogues, the *Protagoras* and two that are named after him (*Greater Hippias* and *Lesser Hippias* – so-called because the first is longer than the second). His portrayal in these works is consistent and for reasons given above[2] I believe it can be taken as generally accurate, allowing for some caricature and exaggeration, and even though Plato seems not to take Hippias very seriously, the information he provides, together with what we learn from other sources, indicates that Hippias was unique among the Sophists for his intellectual breadth and for the number of different fields to which he made important contributions.

In the *Protagoras* he is one of three Sophists present, each portrayed as having his own distinct interests and personality.[3] Not only Protagoras but Prodicus and Hippias too are initially shown each with his own coterie of followers. Hippias' group are asking "both about nature and some astronomical questions about things in the heaven." Protagoras chides the other Sophists for abusing their students, "steering them back again, against their will, into subjects from which they have fled, teaching them arithmetic, astronomy, geometry, music[4], and poetry" (318e).[5] (As Plato puts it, at this point Protagoras gave Hippias a look.) In addition to proving that there was no single standard curriculum for the Sophists, this passage gives us a sense of the competition for students in which the Sophists engaged.

An amusing passage of the *Lesser Hippias* (368b–e) portrays him vividly as a polymath whose range of learning goes well beyond the other Sophists, extending to epic and tragic poetry, prose writing, poetic meters, musical theory and correct spelling. To this list of subjects, we may also add painting, sculpture, genealogy and history as well as the mathematical disciplines mentioned above. The same passage informs us that he boasted of having made a spectacular appearance at Olympia wearing nothing that he had not made himself, including an engraved ring, a signet seal, an oil bottle and his clothing: leather sandals, a woven cloak and tunic and a fancy plaited Persian-style belt. (This is not to suggest that he taught his students these manual skills.) His memory was phenomenal — he boasted that he could repeat a list of fifty names after hearing it only once – and he taught memory techniques as part of his curriculum. Like other leading Sophists he traveled widely and earned a great deal of money from his teaching and from renditions of his performance pieces. One of these pieces included a discussion of "many things of all sorts about both other poets and about Homer."[6] He made a name for himself by speaking at the Olympic festival on a range of prepared topics and like Gorgias he offered to answer any question anyone might put to him.

Hippias contributed to astronomy, and attempted to count the stars in the Hyades star cluster. He was an accomplished mathematician as shown by a significant contribution he made in geometry. One of three problems that were of deep concern to ancient mathematicians was the problem of finding a procedure to trisect any given angle.[7] The curve still known as the quadratrix of Hippias can do this and later on was employed in attempts to square the circle (to construct a square equal in area to a given circle), which was another such problem.[8] It was proved in the nineteenth century that none of these problems could be solved by the techniques available in Euclidean geometry. But this does not mean that Hippias was wrong. Euclid (ca. 300 BCE) limited his geometry essentially to the study of figures that can be constructed only with the use of a straight-edge and a compass – that is, by drawing certain kinds of lines (straight lines and circles), whereas the quadratics of Hippias was conceived in a different way – as the locus of points that satisfy certain conditions. It is of course not certain that it was Hippias who discovered this curve or its properties: the Pythagorean theorem was known to Babylonian mathematicians over 1000 years before Pythagoras lived. However, there are other ways to trisect angles that a clever person like Hippias with some mathematical interests could have conceivably discovered in his time[9] and it is a real possibility that there was a reason for associating Hippias with a solution to that problem.

He compiled the first list of Olympic victors, which was an important contribution to chronology and historiography. According to tradition, the Olympic festival was first held in 776 and was celebrated every four years, thus providing a way of dating events that could be used throughout Greece, for example, the third year of the forty-seventh Olympiad. In some sense this achievement made historical investigation possible, since each city-state had its own calendar and it would be virtually impossible in the absence of any standard reference system to correlate events that took place in different cities in the same month or even in the same year. He made a catalogue of the kings of Sparta, which he presented at Sparta in a performance speech. This catalog was also useful for historical study since the Spartans had two kings simultaneously and they designated years by the regnal year of one or both kings and so Hippias' catalog would have been essential for correlating Spartan accounts of history with those of other cities. He also wrote a work entitled *The Names of Peoples*, which too could have been useful for historical research.

In addition he did pioneering work in intellectual history, claiming to be the first to collect passages of poets and philosophers, which he probably grouped under various headings. The following is his own description of this work.

> Some of these things may have been said by Orpheus, some by Musaeus – in short, in different places by different authors – some by Hesiod, Homer, or other poets and some in prose works by Greeks or foreigners. From all of them I have collected the most important ones that are related, and I will compose out of them this original and multiform account.
>
> (Hippias, fragment 6 DK)

It is hard to underestimate the importance of this collection. The writings of earlier thinkers have entirely disappeared, so that our knowledge of the beginnings of philosophical, scientific and theological speculation among Greek intellectuals before Plato is limited to reports about them and verbatim quotations from them that are found in the surviving writings of later authors. In antiquity there were but few authors who acknowledged their sources, so it is impossible to say how much of the information we possess about the early Greek thinkers is due to Hippias either directly or indirectly. His practice was followed by Aristotle and some of his students, to whom we owe a great deal of our information. Examples of information reported to have come from Hippias are the statements that Thales (early sixth century) believed that amber possesses soul, and that Mamercus, the brother of Thales' contemporary the poet Stesichorus, studied geometry.

He composed speeches like the one he describes in the *Greater Hippias*, which he says made a great impression on the Spartans when he delivered it there. One of these speeches was set after the fall of Troy.

> I have a speech that I put together really finely, and I put the words particularly well. My setting and the starting point of the speech are something like this. "After Troy was taken, the tale is told that Neoptolemus asked Nestor what sort of activities are fine – the sort of activities that would make someone most famous if he adopted them while young." After that, the speaker is Nestor, who teaches him very many very fine customs (*Greater Hippias* 286a–b, Hackett tr. slightly modified).

This work appears to have been a moralizing discourse whose theme resembles Prodicus' *Choice of Heracles*.[10] Where Prodicus' essay concerns a figure of mythology, Hippias takes his theme from the legendary past. Neoptolemus was the son of Achilles, the greatest warrior in the Trojan War, and instead of two goddesses offering opposing views of the good life, as in Prodicus' account, Nestor, the wise and aged adviser of the Greek army, we may suppose, counsels the young man in the ways to live and act that will make him respected and honored in his city. Both Sophists, that is, so far from advocating an immoral life or a system of values contrary to traditional beliefs, will have been reinforcing the *status quo*.

A passage in Plato is suggestive of Hippias' winning ways. It occurs at the dramatic moment in the *Protagoras* described above (p.26). It is Hippias who finally convinces Socrates and Protagoras to continue their conversation, as follows:

> I therefore implore and counsel you, Protagoras and Socrates, to be reconciled and to compromise, under our arbitration, as it were, on some middle course. You, Socrates, must not insist on that precise, excessively brief form of discussion if it does not suit Protagoras, but rather allow free rein to the speeches, so that they might communicate to us more impressively and elegantly. And you, Protagoras, must not let out full sail in the wind and leave the land behind to disappear into the sea of rhetoric. Both of you must steer a middle course. So that's what you shall do, and take my advice and choose a referee or moderator or supervisor who will monitor for you the length of your speeches.
>
> (Plato, Protagoras 337e–338b)

I take it that this model of diplomacy is the kind of speech Hippias was known for. It is brief and to the point, beginning by capturing the interest and favor of his audience, with whom he identifies himself. It raises Hippias above the dispute with an appeal to the circumstances of the conversation. It does not favor one side over the other, but makes a constructive proposal, instructing (not merely suggesting) the disputants to compromise and appoint a neutral referee to keep order. We can see why he was chosen so often to represent the relatively powerless district of Elis in negotiations with Sparta and other powerful states.

Hippias also contributed to the *nomos-phusis* debate (for which see Chapter 12, especially p.12.7–10). Evidence for this comes from Xenophon[11] as well as Plato. Xenophon reports a conversation that took place between Hippias and Socrates, in the course of which Hippias asserts that laws are "what the citizens have recorded after agreement about what they ought to do and what they ought to refrain from." This amounts to the view that members of a society are bound together by what is known as a social contract (or compact), and is perhaps the earliest formulation of the basis of this theory.[12]

The prominence in Hippias' speech of the contrast between *nomos* and *phusis* that was so widespread in discussions of moral, social and political issues in the late fifth century suggests that this topic was particularly associated with Hippias. Some scholars take it as evidence that Hippias was the first to draw the distinction.

Despite these substantial achievements, Plato presents him alone among the Sophists as a proud, pretentious, self-advertising fellow who is out of his depth in a philosophical conversation. How fair an assessment is this? First his vanity.

Aristotle provides an interesting perspective on this matter in his discussion of the virtues in the *Nicomachean Ethics*. Some of the virtues he describes are not what we would expect. Pride (the deadliest of the traditional seven "Christian" deadly sins) for example, is for Aristotle a virtue. Proud people think themselves worthy of great things and are in fact worthy of them,[13] whereas vain people think themselves worthy of great things but are unworthy of them. Elsewhere[14] Aristotle contrasts the vices of boastfulness (where people claim to be better than they are) and mock-modesty (claiming less) with the praiseworthy virtue of truthfulness (which includes among other things owning to what you are, neither more nor less). On this account Hippias would have not the vice of mock-modesty but the virtues of pride and truthfulness. However, Aristotle does add to his account of truthfulness that truthful people tend to understate the truth, for this seems in better taste because exaggerations are coarse and tiresome, and this may be a fair description of Hippias.

Second, philosophy. In the matter of definition Hippias shows himself to be not on same level as Gorgias or Prodicus.[15] The *Greater Hippias* is devoted to the question "what is the *kalon* (beautiful, good, fine)?" Hippias is uncertain what Socrates is asking, and asks in turn, "Doesn't the person who asks this want to find out what is a *kalon* thing?" When Socrates replies that he wants to know what is *the kalon*, Hippias asks "What's the difference?" When Socrates repeats his question, Hippias, to Socrates' disappointment, says "A *kalon* girl is a *kalon* thing." This is not a paradigm definition of the type given by Gorgias, where it is possible to use the given case as a basis for generalizing to cover other kinds of things. There is no way to move to an understanding of beauty as it applies not only to girls but also to sunsets, symphonies and everything else that is beautiful. Throughout the dialogue Hippias fails to get the point and in the end he fights back, describing Socrates' careful and precise questioning as "scrapings and clippings of speeches divided up into bits." And he goes on to state what is really *kalon* in a manner fully in accord with the goals of Protagoras' teaching:

> ... to be able to make a speech well and finely, in a court or in the Council or any other authority for which the speech is destined, to convince them and depart with not the smallest but the greatest of prizes, the successful defense of yourself, your property, and your friends. A person should keep to that. He should give up all this hair-splitting, lest he be thought a total fool for pursuing useless nonsense as he is now." (Plato, Protagoras 304a–b)

It is unsurprising if Hippias was not well versed in philosophical discussion of the Socratic variety and that he could be made to look stupid by the person who had advanced the methods and standards of abstract discussions to an unprecedented level. But this does not mean that Hippias was intellectually valueless in his own time nor does it detract from the importance of the contributions he made to the broad variety of fields we have seen.

Notes

1. Plato, *Apology* 19e.
2. Pp. 17–18.
3. The scene in which the three Sophists are introduced (*Protagoras* 314e–317e) is translated in the Appendix of Translated Texts, pp. 154–6.
4. *Mousikē*, frequently translated as "music," primarily designates poetry performed to music, as was the case with performances of Homer's *Iliad* and *Odyssey*.
5. Hippias' interest in these subjects is reaffirmed at *Lesser Hippias* 363a–368a.
6. Plato, *Lesser Hippias* 363c.
7. That is, to discover a method for finding an angle equal to one-third of a given angle. Bisecting an angle (finding an angle equal to one-half of a given angle) is an elementary matter, but trisection is not so easy. In fact, Hippias' method of trisection can be easily extended to find angles equal to any fractional part of a given angle.
8. The third problem was known as the Delian problem or "duplicating the cube": to construct a cube whose volume is double the volume of a given cube.
9. Reasonable attempts to reconstruct Hippias' method of trisecting an angle that can be understood by anyone with a knowledge of elementary plane geometry are easily found on the internet.
10. Xenophon's summary of this work is included in the Appendix of Translated Texts, pp. 178–80.
11. Xenophon, *Memorabilia* 4.4.14.
12. Despite Xenophon's assertion that "I know that [Socrates] once discussed with Hippias these kinds of issues concerning justice" (*Memorabilia* 4.4.5) it is not at all certain that this conversation took place, but instead was Xenophon's invention.
13. Aristotle, *Nicomachean Ethics* 4.3.
14. *Nicomachean Ethics* 4.7.
15. See below, Chapter 10.

6
PRODICUS OF CEOS

Prodicus was a contemporary of Hippias, one of the principal members of the "second generation" of Sophists, after Protagoras, Gorgias and Antiphon. He is one of the three Sophists present in Plato's *Protagoras* and the mention of him together with Gorgias and Hippias in the *Apology* suggests that he was still alive in 399.[1] He was born on the island of Ceos (modern Kea or Tzia) around 460 BCE. Like Protagoras, Gorgias and Hippias, Prodicus was highly respected and represented his native land on political and diplomatic missions. He visited Athens frequently,[2] where he was widely known and respected long before Plato began to write. Of the Sophists present in the *Protagoras* Socrates singles out him alone as "all wise."[3] Like most other Sophists[4] Prodicus gave presentations of his work for which he charged admission fees. These presentations took place in public settings, such as the Lyceum,[5] which was a large public area just east of the city wall, containing a gymnasium which was a favorite hangout of Socrates and many others. He also lectured and taught in private settings.[6] Like other known Sophists he taught young men and charged fees for his instruction. In fact, he was reputedly very fond of money, charging the surprisingly large sum of 50 drachmas to hear him present a certain well-known performance speech.[7]

To judge by his portrayal in Plato's *Protagoras*, he liked to draw attention to himself and was a popular enough teacher to attract listeners away from Protagoras and Hippias. He also had a lively sense of humor and was ready to contribute to a joke. He did not miss an opportunity to join in a discussion even if he did not have anything very specific to contribute.

Prodicus' intervention in the *Protagoras* is the firmest evidence that the portrayals of all three Sophists present in the dialogue, and in particular their speeches at 333d–334c and 337a–338b, were based in reality.[8] Among the speakers who attempted to persuade Protagoras and Socrates to continue their conversation

Prodicus stands out as saying things that appear pedantic and are only vaguely related to this pressing matter.

> [337a] [Those present] should be common but not equal, for one should listen to both speakers in common but not distribute equal honor to each.... You should agree to argue with each other about your claims, [337b] but not to quarrel, because friends argue with friends, even with good will, while those who differ and are hostile quarrel with each other. [It is best if speakers] gain esteem from the audience, but are not praised. For gaining esteem is from the souls of the listeners without deceit, but being praised is often in the words of those who lie, contrary to their opinions. ...
>
> (Plato, *Protagoras* 337a–b)

The same points could have been made more simply by saying (for example) that Socrates and Prodicus should discuss with goodwill and without hostility.

This original and striking practice of drawing distinctions and defining the terms involved was easy to parody, and as Plato presents it there seems to be no useful purpose behind it. But it is not difficult to show that it had a serious purpose indeed, one that Plato recognized and that has had lasting importance in philosophy and elsewhere.[9]

Prodicus was remembered chiefly for three things: drawing fine distinctions in the meanings of words, his views on the origin of religious belief, which led some to call him an atheist, and a performance speech about Heracles, implicitly recommending a life of virtue rather than pleasure. In addition, there is evidence that he developed a theory about the nature of the physical world.

Prodicus on the Origin of Religious Belief

Numerous ancient sources declare that Prodicus was an atheist. Here is the evidence.

1 Epicurus objected to the total madness of those who eliminated the divine from the things that are, as in book 12 of *On Nature* he objects to Prodicus, Diagoras, Critias and others, declaring that they are deranged and mad, and he compares them with Bacchic revelers, admonishing them not to trouble or disturb us. And indeed by changing the letters they emend the names of the gods. (Philodemus, *On Piety* 1, *PHerc* 1077, fr. 19.519–41)
2 Some who have thought about god's existence declare that there is a god and others that there is not, and still others that god no more is than is not.... Those who are labeled atheists hold that there is no god – such as Euhemerus ... and Diagoras of Melos, Prodicus of Ceos, Theodorus, and very many others.... Prodicus held that what was beneficial for life had been supposed to be a god – like the sun, moon, rivers and lakes, fields, fruits of the earth and everything of this kind. (Sextus Empiricus, *Against the Mathematicians* 9.50–52)

3 He declared that the gods worshiped by humans neither exist nor know, but that they are what the people of old, in astonishment... (Philodemus, *On Piety* 2, *PHerc* 1428, fr. 19)
4 It is clear that Persaeus is really eliminating and abolishing the divine, or that he knows nothing about it, when in his work *On Gods* he says that what was written by Prodicus does not appear implausible – that things that nourish and benefit were first to be considered gods and to be so honored, and subsequently the people who discovered food or shelter and crafts as well, as Demeter, Dionysus and the Dioscuri. (Philodemus, *On Piety* 2, *PHerc* 1428, cols. ii 28–iii 13)
5 ... we will mix into our words the wisdom of Prodicus, who connects all sacred rites of humans and mysteries and festivals and institutions to the goods of farming, thinking that even the conception of gods came to humans from here and so securing all piety. (Themistius, *Oration* 30, 349a–b, Mayhew tr.)
6 Prodicus of Ceos declared that the ancients worshiped the sun, the moon, rivers and springs, and generally everything that benefits our life, because of the benefits we receive from them, as the Egyptians worship the Nile. And this is why bread is worshiped as Demeter, wine as Dionysus, water as Poseidon, fire as Hephaestus, and just so for everything that can be put to good use. (Sextus Empiricus, *Against the Mathematicians* 9.18)
7 What about Prodicus of Ceos, who claimed that the things that benefit human life are numbered among the gods? What religion did he leave room for? (Cicero, *On the Nature of the Gods* 1.118)
8 Prodicus calls the four elements [sc. fire, air, water and earth] gods, and also the sun and the moon, for he said that what is conducive to life belongs to everything because of these. (Epiphanius, *Panarion* 3:507 Hall)
9 Prodicus says that those who in their wandering benefited the interests of humans by means of newly discovered crops were elevated to the status of gods. (Minucius Felix, *Octavius* 21, Mayhew tr.)

Some of these texts display confusion, most notably the claim in text 3 that the gods worshiped by humans neither exist nor know, which appears hardly more sensible than if I were to say that I do not have a brother and he has no hair. Texts 1, 2 and 3 are the only ones that straightforwardly state that Prodicus denied that gods (or the gods worshiped by humans) exist. The remaining texts associate him with particular views on the origin of beliefs in gods. In fact all the texts except for texts 1–3 point to an account of the origin of belief in gods and of their worship stemming from the recognition that the world has features advantageous to humans. Texts 4 and 5 clearly assert this. Text 3 breaks off, but may have continued along the same lines as these others, to the effect that the gods worshiped by humans are just the things that people of old deified in astonishment at the benefits they conferred. Text 6 with its reference to "the ancients" is probably another expression of this idea, which texts 7 through 9, speaking of things that benefit human life, support as well.

In evaluating this material we need to observe the obvious but easily overlooked distinction between believing in God and holding beliefs about the origin of religious belief in general. Jews, Christians and Muslims believe in one God but they recognize that the people who lived before these "peoples of the Book" held other religious beliefs that were not based on revelation. A Jew, Christian or Muslim speculating about the origins of earlier religious beliefs might well make the kind of guesses that we find in Prodicus without being charged with atheism.

For this reason I believe that Prodicus' views on the origin of religious belief do not necessarily reveal anything about his own attitude towards the divine. (This is not to deny that he may have been an atheist, although atheism was rare in ancient Greek lands.) It is also significant that the reliability of the sources of most of these texts is suspect. The earliest reference to his atheism, in Epicurus (cited in text 1), is part of a smear campaign with little historical value. Epicurus and his followers attacked ideas of rival philosophers and philosophical schools in order to show the superiority of their own philosophy. Their attacks were not always fair or faithful to the thought of their opponents, most of whom (being dead) were not in a position to reply. Later sources may have taken their cue from Philodemus, an Epicurean philosopher of the first century BCE, or Cicero, Philodemus's well-known contemporary. Texts 1, 3 and 4 are taken from polemical texts of Epicurus and Philodemus. Cicero was not an Epicurean but text 7 is taken from a speech in Cicero's *On the Nature of the Gods* that is influenced by Philodemus and spoken by an enthusiastic and prejudiced Epicurean who makes wild and distorted accusations against many Greek philosophers. It is obviously wrong to suppose without further ado that someone does not believe in any god simply because she holds that belief in gods originated from noticing that certain features of the natural world seem to have been designed for the advantage of humans. But such mistakes happen often enough. In any case reasoning like this does not establish the truth of its conclusion.

Leaving the question of Prodicus's atheism aside, the testimonia cited above make it possible to situate him in a discussion of the nature of the divine and the origin of religious belief that went back to Protagoras[10] and further. Certain earlier Presocratic philosophers[11] cast doubt on the existence of the Olympian gods worshiped by the Greeks while believing in the divine. And even if it is true that Prodicus believed that the sun and moon and some things related to farming are divine, that should be enough to show that he is not an atheist, only that he did not worship the Olympian gods worshiped by the Greeks. Indeed, it does not even show this much. Text 7 says that "things that benefit human life" are gods, but not that they are the only gods. Given the nature of Greek polytheism and the practice of introducing the worship of new gods even as late as Prodicus' time, it is conceivable and I think highly probable that Prodicus attended religious celebrations of the Olympian gods along with the rest of the populace.

Heracles' choice

We are fortunate to have a long extract from a performance speech of Prodicus which was known and admired in antiquity.[12] It is found in a work of Xenophon, a younger contemporary of Prodicus, who may actually have heard the speech and/or have had a copy of it to refer to. In a work known as the *Memoirs of Socrates*[13] Xenophon introduces it at a point where Socrates is recommending a life of virtue in a conversation with Aristippus who favors a life of pleasure. The first sentence of the passage refers explicitly to "Prodicus the wise in his treatise on Heracles, which he performed for very many people" and says that he "presents his views on virtue … speaking something like this, as far as I remember." This indicates that Xenophon has not transcribed Prodicus' speech, but that he has made an effort to report the contents of the speech and perhaps even Prodicus' style. Philostratus (third century CE), the author of biographies of the Sophists, supports this interpretation, saying that he will not take the trouble to describe Prodicus' language since Xenophon has done such a good job. Although we have no way of knowing how much of Prodicus' famous speech Xenophon reports, what he gives us is precious evidence for the content and style of the speech, from which we can make inferences about the moral beliefs and attitudes of his intended audience.

The theme is one we can understand. Adolescents need to make life choices, and among the most important are the choice of what kind of person they want to be and what they want most out of life. Money? Pleasure? Fame? Honor? Power? Esteem? A happy family? Friendship? Achievement? Prodicus depicts Heracles at this critical moment. He conveniently overlooks the traditional story that Heracles did not choose to endure his famous labors, but was compelled to do so as punishment for a terrible crime he committed during a period of temporary insanity. Instead, he shows him as an adolescent who did not know what he would become, deliberating alone about his future, not asking the advice of family or friends. He is presented as making a choice between a life of virtue and one of vice.

During his deliberations he is approached by two female figures, later identified as personifications of Virtue and Vice, who take turns describing the two lives. The appearance and behavior of the two women correspond (according to the standards Prodicus supposes his audience accepts) to the lives they champion. Vice speaks first, promising a life of pleasure (not of vice). She later says that her friends (those who follow her) call her Happiness (*eudaimonia*), while those who hate her call her Vice. Now *eudaimonia* sounds like a reasonable goal in life; Aristotle would declare that everyone wants it and that it is the only thing that is desired for itself and only for itself. Aristotle goes on to conclude that *eudaimonia* consists in a life of virtuous activity. So there needs to be nothing bad about adopting *eudaimonia* as one's life goal. But, as he recognizes, different people have different views of what *eudaimonia* consists in, and one of the most commonly held views is that it consists in pleasure. Prodicus' Vice promises Heracles a carefree life, without civic responsibilities or work but full of the pleasures of the senses. But such a life requires resources and Vice promises Heracles that he will get what he needs for his pleasures from the work of others and by doing whatever it takes to profit.

Virtue (who, in her modesty, never names herself) next promises Heracles a life of labor and diligence in whatever he does. She gives a list of possibilities: if you want the gods to be gracious to you, you must worship them, if you want to be admired by your friends, you must do good to them, if you want the land to produce plentiful crops, you must tend the earth, etc. She does not say that a virtuous life consists in engaging in all these activities: one need not be a farmer, a livestock breeder and a warrior too, and Heracles himself did not do everything Virtue mentions. But it is certain that some of the things mentioned would normally be considered necessary ingredients of a virtuous life: correct behavior towards the gods, one's friends and one's city.

Next come the rebuttals, as is appropriate in a debate at which each both competitors aim to win by making the strongest possible case for their respective sides and showing the weak points in the opposition – the kind of debate ("antilogic") at which the Sophists trained their students to excel.[14] Vice has little to say, simply pointing out that the life of virtue is a long and difficult path to enjoyment (*euphrosunē*), while her own life is a short and easy path to happiness. These are important practical considerations, since many people do not want to spend their lives in hard labor, and instead prefer to take an easier way. On the other hand, it is interesting that even Vice recognizes that ultimately the life of virtue can bring enjoyment.

Virtue's rebuttal is much longer and falls into two parts. First, she objects that the life of sensory pleasure is not as pleasant as it is cracked up to be. She abuses Vice as an outcast from the gods who is dishonored by good people, who have done nothing to be proud of, is untrustworthy and shunned, and she describes the sordid old age of those who choose vice instead of virtue. Second, she describes herself and the life of those who follow her in pointed contrast to what she has just said about Vice. Virtue concludes by saying that Heracles, whom she earlier described as having the potential for greatness, is capable of achieving the most blessed happiness (*eudaimonia* again) through a life of hard work.

Even if we assume that the text as it stands is faithful to Prodicus, it invites several questions of interpretation. Two things are noticeable: it does not reveal the choice that Heracles made, and it is unclear whether it is meant to recommend that those who hear the speech should choose one path rather than the other. Of course the audience knew perfectly well about the labors of Heracles, that his life was one of great effort and that after his death he is one of those who "do not lie forgotten without honor, but flourish remembered, celebrated in song for all time" exactly as Virtue promises. But to bring this into Prodicus' speech would undermine its effectiveness, which consists in presenting Heracles *before* his choice, with the two very different lives, each with its own advantages and disadvantages, both short-term and long-term, laid out before him more clearly than most of us facing a corresponding choice about our own future ever see them. And this is why

Prodicus does not preach for either life – he encourages us all to think for ourselves and make our own choices. On the other hand, that Prodicus favors the virtuous life as he describes it is obvious enough from Virtue's second speech. Eating, drinking and having sex in moderation bring pleasure without the pain and discomfort that comes from excess; the life of idle luxury brings cares and expenses; still worse, the life of vice brings disrepute and distrust; and worst of all, the long-term prospect of such a life is a miserable old age – whereas a life of effort and virtue brings the opposite: all kinds of pleasures unmixed with pain, including not only the bodily pleasures but also the pleasure that comes from knowing that you have the love and respect of others, from satisfaction at your accomplishments and from the sure belief that you will be remembered favorably after your death.

Where Vice promises an easy and short path to happiness, Virtue offers the possibility (not the certainty) of achieving "the most blessed happiness" through a life of hard work, thus claiming that the happiness she has in mind is superior to that which Vice promises. Aristotle acknowledges that there are different ideas about what constitutes a happy life, but does Virtue recognize the life of Vice to be happy at all? Does her offer of "the most blessed happiness" imply that there are other kinds of happiness, perhaps even including Vice's life of pleasure, or does "most blessed" mean that hers is the only life that brings happiness? I am inclined to think that the former view is correct. If you say that you are happy with a life that would make me miserable, who am I to say that you aren't happy? I might point out that if you keep going like that you will have a miserable old age or that you are taking risks that could lead to great harm or future unhappiness, and to say that your life wouldn't make me happy, but if you continue to say that you are happy as you are, it is not easy to prove that you are mistaken. And if you get away with it – if you live to a ripe old age and do not suffer any bad consequences of your lifestyle (think of all the heavy smokers who never suffer the ill effects associated with smoking) – how can I say that you were wrong?

To judge that one notion of happiness is superior to another requires taking some distance from both and judging them according to the same criteria – something that goes beyond one person saying that happiness consists in sensory pleasure and another saying that it consists in hard work. This is what Virtue does in her rebuttal, pointing out that the happiness Vice recommends involves discomfort, pain, being despised and distrusted by others, and so on, whereas the life of virtue does not involve any of these disadvantages and it brings some advantages that Vice cannot promise. In such a discussion it would be open to Vice to offer a different set of criteria that favor her own conception of happiness (perhaps that intense but brief pleasure is all that counts, regardless of its consequences), and to remain unconvinced. In any case, the point of the debate in Prodicus' speech is not to convince Vice to change her ways, but to convince Heracles to make the right choice, and the purpose of Prodicus's speech is presumably to encourage his audience to think about the criteria of happiness set out by Virtue, to recognize their importance, and to act accordingly.

This was a performance speech meant to be presented before an audience. He gave it in order to make money, acquire students and increase his fame (not necessarily in that order). These would be strong reasons for him not to offend against the views he could expect his audience to share. And in fact there is nothing in the speech to cause offense – no suggestion that he is promoting the life recommended by Vice, no subversive ideas or challenges to traditional morality, nothing that parents would not encourage their children (potential students of Prodicus) to learn.

To those of us who are used to questioning traditional views the speech may appear banal and trite, but its contemporary fame and the enthusiastic reception it received at least until the nineteenth century should caution us from dismissing its value out of hand. Finally, in evaluating it we need to bear in mind that it is perhaps the earliest surviving work which brings to the fore the stark contrast between the lives of virtue and of vice,[15] sets out the pros and cons of pursuing each and presents positive and plausible reasons for choosing the one over the other.

The Physical World

The earliest surviving references to Prodicus are found in two comedies by Aristophanes: *Clouds* (produced in 423 BCE and revised between then and 417) and *Birds* (produced in 414). Prodicus is not presented as a character in either play, but it is clear from the way his name is used that he was well known in Athens and he held views about the nature of the cosmos to which the plays allude.

In *Clouds* he is called a "meteorosophist" – a word evidently coined by Aristophanes that identifies him as a Sophist and also as someone who investigates *ta meteōra* "the things up in the air" – a phrase used to refer to the heavenly bodies as well as weather and other atmospheric phenomena. Aristophanes is evidently identifying Prodicus as someone celebrated for his wisdom and intelligence, who investigates the mysteries of nature, just like Socrates, who first appears in the same play suspended in a basket high above the earth in order better to observe the heavens.

Likewise in *Birds* he is mentioned once, in the following passage, spoken by the chorus of birds.

> Harken men, by nature living in darkness, with all the nobility of fallen leaves, helpless, moulded from clay, shadow-like feeble race, wingless ephemeral things, wretched mortals, dream-like men, turn your mind to us, we who are immortals, who exist always, who live in the air, who never age, with imperishable counsels, you'll hear from us everything that is correct concerning what is on high: the nature of birds and the genesis of gods and rivers and Erebus and Chaos, and once you know what's correct, you may tell Prodicus from me to weep for the rest of his days.[16]

It is disputed how much these references tell us about the "meteorosophistic" theories Prodicus actually held. Some have claimed that his theories must have resembled the bird's account, which goes on for another thirty lines recounting the origin of the world out of Chaos and Night, how birds were the first living creatures, older even than the Olympian gods, and how birds bestow the most important things upon mortals. The birds' account is a spoof of Hesiod's presentation of the origin of things, written centuries earlier, and with all its humor it is not intended to be taken at all seriously. It is not the kind of account that intellectuals were composing in the late fifth century, and I believe that it provides no basis for imagining what Prodicus' account might have contained.

"It Is Impossible to Contradict"

This assertion is attributed to Prodicus by an author known as Didymus the Blind (fourth century CE). Since it resonates with so-called Protagorean relativism[17] and with some of the arguments in Plato's *Euthydemus*,[18] some have doubted the accuracy of Didymus' attribution. The alleged fragment, far from being taken from a book on the history of philosophy, is part of a commentary on *Ecclesiastes* (a book of the Old Testament). In fact the commentary does not survive; the information about Prodicus is part of a scrap of papyrus discovered in 1941, containing only 10 lines of text, which can be translated as follows:

> A certain paradoxical thought of Prodicus has been passed down: that 'it is not possible to contradict.' How can he say this? It is against the thought and the opinion of all people; for all people engaging in conversation contradict, both in their everyday affairs and in matters of thought. Yet he says dogmatically that 'it is not possible to contradict.' For if (two people) contradict, they both speak. But it is impossible for both to speak with respect to the same thing. For he says that only the one saying what is true and proclaiming things as they are is speaking of them. The one opposing him does not speak of the [same] thing.
>
> (tr. Mayhew)

The passage is problematic in several ways. First, the Prodicus fragment is taken out of context; if in fact Prodicus did assert it, we are not given any idea of his reasons for making the assertion, of how he thought it could be applied, or of what precisely he took it to mean. Second, we have no indication of Didymus' sources for this information. There could well have been some slippage in the many centuries that separated Prodicus from Didymus. For example, the original claim may have mentioned Protagoras and at some point in the transmission (making copies of an earlier text) a careless or ignorant scribe could have substituted Prodicus' name. Third, the passage quotes this fragment simply to attack it; it is a hostile witness. But hostile witnesses are notoriously unreliable.

This is not to say that Prodicus did not write these words, but even supposing that he did, it remains unclear what he meant by them, why he stated them, and what role they played in his thinking overall, let alone how anyone who believed them could also hold the other views that are more securely attributed to Prodicus.

Notes

1. Plato, *Apology* 19e.
2. Plato, *Greater Hippias* 282c.
3. *passophos*, a rare word, first used by Homer to describe Odysseus. In Plato's *Symposium* he is called "most outstanding" (*beltistos*).
4. Antiphon is an exception. See above, p.50.
5. Plato, *Eryxias* 397c.
6. Plato, *Greater Hippias* 282c.
7. In the *Cratylus* Plato makes Socrates say that he did not attend the 50 drachma lecture about names, which Prodicus claimed to be a full treatment of the topic, because could afford only the one drachma lecture on the subject (384a–c). This may well be a joke or an example of Socratic irony.
8. See above pp. 61 and 99–104.
9. This will be taken up in Chapter 10.
10. See above, p.22.
11. Most prominently Xenophanes.
12. Xenophon's version is included in the Appendix of Translated Texts, pp. 178–80.
13. This work is also known by the Latin title *Memorabilia*.
14. "Antilogic" is the subject of Chapter 11.
15. Hesiod's *Works and Days* shows similarities, contrasting the life of hard work with the life of laziness.
16. Lines 685–692, tr. Mayhew.
17. For an argument that this doctrine was Plato's invention, see above, p. 27–30.
18. *Euthydemus* 283e–286d, especially 284b–c.

7
THRASYMACHUS OF CHALCEDON

Anyone who has read the first book of Plato's *Republic* will have an indelible impression of Thrasymachus, the man who violently interrupts the conversation about the nature of justice (336b), declaring that justice is simply the advantage of the stronger (338c), a thesis he considers so obviously borne out by the behavior of individuals and countries that it needs no further proof. When Socrates asks for clarification and detects inconsistencies or at least unclarities in Thrasymachus' views, Thrasymachus calls him a trickster who is out to win the argument unfairly (341b), he insults Socrates in a childishly vulgar way (343a), and after delivering a lengthy harangue in favor of his thesis he angrily stands up to leave the discussion without giving the others present the opportunity to understand his position (344d).

Fewer readers of the *Republic* recall Thrasymachus' appearances later in the dialogue. There it is apparent that he has attentively followed the conversation, and that he wants it to continue and encourages further discussion of the nature of justice (450a–b). Elsewhere Socrates declares that he and Thrasymachus were never enemies and have in fact become friends (498c). In introducing the topic of book 8 Socrates effectively declares that he is still concerned with Thrasymachus' thesis (545a). Most importantly at the very end of his lengthy treatment of justice Socrates admits that in a way Thrasymachus was correct (590d). This is a reasonable interpretation of Socrates' ideal state in which the rulers' rule for the benefit of the city as a whole (519e–520e), which is identical with the benefit of all its citizens. This is especially true for the rulers (the philosopher kings) who could not live a happier life in any other city.

How accurate a portrayal this is of the actual Thrasymachus is unclear. The name "Thrasymachus" is a compound of the adjective *thrasus* (bold, rash, arrogant) and the noun *makhē* (fight or battle), which so well fits the character in book 1 that we

DOI: 10.4324/9781003493259-7

might suppose that he is simply fictional. But other references to Thrasymachus in Plato, Aristotle and elsewhere make it certain that he did exist. Still, little is known about him.

He was a native of Chalcedon, a Greek city on the Bosporus. Plato describes him as a master of the craft (*tekhnē*) of speaking (*logos*) who is capable of teaching it to others.[1] Like Protagoras and some other Sophists he claimed to teach *aretē*.[2] In the *Republic* he demands payment for teaching Socrates and the others what justice is.[3] This information establishes his pedigree as a Sophist.

Plato names him alongside Gorgias as the author of rhetorical treatises[4] and Aristotle provides a genealogy of the development of rhetoric: first "the founders" (whose names he does not give), then Tisias, followed by Thrasymachus.[5] Aristotle mentions his contributions to rhetoric in matters of delivering speeches, for his rhythmic prose and his use of similes,[6] and later authors discuss other stylistic features of his writings. He received praise for being

> pure, subtle and inventive, and able, according to his wishes, to speak either with terseness or with an abundance of words; but he occupied himself entirely with the writing of handbooks and performance pieces and has left no court speeches.[7]

A brief history of rhetoric found in Plato's *Phaedrus* refers to "the powerful man of Chalcedon, skilled both at enraging many people and then when they are seething with anger to soothe them as if by magical incantations."[8]

In fact, virtually all that remains of Thrasymachus' writings are two fragments. One belongs to a speech addressed to the Athenian Assembly on a political matter.[9] The situation for which it was written and the cause it advocates are not clear from the fragment, which is apparently the opening part of the speech and confines itself to generalities. Since like Antiphon Thrasymachus wrote political speeches for others to deliver, there is no reason to suppose that he delivered this speech himself or that it expresses his own views.

The second is a single sentence quoted from his speech *For the People of Larissa*: "Shall we, who are Greeks, become slaves to Archelaus [king of Macedonia] – to a barbarian?"

This leaves the material in the first book of the *Republic*. Many have thought that the thesis presented there, that justice is the advantage of the stronger, and the arguments he brings in its favor are genuinely Thrasymachean, but this interpretation is uncertain in view of Plato's very free treatment of the views of other thinkers, such as Protagoras' genuine fragment "A human being is the measure of all things." I argued earlier[10] that Plato attributes to Protagoras ideas alien to his stated views on his profession and his approach to education and so it is unlikely that he held the radical interpretation which Plato gives to the fragment. Likewise, I believe that even if Thrasymachus did hold the thesis in question, it is almost certain that the series of arguments and views that Plato puts in his mouth are due to Plato himself, developing Thrasymachus' thesis in a way that suits his own philosophical purposes.

If this is the case, then all we have left is the thesis itself. Unfortunately, there is no agreement as to what it means. Is Thrasymachus advocating this view? When he speaks of the stronger and the weaker is he referring to individuals, or to groups of individuals within a state (political parties, for example, or the wealthy)? Does he believe that the stronger *should* use their strength to dominate and exploit the weaker? Or does he intend it as a factual description of how things are: that *in fact* the stronger dominate and exploit the weaker? If the latter is true, does he think that this is good or bad? Does he advocate this behavior or does he lament it? There is no way to tell. This has not deterred scholars from preferring one possibility to the rest and developing the thesis in interesting and philosophically important ways, but it is beyond the scope of this book to engage in such speculation, much of which has more to do with Plato than with Thrasymachus.[11]

Notes

1 Plato, *Phaedrus* 266c.
2 Plato, *Clitophon* 410b–c.
3 Plato, *Republic* 337d.
4 Plato, *Phaedrus* 261c.
5 Aristotle, *Sophistical Refutations* 183b32. Aristotle's omission of Gorgias as the successor of Tisias is surprising given that Tisias and Gorgias were both from Sicily.
6 Aristotle, *Rhetoric* 1404a14, 1409a2, 1413a8.
7 Dionysius of Halicarnassus, *On Isaeus* 20.
8 Plato, *Phaedrus* 267c-d.
9 Translated in DG, pp. 210–12.
10 Chapter 2 pp. 19–22.
11 For example, Guthrie (1969, 297–8) appears to accept that the *Republic* presents Thrasymachus' actual view on the very weak grounds that it is not inconsistent with the views expressed in the surviving fragment of the speech to the Athenian assembly, while Kerferd (1981, 120–22) argues that the various statements of Thrasymachus in the *Republic* are consistent with one another. Annas (1981, pp. 34–7) gives a clear summary of the problem.

8
EUTHYDEMUS AND DIONYSODORUS OF CHALCEDON

These two brothers were of the same generation as Socrates, younger than Protagoras and Gorgias and older than Hippias and Prodicus. They emigrated from the island of Chios, where they were born, to the pan-Hellenic colony of Thurii in Italy, from which they were subsequently exiled for reasons we do not know. Afterwards, they traveled through the Greek world making their living first as teachers of martial arts and later as Sophists. Aside from this, we are told little else about them except that Euthydemus made a large collection of texts written by wise men of the past.[1]

The principal source for the two brothers is Plato's dialogue *Euthydemus*, which gives an unfavorable but lasting impression. They are described as "newfangled (*kainos*) Sophists" (271c) and Plato presents them in an entirely different light than Protagoras, Gorgias, Hippias and Prodicus. The dialogue's setting is the Lyceum, the gymnasium where later Aristotle would find his school. The purpose of the brothers' visit to Athens was to give a demonstration of their teaching in hopes of drumming up some business and the Lyceum was an excellent location for a display of their talent since it was a place where men both young and old congregated. The brothers claimed to teach *aretē*, which as we have seen is a general term for excellence that can be applied to whatever a person supposes excellence consists in. Their notion of excellence can be understood through the teaching demonstration that occupies the rest of the dialogue. Briefly, it is the ability to defeat people in discussion, "refuting whatever may be said, no matter whether it is true or false" (272b).

In fact they do not teach any particular doctrines but rather a method of debate that consists in refuting other people's views without any commitment to the truth of any opposing view – in effect leaving no opinions standing. They operate together like tag-team wrestlers. One of them asks a student which of two

DOI: 10.4324/9781003493259-8

alternatives he believes, and then proceeds to refute it, and then when the student accepts the remaining alternative, the other Sophist joins in and refutes that too. The arguments they use are faulty in a number of ways, but leave the student dumbfounded. Plato calls this practice eristic (*eristikē*) – a word that he may have invented[2] that means something like "the art of disputation" – a competitive practice in which the aim is not to learn the truth (as in philosophy or what Plato calls dialectic) but simply to reduce others to silence. The following passage is typical of this technique.

(275d) Well, as I [Socrates] remember, Euthydemus began something like this:

"Cleinias, which are the men who learn, the wise or the ignorant?"

Being confronted with this weighty question, the boy blushed and looked at me in doubt.

And I, seeing that he was troubled, said, "Cheer up, Cleinias (275e) and choose bravely whichever seems to you to be the right answer – he may be doing you a very great service."

Just at this moment Dionysodorus leaned a little toward me and, smiling all over his face, whispered in my ear and said, "I may tell you beforehand, Socrates, that whichever way the boy answers he will be refuted."

While he was saying this, Cleinias gave his answer, so that I had no chance to advise (276a) the boy to be careful; and he answered that the wise were the learners.

Then Euthydemus said, "Are there some whom you call teachers, or not?"

He agreed that there were.

"And the teachers are teachers of those who learn, I suppose, in the same way that the music master and the writing master were teachers of you and the other boys when you were pupils?"

He agreed.

"And when you were learning, you did not yet know the things you were learning, did you?"

"No," he said.

(276b) "And were you wise when you did not know these things?"

"By no means," he said.

"Then if not wise, ignorant?"

"Very much so."

"Then in the process of learning what you did not know, you learned while you were ignorant?"

The boy nodded.

"Then it is the ignorant who learn, Cleinias, and not the wise, as you suppose."

When he said this, the followers of Dionysodorus and Euthydemus broke into applause and laughter, (276c) just like a chorus at a sign from their director. And before the boy could well recover his breath, Dionysodorus took up the argument and said,

"Well then, Cleinias, when the writing master gave you dictation, which of the boys learned the piece, the wise or the ignorant?"

"The wise," said Cleinias.

"Then it is the wise who learn, and not the ignorant, and you gave Euthydemus a wrong answer just now."

(276d) Whereupon the supporters of the pair laughed and cheered very loudly indeed, in admiration of their cleverness. We, on the other hand, were panic-stricken and kept quiet.

Euthydemus, observing our distress and in order to confound us further, would not let the boy go but went on questioning him and, like a skillful dancer, gave a double twist to his questions on the same point, saying, "Do those who learn learn the things they know or the things they do not know?"

And Dionysodorus again whispered to me in a low voice, (276e) "This is another one, Socrates, just like the first."

"Mercy on us," I said, "the first question certainly seemed good enough!"

"All our questions are of this same inescapable sort, Socrates," he said.

"And this, no doubt, is the reason why your pupils admire you so much," I said.

Just then Cleinias answered Euthydemus that the learners learned what they do not know, (277a) whereupon Euthydemus put him through the same course of questions as before.

"What then, he said, don't you know your letters?"

"Yes," he said.

"Then you know them all?"

He agreed.

"Whenever anyone dictates anything, doesn't he dictate letters?"

He agreed.

"Then doesn't he dictate something you know, if you really know them all?"

He agreed to this too.

"Well then," he said, "you are not the one who learns what someone dictates, are you, but the one who doesn't know his letters is the one who learns?"

"No," he said, "I am the one who learns."

"Then you learn what you know," he said, (277b) "if you in fact do know all your letters."

He agreed.

"Then your answer was wrong," he said.

Euthydemus had barely said this when Dionysodorus picked up the argument as though it were a ball and aimed it at the boy again, saying,

"Euthydemus is completely deceiving you, Cleinias. Tell me, isn't learning the acquisition of the knowledge of what one learns?"

Cleinias agreed.

"And what about knowing? he said. Is it anything except having knowledge already?"

He agreed.

"Then not knowing (277c) is not yet having knowledge?"

He agreed with him.

"And are those who acquire something those who have it already or those who do not?"

"Those who do not."

"And you have admitted, haven't you, that those who do not know belong to the group of those who do not have something?"

He nodded.

"Then the learners belong to those who acquire and not to those who have?"

He agreed.

"Then it is those who do not know who learn, Cleinias, and not those who know."
(Plato, *Euthydemus* 275d2–277c8, Hackett tr.)

It is apparent to us as well as to Socrates and the audience for whom Plato wrote the *Euthydemus* that the arguments used against Cleinias are faulty – they do not really prove the conclusion. On the other hand, to identify precisely what the errors are and explain why they are errors is not so simple, at least for people who have not studied logic. This is an important consideration, since logic did not exist as a field of study when Euthydemus and Dionysodorus lived; it was invented by Aristotle, who would have had no difficulty detecting the fallacies in the passage quoted above. In fact in his work *Sophistical Refutations* he discusses fallacies like these, making them objects of study, focusing on the form that the different fallacious arguments have, so that what he says applies to entire classes of arguments rather than just to individual ones. During the lifetimes of Euthydemus, Dionysodorus and Socrates and also at the time when Plato wrote the *Euthydemus* this kind of diagnosis of fallacies was nonexistent and consequently it was harder to put your finger on just what was wrong even if you could detect that the argument was faulty. From a rhetorical point of view, you are in a weak position if you cannot say what is wrong with an argument. The burden of proof is on you. If you can do no more than simply assert that it does not go through, your opponent can equally well assert the opposite and it remains unrefuted, which means that you have not established either that your own position is correct or even that the opposite is wrong.

After a long series of this sort of refutations the conversation ends. The fans of Euthydemus and Dionysodorus enthusiastically cheer for their success, but Socrates and others disagree.

> (304d) When I [Crito, the narrator of the conversation] was taking a walk, one of the men who was leaving your discussion came up to me (someone who has a high opinion of himself for wisdom and is one of those clever people who write speeches for the law courts) and he said, "Crito, aren't you a disciple of these wise men?"
>
> "Heavens no," I said, "there was such a crowd that I was unable to hear, even though I stood quite close."
>
> "And yet," he said, "it was worth hearing."
>
> "What was it?" (304e) I asked.
>
> "You would have heard men conversing who are the wisest of the present day in this kind of argument."
>
> And I said, "What did they show you?"
>
> "Nothing else," said he, "than the sort of thing one can hear from such people at any time – chattering and making a worthless fuss about matters of no consequence." (These are his approximate words.)
>
> "But surely," I said, "philosophy is a charming thing."
>
> "Charming, my (305a) innocent friend?" he said, "Why it is of no value whatsoever! And if you had been present, I think you would have been embarrassed on your friend's account, he acted so strangely in his willingness to put himself at the disposal of men who care nothing about what they say, but just snatch at every word. And these men, as I was just saying, are among the most influential people of the present day. But the fact is, Crito," he said, "that both the activity itself and the men who engage in it are worthless and ridiculous. Now as far as I am concerned, Socrates, the man is wrong to criticize the activity and so is anyone else who does so. But to be willing to argue with such people in front of a large crowd does seem to me worthy of reproach.
>
> (Plato, *Euthydemus* 304d4–305b3, Hackett tr.)

From Socrates' point of view the real danger that these men posed was that their worthless activity, which has no regard for the truth, could be confused with philosophy and so lead people to feel disgust at what Socrates considered the most important activity a human can undertake. The confusion is especially possible in the case of Socrates, whose practice was to investigate the opinions of others, a process that almost always ended in refutation. The crucial difference was that, unlike Euthydemus and Dionysodorus, Socrates aimed at finding the (elusive) truth and intended the arguments he constructed to be valid.[3]

Plato presents these Sophists as intellectually harmful, but from another point of view, the kind of exercise they engaged in can be philosophically useful. Consider one of the arguments in the lengthy passage quoted above (276d–277b). The chain of reasoning is unclear, but concludes in effect that if you know the alphabet, you know anything the letters spell, therefore you are unable to learn (or perhaps learn from anyone else or from anyone who is speaking). Nonsense, of course. But it raises important philosophical issues that are still being explored: What is the relation between written and spoken words? What is the relation between words and things? What are the ways in which something can be known? How and in what sense does teaching actually impart knowledge? More generally, how does interpersonal communication work? The same can be said of the other arguments that the brothers deploy.

From this point of view, the public display of the brothers can be seen as an advertisement: study with us and we will teach you how to defend yourself against questioning of this kind, for example by detecting flaws in your opponents' case and exposing them as ignorant or intellectual frauds. One can imagine an introductory class in philosophy beginning with the *Euthydemus*, showing students how to recognize and deal with fallacies and also detect philosophical problems that some fallacies raise. This is not to say that this was the brothers' intention.[4] Plato gives no hint that it was and we have no further information.

In fact since Plato is our only source for their manner of teaching and since Plato is a prejudiced and suspect source, we need to be extremely careful in interpreting what he says. In the case of some other Sophists, we have enough collateral information to confirm that Plato's account of their doctrines is based in reality even though his manipulation of those doctrines may stray far from their authors' original intent. Likewise, as the *Protagoras* witnesses for Protagoras, Prodicus and Hippias, Plato's presentations of the personalities of Sophists are quite likely to be reasonably accurate.

If we use these conclusions as a guide to his presentation of Euthydemus and Dionysodoros, we can infer that the brothers (uniquely among known Sophists) worked as a team rather than as individuals, that they developed a technique of refutation that is very unlike antilogic. Where antilogic involves making the strongest case for one's own position and the strongest case against the opponent's, the brothers took no position of their own in their discussions; their goal was simply to refute, and to refute not by showing that other positions are preferable but by reducing their opponents to dumbfounded silence, having been forced to admit that they could not defend either their original view or its denial. The obvious errors in the brothers' refutations make it plausible that they could have imparted a certain proficiency in this technique in a reasonably short time simply by training their students in a number of argumentative tactics.[5]

Even if we are willing to go this far, I see no reason not to think that the conversation between the brothers and Cleinias is entirely due to Plato and as such is not a safe guide to the topics that the brothers used in their teaching. Of course, it would not be surprising if they dealt with issues related to teaching, as we find in the quoted passage, but the philosophical issues raised explicitly in some of the refutations that occur later in the dialogue may have no more to do with what the brothers actually discussed than the "Protagorean" relativism of the *Theaetetus* has to do with the historical Protagoras.[6]

That the brothers engaged in the kind of sophisms Plato puts in their mouths is supported by two references in Aristotle[7] that declare that Euthydemus argued something to the effect that a person who happens to be in Sicily and knows a trireme and also knows the Peiraeus,[8] knows that there is a trireme in the Peiraeus. Aristotle gives this as an example of a fallacy that combines things that are separate.

If Plato is right that all that the brothers did was this, that they had no positive doctrines to teach, then he is certainly right to describe them as newfangled Sophists. Unlike the other Sophists we have treated, they will have made no contribution to the intellectual issues of the day but they may have spurred Aristotle on to study the nature of fallacies and the means to refute them – a not inconsiderable achievement.

Appendix: Eristic and the Socratic method

Plato sees no value in the eristic techniques of Euthydemus and Dionysodorus, but he sees great value in Socrates' teaching, which as Plato presents it has a lot in common with the two brothers' method. Both methods proceed by question and answer, where each answer is subjected to further questions, and eventually, the student contradicts himself and ends up in a state of bafflement.

There are also some important differences. In most of Plato's "Socratic's" dialogues the initial question arises naturally from a conversation, while Euthydemus and Dionysodorus begin the conversation by asking a question of their own devising. Euthydemus and Dionysodorus seem to have rehearsed their questions and answers beforehand and they deliberately set out to produce contradiction, while Socrates' conversations are not predetermined and are focused on the genuine opinions of the student. Euthydemus and Dionysodorus's conversation is staged in a public setting before a large crowd, while Socrates' conversations are private. Euthydemus and Dionysodorus aim to confuse and humiliate their students while Socrates' goal is to clarify his students' thoughts and make them better persons.

Plato labels the techniques of Euthydemus and Dionysodorus as "eristic" (*eristikē*)[9]. This word is derived from *eris*, whose original meaning was "quarrel" or "strife" but later came to mean "wordy wrangling" and "disputation."[10]

The word "eristic" is first found in Plato and he may have invented it, just as he invented other words ending in *ikē* to designate various practices and fields of expertise.[11] For Plato the word "eristic" is negatively charged. His student Aristotle would later describe eristic arguments as those that have premises that seem to be plausible, but are not really such, or again that merely seeming to reason from premises that are or seem to be plausible.[12] In contrast to scientific demonstrations that have true premises and valid reasoning, eristic arguments employ either one or more false premises, or invalid reasoning or both. In effect Aristotle's definition concerns the logical aspects of eristic arguments, while Plato is more concerned with the intentions of the people who use them, which in the case of Euthydemus and Dionysodorus amount to the ability to refute a person's answers to their trick questions no matter what answer is given, with no concern either for the truth or for improving the mind of their victims.

Notes

1. Xenophon, *Memorabilia* 4.2.
2. Its appearance at *Euthydemus* 272b may be the earliest recorded instance of its use.
3. For more on the difference between Socrates and the two brothers, see the appendix to this chapter, pp. 84–5.
4. In the dialogue (277d–278d) Socrates (perhaps over-generously) suggests that this was in fact the brothers' intention.
5. This point is made 303c–304a.
6. See pp. 26–30.
7. *Sophistical Refutations* 177b12ff. and *Rhetoric* 1401a25–29.
8. The harbor of Athens.
9. Plato, *Euthydemus* 272b.
10. These definitions are taken from Liddell and Scott's Greek-English Lexicon.
11. See xsc, pp. 137–8.
12. This is a loose translation of Aristotle's *Topics* 100b23–26.

9
LOGOS

If any single word encapsulates the work of the Sophists, it is *logos*. Protagoras' "two opposed *logoi*" doctrine[1] and Gorgias' *Encomium of Helen*[2], which might just as well be considered an encomium of *logos*, contain the best-known occurrences of the word in the extant texts written by Sophists, but it is no exaggeration to say that *logos* formed the core of the activity of all the Sophists. The word has a conveniently broad spectrum of meanings that ranges from words both spoken and written to thoughts to things and facts. On the "words" side it can mean word, phrase, sentence and even language; when referring to spoken words in particular it can mean utterance, statement and speech (both the kind of speech one makes before an audience and speech in general). On the "written words" side it can mean book, treatise and text. On the "thought" side it can mean anything from discourse, discussion and reasoning to doctrine, theory, formula, concept, meaning and definition. Yet other meanings, such as principle, proportion, ratio and relation seem to be most closely related to things and facts. Other translations such as "account," "argument," "description," "explanation" and "story" bridge two or more of these categories.

The Sophists were interested in *logos*. They taught their students to speak effectively, which included teaching matters of style, organization and delivery as well as how to speak on different types of occasions. Some of them went further and reflected on the nature of *logos* itself, in effect initiating the study of language or at least of the Greek language.

It may not be surprising to us that intelligent teachers like Protagoras should have inquired into the nature and characteristics of the subject they taught and not have been content simply to impart techniques and offer guidance in the practical application of their subject, but surely the move from simply learning and using a language to reflecting *for the first time* about the language itself and analyzing how it works was an enormous intellectual advance.

Some Sophists went further and theorized about *logos*. Protagoras' assertion that on every subject there are two opposed *logoi* is a general statement about the nature of language and its relation to reality as well as a way of describing his own teaching. Gorgias' presentation in his *Encomium of Helen* of *logos* as "a powerful master which by means of the smallest and most invisible body accomplishes the most divine deeds" and the impressive support that he marshals for this claim, whether intended seriously or not, not only grabbed people's attention and advertised Gorgias' profession, but also even now presents a way of thinking about speech and its effects that has some plausibility and that is fresh and new to most of his readers today.

It is unfortunate that we have only scanty evidence about the early stages of the Sophists' investigation of *logos*. However, the information we have is important, indicating that Sophists and especially Protagoras were at the very beginning of the study of language. Protagoras is credited with identifying the three grammatical genders of Greek nouns and adjectives, which are known as masculine, feminine and neuter (which means "neither," that is, neither masculine nor feminine). The first two of these names go back to Protagoras himself; instead of "neuter" whose Greek equivalent became the standard word in later grammarians, Protagoras referred to this third gender as *pragmata* (things or objects).[3] Protagoras also identified several different types of sentences: request/prayer, question, answer and command.[4]

He used these distinctions in analyzing and criticizing Homer, calling attention to what he regarded as grammatical mistakes in the first two lines of the *Iliad*, "Sing, goddess, of the raging wrath of Peleus's son Achilles." He complains that this is a command, whereas a human is in no position to command a goddess to do anything; Homer should have stated this as a request/prayer. He also complained that Homer wrongly made the word "wrath" (*mēnis*) feminine, whereas it should be masculine, presumably because he regarded wrath as a masculine emotion and so the adjective "raging" should have a masculine ending instead of the feminine ending in the text of Homer. (In fact, the grammatical gender of *mēnis* is feminine.[5]) In effect, Protagoras (who evidently had not heard the saying that hell has no fury like a woman scorned) appeared to be advocating language reform, to change it and make it more rational. He was also challenging authority in a stunning manner. The Homeric epics were universally known and widely revered among the ancient Greeks, and Protagoras' suggestion that Homer made elementary mistakes in his use of the language of which he was considered a master would have attracted attention and comment. (We should not neglect the likelihood that Protagoras' proposal was not serious.) It would be anachronistic and misleading to call Protagoras a grammarian. The field as such did not exist in his time and his intent was not to discover and systematically catalog all the grammatical forms and constructions of ancient Greek, but to examine his native language in general.

Plato makes Protagoras say that he considers that the most important part of anyone's education is being clever[6] about poetry, which, he continues, consists of

88 *Logos*

three things: (1) to be able to understand what the poets are saying, (2) to know what has been composed correctly and what has not and (3) to know how to analyze a poem and when asked about it to provide a *logos* – to give reasons for your interpretation.[7] He then goes on to give a sample of his style of literary criticism by analyzing a poem by Simonides (beginning at 339b), claiming that Simonides contradicts himself in it. Again, this would be an excellent device for drawing attention to oneself as a clever thinker and speaker and also for encouraging thought about the content and meaning of poetry instead of mere familiarity.

In this connection it is worthwhile to note that before the time of the Sophists, literacy was quite rare in Greece. This situation changed during the fifth century, partly because of the Sophists and the conditions that gave rise to sophisticated education. Before this, almost all Greek literature was poetry, whose metrical structure made it relatively easy to memorize. This is typical of "oral" societies. Learning poetry, Homer's *Iliad* and *Odyssey,* in particular, was a major part of one's education. But mere memorization does not encourage critical thought; the emphasis is on getting every word right, not on understanding or analyzing the content. And even if some people did think about the content of poetry, their thoughts would not be preserved unless they wrote them down (presumably in prose) and writing them down would require writing materials, which would not have been readily available. It would be overstating the case to call Protagoras the first person to criticize Homer. Heraclitus (who wrote prose), born around 540 BCE, two generations before Protagoras, reproached Homer and Xenophanes (who wrote verse), born a generation before Heraclitus, did the same.

> Homer deserved to be expelled from the contests and flogged.
> (Heraclitus, fragment 42 DK)

> Both Homer and Hesiod have ascribed to the gods all deeds which among men are matters of reproach and blame: thieving, adultery, and deceiving one another.
> (Xenophanes, fragment 11 DK)

Significantly, these criticisms do not amount to the kind of textual analysis that Protagoras gives of Simonides' poem, quoting it and finding inconsistencies in verses some distance apart.

The advent of literacy made it possible to preserve one's thoughts and also to have texts (of poetry as well as prose) that could be referred to, cross-referenced and studied in much the same ways as they have been studied ever since, and Protagoras' opinion that the ability to be clever at criticizing poetry is an important part of education implies that this was part of what he taught his students[8]: to pay attention to (presumably written) texts and find interesting and new things to say about them.

This critical approach to poetry would be an excellent way to introduce the practice of rebutting opponents' arguments in courtrooms and public assemblies, since for his students, who had grown up hearing poetry, it would be a new, exciting and fun way to approach what they already knew by heart. They would have the wonderful experience of learning for the first time how to think about and criticize instead of merely parroting.

Unsurprisingly the Sophists wrote in prose. There are entire surviving works by Gorgias and Antiphon and quotations from or summaries of works by Protagoras, Hippias, Prodicus and Thasymachus that establish this beyond any doubt. It was during this time (second half of the fifth century BCE) that prose became dominant, as books devoted to history (notably those of Herodotus and Thucydides), books containing political and forensic speeches, and writings with philosophical content joined lyric poetry and drama (both tragedy and comedy were written in verse) as leading literary genres.

Gorgias and Prodicus made important contributions as well. Gorgias was famed for his amazing style, which stunned the Athenians when he performed one or more display speeches during a visit to Athens on a diplomatic mission in 427 BCE. The most impressive surviving example is his *Encomium of Helen*, which employs a formidable array of literary devices, such as rhythm, rhyme (which is unusual in Greek prose and poetry), alliteration, striking similes and metaphors and other figures of speech as well.[9]

As we have seen, the Sophists trained their students to succeed in the principal venues for public speaking, the Assembly and the lawcourts, where decisions on controversial matters had to be made and your success depended largely on your ability to persuade the jurors or assemblymen to vote for the side you advocate. It is easy to suppose that many a Sophist made the kind of claims that Plato puts in Gorgias' mouth at *Gorgias* 452d–453a.[10]

A successful speech will take many things into account, some relevant to the matter at issue and some irrelevant, some personal and some impersonal, some depending on the assumptions and prejudices of the individuals that constitute the voting body and some more objective. Unsurprisingly we have little information about how the Sophists taught these matters.

An important source of information about their teaching of the techniques of public speaking is the following passage from Plato's *Phaedrus*, which refers to "written books on the art (*tekhnē*) of *logos*,"[11] and mentions most of the Sophists discussed earlier as well as a few more about whom very little is known and gives evidence of the range of rhetorical techniques and terminology.

[266d] [Socrates] We need to say what part of rhetoric is left.

[Phaedrus] In fact there are very many things in the books about the art of speech.

[Soc] You did well to remind me. I think that the introduction is the first thing since it has to be said at the beginning of a speech. Is this what you have in mind – the fine details of the art?

[266e] [Ph] Yes.

[Soc] The second thing is a narrative and testimonies of witnesses to confirm it; the third is evidence; the fourth, likelihoods. I think that the cunning artist in words from Byzantium speaks of confirmation and supplementary confirmation.

[Ph] Do you mean that worthy man Theodorus?

[267a] [Soc] Who else? He also speaks of refutation and supplementary refutation in both prosecution and defense. But we are not bringing forward Evenus of Paros who was the first to invent insinuation and seeming praise (some say he also spoke seeming blame in verse to help his memory), for he was a wise man. Will we ignore Tisias and Gorgias, who saw that likelihoods must be honored above the truth, who with the strength of their speech make small things appear large and large things small, [267b] who say new-fangled things in old-fashioned ways, and the opposite things in new-fangled ways, and discovered both brevity and endless length of speeches on any subject? In fact, once when Prodicus heard me saying these things he laughed and said that he was the only one who had discovered the art of what speeches are needed: they need to be neither long nor short but just the right length.

[Ph] Brilliant, Prodicus!

[Soc] Will we not mention Hippias? I think that our friend from Elis would vote the same way as him.

[Ph] Why not?

[Soc] And how are we to describe the gallery of Polus's terminology, like [267c] "word-repetition," "maxim-speaking," and "figurative speaking" – terms for the production of beautiful diction that he borrowed from Licymnius?

[Ph] But weren't some terms like this used by Protagoras?

[Soc] "Correct diction" was, my boy, and many other fine terms. But when it comes to tear-jerking speeches about old age and poverty, in my opinion the mighty Chalcedonian [Thrasymachus] has won the prize. He has a marvelous ability to enrage a crowd [267d] and then to charm and soothe them when they are angry, as he said himself. And he is very strong at both slandering and refuting slander from any source. The end of speeches appears to be universally agreed by all. Some call it recapitulation and others use other names.

[Ph] Do you mean reminding the audience in a summary at the end of the speech of all that has been said?

[Soc] That is what I mean.

(Plato, *Phaedrus* 266d5–7d7)

In addition to making appropriate use of these techniques, a speech must aim to convince the audience, typically through arguing in support of one's own side and against the opposition. Unsurprisingly one of the subjects associated with the Sophists was expertise in forms of argument. Gorgias' *Encomium of Helen* and *Defense of Palamedes* consist of arguments aimed to exonerate Helen from the hatred people still held for her and Palamedes from the charge of treason for which he was put to death. The argumentative structure of these works was discussed above.[12]

A type of argument associated with the Sophists is the argument from likelihood (*eikos*).[13] The following comic fictional example of this kind of argument is variously reported in a number of ancient texts.[14]

There was a fight between two men, one big and strong, the other small and weak. The case came to court with the small man saying that the big man was the aggressor. There were no witnesses to the fight so the jury had to base its decision on the testimony of the two men and their appearance. The small man argued that it was unlikely that being so small and weak he would have picked a fight with so big and strong an opponent. The big man replied that it was unlikely that *he* was the one that started the fight because everyone would suppose that it was likely that he had done so.

Several other *eikos* arguments are prominent in a speech in one of Antiphon's *Tetralogies* that is concerned with a murder trial. A man is found dead in the street and his servant is badly wounded and on the point of death. The dead man still has his cloak on. The murderer has disappeared. Just before he dies the servant tells some passers-by that the murderer was a certain man (the defendant in the trial), who was a known enemy of his master and who was about to take him to court on a charge of embezzlement. Friends of the dead man have brought this person to trial on a charge of murder. Since there are no living witnesses to the event, *eikos* arguments play a large role in the speeches of both the prosecutors and the accused.

The[15] prosecutors begin by saying that in the absence of the testimony of eyewitnesses the jurors "must give the utmost weight to any indication whatever of what is likely (*eikos*)." Since the dead man's cloak had not been stolen, theft was not the purpose. "Who is more likely to have committed the murder than someone who had already suffered great injuries at his hands and who could expect to suffer greater ones still? That man is the defendant."

The defendant replies in terms of likelihood. "If you find me guilty on the grounds of what is likely, it is even more likely for me to have figured out before committing the crime that I would be the suspect, as has happened, and if I knew of anyone else who was plotting the murder it would have been likely that I would have tried to stop them rather then knowingly become the obvious suspect.... As the prosecution alleges it is not unlikely but likely that a man wandering about in the middle of the night should be murdered for his clothes, but the fact that he was still wearing his cloak means nothing. The attackers could have run off because they were scared away by passers-by." Also since the dead man had other enemies, "is it not more likely that they murdered him rather than I? It would have been obvious to them that I would end up as the prime suspect." As to the testimony of the dead servant, "frightened by the danger he was in, it is hardly likely that he would have recognized the murderers; rather, it is likely that he would have gone along with whatever his master suggested... If one grants likelihoods the status of facts when they tend towards convicting me, one must on the same principle consider the following as confirming my innocence: it was more likely that, in order to be safe I would be especially careful not to be found at the scene of the crime rather than taking the risk that the slave might identify me just when he was being murdered.... My accusers claim that it was more likely that the witnesses would ask who the attackers were and then bring the information to the victim's home rather than running off. But I do not believe that anyone is so foolhardy or brave that, after finding someone breathing his last in the middle of the night he would not turn and run away rather than put his life in danger by stopping to inquire who had committed the crime. Now since it is more likely that the passers-by did the natural thing, those who murdered these people for their clothes can no longer reasonably be let off, and I am free and clear of suspicion."[16]

The success of a likelihood argument depends on what the audience (in this case, the jurors) think is likely, and that in turn depends on their beliefs and their experience, which includes their social and educational background, their exposure or lack of exposure to different ways of life and thought, and other aspects of their experience. One person might think that a big man is more likely to be aggressive than a small man but another might take other things into account before deciding who is more likely to be the aggressor. A consequence of this is that likelihood arguments do not usually have the form of logical deductions where the premises are stated explicitly. Stating them calls attention to them and so invites reflection and doubt about their truth. If someone were to produce an argument to prove that the big man attacked the small man and as one of his premises he said "as a rule big men are aggressive towards small men" anyone might quickly think of many big men who are not aggressive, and the argument would lose much of its force.

This is not to say that political and forensic advocacy should consist of deductive proofs. Rather it points to the uncertainty and indefiniteness inherent in political discussion and in the courtroom, where the nature of the case requires us to evaluate a number of separate factors, take many considerations into account and reach the best decision we can. In such conditions, a strictly logical argument may not even be possible.

Plato vigorously objects to *eikos* arguments which, he says, do not rely on the truth and do not even care about the truth. In the *Phaedrus* passage quoted above Plato refers to this kind of argument when he says that Tisias and Gorgias held that "likelihoods must be honored above the truth."[17] Elsewhere he attacks it more viciously:

> [272d] One who intends to be an able rhetorician has no need to know the truth about the things that are just or good or yet about people who are such either by nature or by upbringing. No one in a law court cares at all about the truth of such matters. They only care about what is convincing. [272e] This is called "the likely," and that is what a man who intends to speak according to art should concentrate on. Sometimes whether you are prosecuting or defending a case you must not even say what actually happened, if it was not likely to have happened – you must say something that is likely instead. Whatever you say, you should pursue what is likely and leave the truth aside: [273a] the whole art consists in sticking to that throughout your speech.
>
> (*Phaedrus* 272d6–3a1 – Hackett tr.)

Plato is right to say that likelihood is an inappropriate standard when certainty is possible. Since he believed that certainty is possible in philosophy (although we may not be convinced of this) he was justified in holding that likelihood arguments are inadequate for *his* purposes. But certainty is rarely found in the circumstances for which the Sophists prepared their students. In arguing for or against a proposed policy or law, for example, arguments will tend to be in terms of expected results: if we adopt the proposal then it is likely that such and such will occur. But in most cases it is not certain that it will occur: the facts are not yet in and since the measure either will be adopted or it will not, the only results that will ever be known are the results that actually occur later on, when the measure either has or has not been adopted. In court cases, jurors typically do not know whether or not the defendant committed the alleged crime, and the cases made on either side may well rely on *eikos* arguments. Witnesses who testify to the defendant's good character are contributing to such arguments. Implicitly if not explicitly the point of bringing them in is to convince the jury that the defendant is unlikely to have committed the crime. When the jurors or members of the Assembly cast their votes the best they can do is vote for whatever appears most likely to them. Philosophers may spend their entire lives without reaching the knowledge they seek, but juries and legislators do not have that luxury.

Another type of argument associated with the Sophists was later given the label *peritropē* ("reversal"). This is a species of likelihood argument that consists of responding to an argument against you by using one or more of your opponent's claims to construct another argument that makes the same point against him or her.

94 Logos

The best-known example of this is a fabricated story about the two men who according to tradition were the first teachers of rhetoric.

> Tisias, a poor young man, approached Corax (reputedly the founder of rhetoric; his name means "crow") and said that he wanted to learn rhetoric from him but that he could not afford his fees. However, he would pay him double later. Corax agreed and taught him, but Tisias never paid. When Corax eventually confronted him Tisias asked him what rhetoric is. Corax answered "the creator of persuasion." Then Tisias put up the following argument: "I will sue you over the fees, and if I persuade the jury I won't have to pay, and if I don't succeed in persuading them I still won't have to pay because it will prove that you failed to teach me to persuade." Corax overturned the argument saying "I will sue you too, and if I persuade the jury I will get the fees since I have persuaded them, and if I don't persuade them I am still owed my fees for having trained students so well that they can outdo their teacher." At this the bystanders shouted "The bad crow has laid a bad egg!"

This is an extreme example of a reversal argument and it is hard to imagine that occasions of this kind arise very often.[18] However, there are other kinds of reversal arguments in existing texts of Sophists, particularly in Antiphon's *Tetralogies*, in which the defendant argues that the evidence that the prosecution has presented to show him guilty actually tells for his innocence.

Another rhetorical feature that was associated with some of the Sophists was known as *kairos* (the right moment). In public speaking, this was a matter of saying the right thing at the right time, and it is specifically associated with Gorgias. Gorgias recognized that success in persuasion was not simply a matter of presenting strong arguments but of making your case in a way that would appeal to the audience. This required orators to be sensitive to the audience's mood and to extemporize as the moment required. Gorgias presumably trained his students in this art and he wrote a treatise on this subject, which unfortunately is no longer extant. The following verdict on his treatise is instructive.

> I hold that in all cases it is necessary to observe *kairos*. This is the soundest standard of what is pleasant and unpleasant. However no rhetorician or philosopher has succeeded in defining this art up to the present time. Even the first person who undertook to write on it, Gorgias of Leontini, wrote nothing worthwhile. In fact the nature of the subject is not such that it falls under any universal and technical study, and in general it cannot be attained through science but rather by judgment.[19]

Study of Antiphon's *Tetralogies* and also of Gorgias's works and the long summary of Prodicus's *Choice of Heracles*[20] (the only lengthy texts left from fifth-century Sophists) will reveal more techniques of persuasion, including other kinds of argument, but we do not have enough information to say how they were conceived and discussed, or even whether they were identified by Sophists as specific techniques.

The next two chapters will treat aspects of sophistic teaching that were philosophically influential: the topic of definition as originated by Gorgias and Prodicus, which is the subject of Chapter 10 and the practice of antilogic, which began with Protagoras, which is treated in Chapter 11.

Notes

1. This doctrine is discussed in Chapter 11.
2. 'This work is included in the Appendix of Translated Texts, pp. 171–4.
3. Aristotle, *Rhetoric* 1407b7–8.
4. Another source gives seven: narration, question, answer, command, report, request, summons (Diogenes Laertius 9.53–4).
5. Some have held that Protagoras was proposing to *change* the grammatical gender of *mēnis* from feminine to masculine because most nouns ending in *-is* are masculine. In fact it is not true that most nouns ending in *-is* are masculine. See Bluck and Peterson 1947, 14–18. Protagoras also held that the feminine noun *pēlēx* (helmet), also found in Homer, should properly be masculine. The source of this information is Aristotle, *Sophistical Refutations* 173b19–20.
6. The Greek word is *deinos*, which can also mean "skilful."
7. Plato, *Protagoras* 339a.
8. See above, p. 19.
9. For further discussion of Gorgias' prose style see Schiappa 1999, 86–105. And for a successful attempt to convey Gorgias's over-the-top style see the translation of the *Encomium of Helen* in DG, pp. 76–84.
10. Quoted above, p. 3.4.
11. This is an excellent instance of the use of this word, since the Sophists taught matters having to do with speech in general, and also with the correct use of language, speech-making, explanation, argument and the correct use of language all of which are possible translations of *logos*.
12. Pp. 3.7–9 and 3.10–11.
13. This word is usually translated "probability," but nowadays probability is frequently associated with percentages (for example, the probability of a tossed coin coming up "heads" is 50%), which is alien to the thinking of antiquity, so it is preferable to use a different word in translating it.
14. These include Plato, *Phaedrus* 273b–c and Aristotle, *Rhetoric* 1402a17.
15. For purposes of the present exposition, this and the following quoted passages are paraphrases, not exact translations, of relevant sections of the first *Tetralogy*.
16. Translation adapted from DG.
17. Plato, *Phaedrus* 267a.
18. Plato uses this technique in the *Theaetetus* dialogue (170a–1c) to good effect against the doctrine known as Protagorean relativism.
19. Dionysius of Halicarnassus (1st century BCE–1st century CE), *On Literary Composition* 12.
20. This work is included in the Appendix of Translated Texts, pp. 31–34.

10
DEFINITION

Part 1: Gorgias

Definition by Paradigm

Although much more original text survives from Gorgias than from any other Sophist, virtually none of it is definitional. Even so, there is good evidence that Gorgias was interested in matters related to definition, which with Socrates would become a central focus of philosophical work, and that he had a distinctive approach.

The principal evidence comes from Plato's *Meno*. Meno wants to know whether it is possible to teach *aretē* (virtue or excellence). This is an appropriate question for someone who associates with Sophists and in particular for someone associated with Gorgias who said that he did *not* teach it. Socrates declares that he does not know what *aretē* is, and so cannot say whether it can be taught; in fact he has never known anyone who does know what *aretē* is. Meno expresses surprise: "How so? Did you not meet Gorgias when he was here?" (71c) Socrates says that he did, but that he does not remember what Gorgias said. He asks Meno to remind him: "You tell me yourself, if you are willing, for surely you share his views." Meno replies "I do." This entitles us to interpret what follows as Gorgianic in content. This is confirmed by Socrates' statement later on that in defining color he will proceed *à la* Gorgias (76c).

Meno has no trouble saying what virtue is:

[71e] First, if you want the *aretē* (pl. *aretai*) of a man, it's easy, because this is the *aretē* of a man: to be capable of managing the affairs of the city and benefiting his friends and harming his enemies, and making sure not to suffer any such harm himself. If you want the *aretē* of a woman, it's not hard to tell: running

DOI: 10.4324/9781003493259-10

the household, keeping the family's possessions safe and being obedient to her husband. There is a different *aretē* for children, both girls and boys, and for an old man, whether free or [72a] slave. And there are a great many other *aretai* so that there is no difficulty about saying what *aretē* is. For every one of our actions and ages regarding everything we do there is an *aretē* and likewise, I think, a deficiency.

(Plato, *Meno* 71e1–72a4)

Socrates objects: Meno has provided a whole swarm of *aretai*, while he is looking for only one. Gorgias aims to identify different *aretai* and define each separately, whereas Socrates is interested in what all the different *aretai* have in common. Where Socrates wants to know what *aretai* have in common and in particular what constitutes the different *aretai* as *aretai*, Meno tells us what (some of) the different *aretai* are and gives brief accounts of them. Further, the accounts he gives of the *aretai* of a man and woman are superficial and based on traditional values. It is clear that Gorgias has not given much thought to the nature of these *aretai* – his concern is to give a list of several virtues, not to show what they have in common, much less to explain why his accounts are correct.

When Socrates presses Meno to give an account of *aretē* that holds for all humans, not separate ones for men, women, etc. Meno disappoints him by saying that this one *aretē* is "to be able to rule over people – if you are seeking one description to fit them all" (73d). This does not satisfy Socrates' demand for a definition that covers all humans, not just men. But it is not as unsatisfactory as it appears. I take it to be an instance of a kind of definition by example which I call a paradigm definition.

Suppose a child asks me what *aretē* is. Since there are many different *aretai* and they don't seem to have much in common it is not easy to find a single expression that captures them all, so I might decide to answer by describing an *aretē* that I take to be obvious, important or at least familiar and easy to understand, and then leave it to the child to use this case as a guide or paradigm for working out what other virtues are. Meno thinks that men (not women or children) rule over people and that ruling over people is an activity that is the most important thing that a man can do, and that men who do this well are the best or most successful men. So it is reasonable for him to identify this activity as the *aretē* of a man.

Meno recognizes that there are other categories of people – women for example – and he specifies what the *aretē* of a woman is. Again, in his society, it is likely that many people thought that women who successfully performed the activities he included in womanly *aretē* were the best and most successful women.

It is significant that he does not give definitions of the *aretai* of children, etc. He is not out to give a complete inventory of things and their *aretai*, but rather to use one or two clear examples (The Greek word for "example" is *paradeigma* – our word "paradigm.") In other words, the notion behind the paradigm definition of man can be applied to other cases and give insight into the nature of the things

98 Definition

thus defined. In many cases, it will be more useful than a more abstract and general definition that a child might not understand.

That Gorgias employed this kind of definition is borne out by the opening of his *Encomium of Helen*, which can be taken as a Gorgianic definition of *kosmos*.[1]

> Having strong men brings credit (*kosmos*) to a city, as beauty does to a body, wisdom to a soul, excellence to an object and truth to a speech. Their opposites bring discredit (*akosmia*, literally "lack of *kosmos*").

The additional examples (beauty, etc.) are important since the first example is so specific that by itself it is unclear how it is meant as a good example of *kosmos* and unclear how it might apply to other kinds of things. *Kosmos* has an opposite, *akosmia*, and the absence in a city, a body, a soul or a speech of the defining property of *kosmos* is the defining property of the corresponding *akosmia*.

It is not surprising that Socrates finds fault with Gorgianic definitions: they are not the kind of definitions he is looking for. But the fact that Socrates is not satisfied need not entail that Gorgianic definitions have no value. Whether they are successful depends at least partly on what Gorgias expected them to do.

The few examples we have seen suggest that he was on to something important: acknowledging that language can be misleading and elaborating a technique for avoiding being led astray. Take the case of *aretē*. We begin by noticing that although many terms seem to mean the same thing in all cases ("dog" for example), *aretai* seem to be quite different in different cases. There is ordinarily no need to go to the trouble of defining dog; we can do well enough by relying on familiar instances. But *aretē* is something else since it seems impossible to find any commonality among all the different *aretai*. In this situation it is reasonable to survey the wreckage – to locate at least some of the different *aretai* and sketch them out roughly, in the hopes of finding something to go on. This is particularly true if we agree with Meno that not only do different kinds of people have different *aretai*, but actions and tasks have *aretai* as well.[2] It may seem impossible to find any common feature of them all. At this point, rough sketches may be all we can hope for, at least as a starting point. This will give a general idea of what we are looking for before we attempt to go into detail or worry about borderline cases. And in many instances, we will never feel the need to take these further steps. In these circumstances it is reasonable to focus on the differences as well as the commonalities: they may prove more important in the end.

Gorgias seems to do more. He sketches out a couple of kinds of *aretē* that can be used as paradigmatic for other analogous accounts. He looks at the social roles of men and women in his own society and does not question them. If you accept those accounts of manly and womanly *aretē* you may even agree that the *aretē* of a man or woman involves, includes or even consists in or is due to behaving in the ways Gorgias specifies. From this someone might go on to find analogous accounts for the *aretē* of humans in other age brackets and other social roles, and beyond that to talk about the *aretai* of activities and tasks, and so on.

We may dispute Gorgias' offhand accounts of the *aretai* of men and women, but (and I think that this is significant) that makes no difference for Gorgias' purposes. If we can understand why someone else might think that these are the manly and womanly *aretai*, we can simply substitute the same kind of rough description of our own views and proceed in the same way. If, for example, Gorgias' manly and womanly *aretai* are what he supposed his fellow Greeks would roughly agree to be the characteristics of an ideal man and woman, we can substitute our own views and go on from there.

It is worth bearing in mind that there was no clear notion of definition in Gorgias' time – no imperative to find a single one-fits-all formula that accounts for all cases. For some purposes, it is more important to investigate the variety of a phenomenon in its several occurrences and to characterize them than to look for a single key to them all.

In this connection it is useful to note that Meno's list of *aretai* is a reply to Socrates' question in which the Greek can mean either "What do you say *aretē* is?" or "What do you say is an *aretē*?" Socrates intended it in the first way, and Meno took it in the second. Reasonably so, since that is a sensible question and it is also a question for which he had a ready answer. And since Meno extends the notion of *aretē* beyond its familiar application in which it refers only or primarily to various human characteristics – so that now every action has its *aretē* as well – he may well believe that his answer makes some kind of progress towards understanding the nature of *aretē* in general.

Part 2: Prodicus

Distinctions and Definitions

Prodicus was famous for drawing fine distinctions, a practice that was known variously as precision in speech (*akribologia*[3]), the precise use of names (*onomatōn akribeia*[4]) and correctness of names (*orthotēs onomatōn*[5]). This practice is prominent in Plato's presentation of Prodicus in the *Protagoras* and in several other dialogues. In the *Charmides* Socrates says "I have heard Prodicus making distinctions among words thousands of times"[6] and it is borne out by other ancient authors including Plato. Consider the opening of Prodicus' cameo speech in the *Protagoras*.

> [337a] Those who are present at such conversations should be common but not equal, because it is not the same thing. One should listen to both speakers in common but not distribute equal honor to each. Instead one should grant more to the wiser speaker and less to the one who is more ignorant. Now I myself, Protagoras and Socrates, think it is right for you to agree to dispute with each other about your claims, [337b] but not to quarrel, because friends argue with friends,

even with good will, while those who differ and are hostile quarrel with each other. This way our gathering will be most delightful, since you, the speakers, will be esteemed and not praised – for esteem is in the listener's souls without deceit, but being praised is often in the words of those who are lying contrary to their opinions. But we, your listeners, will feel good cheer but will not feel pleasure, since feeling good cheer is learning something [337c] and partaking in reason through thought itself, while feeling pleasure is eating something or experiencing something else that's pleasant in the body.

(Plato, *Protagoras* 337a2–c4)

Notice that Prodicus does not simply assert that disputing and quarreling are different; he explains how. This holds for the other distinctions he makes in the passage quoted. Prodicus points out that words have different meanings and encourages people to pay closer attention to the words they use so as to express precisely what they want to say. Elsewhere Plato refers to Prodicus as "the finest of the Sophists in distinguishing such names"[7] and refers to this practice as his "special art."[8] Hermias states that he "discovered" the accurate use of names, which if true would give Prodicus a claim to be the founder of lexicography and taxonomy and to have originated a technique that led to the notions of Socratic definitions, Platonic Forms and Aristotelian essences and that continues to be one of the basic practices of contemporary analytic philosophy.

Indeed Prodicus was doing something new – something that earlier thinkers had not developed systematically. The best-attested distinctions of Prodicus involve pleasure. According to Aristotle, he drew distinctions between pleasure, enjoyment, delight and good cheer, maintaining that enjoyment, delight and good cheer are different kinds of pleasure. Plato gives him credit for recognizing that although these distinctions are sometimes useful, there are occasions where the generic word "pleasure" is the right term to use.

[358a] "So you agree that what gives pleasure (*hēdu*) is good and what causes pain is bad. I am avoiding the distinction of words practiced by Prodicus here; for whether you call it pleasure-giving (*hēdu*) or delightful (*terpnon*) or enjoyable (*kharton*),[9] or however you enjoy [358b] naming these kinds of things, my excellent Prodicus, please respond to what I am trying to ask." – Prodicus laughed and agreed, and so did the others.

(Plato, *Protagoras* 358a5–b3)

For example, someone who knows all the different breeds of dogs will frequently say "dog" rather an specify any particular breed. Indeed, one of the requirements for the precise use of language is to know how precisely something needs to be described or otherwise located. Sometimes, depending on the context, the question "where do you live" is appropriately answered by "in Greece," other times by "in Athens" and other times "in the third floor apartment of 4 Akademias

Street." Likewise, knowing that some bugs are poisonous and others are not is useful but not particularly helpful. You want to know which kinds of bugs are poisonous and which kinds are not – that is, to distinguish among them. And in order to communicate this knowledge to others it will be helpful to have a vocabulary that is adequate for the job. Even then you will need to be able to explain or at least point to what the different words mean – what bugs they refer to. You will need to tell spiders from insects, for example, which spiders are poisonous to humans and which are not. Some ancient authors considered Prodicus' practice to be pedantry, but it is more justly seen as an important first move towards what soon became the standard philosophical practice of drawing distinctions where needed to solve problems, avoid contradictions and expose fallacies.

To judge by the *Protagoras* passage quoted above, Prodicus justified his distinctions and did so in a number of ways. He distinguishes "impartially" from "equally" by giving an example of a situation in which a person might do something that is impartial but not equal. We might suppose that there would be no point in making this distinction since the words mean such different things, but in fact "equal" is one of the meanings of the Greek word here translated as "impartial" (*koinos*), and ignorance of the distinction can lead to confusion or fallacious reasoning. This is related to Gorgias' manner of using paradigm cases to define.

The second distinction made in the speech quoted above (Plato, *Protagoras* 337a–b) differentiates debating from engaging in eristics, and it is to the point. Socrates and Protagoras began by engaging in a philosophical debate but wound up squabbling about the ground rules for their discussion. Prodicus calls them to order: they are behaving not like friends – who can debate matters on which they disagree by articulating their own views, criticizing each other's views and being willing to alter their own position or even accept their friend's view if the discussion convinces them that their own initial views were incorrect – but like enemies who quarrel when they disagree and aim for victory at all costs.

Respect and praise are proved different by displaying a case where praise can occur without respect. This discussion may appear unneeded since praise and respect seem to be different kinds of things: praise is something that we do and respect is something that we feel. I suppose the idea is that we are inclined to praise people we respect, but sometimes we may praise people we do not respect. The former praise is sincere and the latter may be insincere, so there is such a thing as insincere praise but not insincere respect. Therefore people should prefer to be respected rather than praised.

These three cases present different types of situations that show that the pairs of items involved are not (always) the same. This is Prodicus' goal in the passage, but it is not enough simply to assert that this is the case; he needs to justify his claim and he uses examples he supposes will be readily understood and accepted.

The fourth case is different. As in the earlier cases, feeling pleasure and feeling good cheer are initially differentiated by reference to the present situation in the dialogue, declaring that if Socrates and Protagoras behave as he has proposed, the listeners will feel good cheer but not pleasure. This time he justifies the distinction by assigning good cheer and pleasure to different sources – the one to bodily feelings, the other to reason and thought. He supplements this assignment by generalization: the good cheer that the listeners will experience comes from the experience of learning from Socrates and Protagoras and partaking in reason. Feeling pleasure is different: it comes from eating something (a specific example) or "experiencing something else that is pleasant in the body itself" (a generalization). This justification through examples is related to Gorgias' paradigm definitions, but unlike Gorgias, Prodicus suggests how to generalize, and this is the first move towards an explicit definition.

The definitions of pleasure as bodily and enjoyment as intellectual appear implausible, and we may wonder how closely Plato was following Prodicus in this and also in the other examples. In fact, there is ample evidence from other ancient authors that Prodicus did make distinctions in this range. Aristotle confirms that

> Prodicus divided pleasure (*hēdonē*) into enjoyment (*khara*), delight (*terpsis*) and good cheer (*euphrosunē*).[10]

Aristotle disagrees, declaring that these are all names for the same thing: pleasure. But Aristotle's disagreement does not affect the value of his testimony that Prodicus did make this distinction among kinds of pleasure.

Alexander in his commentary on this Aristotelian passage informs us that the Stoic philosophers followed Prodicus.

> Prodicus attempted to assign to each of these names something peculiar signifying [its meaning], just like the Stoics do, who say that enjoyment (*khara*) is rational elation, pleasure (*hēdonē*) irrational elation, delight (*terpsis*) the pleasure that comes from hearing, and good cheer (*euphrosunē*) the pleasure that comes from speech.

But, Alexander adds,

> This is from those who legislate [i.e., stipulate], not those who say what is sound.[11]

Aristotle does not say that Prodicus defined the four terms in question, but Alexander declares that he marked them off from one another, while Hermias says how he did so.

> Prodicus discovered the difference between delight (*terpsis*), enjoyment (*khara*) and good cheer (*euphrosunē*): delight is the pleasure (*hēdonē*) that comes from hearing what is beautiful, enjoyment is the pleasure of the soul, and good cheer the pleasure that comes from the eyes.[12]

Since Hermias, unlike Alexander, is commenting on Plato, not Aristotle, and since he goes beyond what Plato says, he seems to have had access to information about Prodicus that is no longer available, which contained the information he reports, specifically the accounts of what delight, enjoyment, good cheer are, including that they are all different kinds of pleasure. This is good reason to think that Prodicus did distinguish these four feelings and identified delight, gratification and enjoyment as different kinds of pleasure, just as Aristotle had reported and distinguished them more or less in the way he is presented by Plato.

This takes Prodicus two steps beyond Gorgias. Not content with examples (which have the disadvantage of not being precise and being able to be taken differently by different people), Prodicus offers accounts that provide ways to distinguish one thing from another. Further, by identifying different kinds of pleasure, he provides the means to select the appropriate degree of generality, as the passage from Aristotle quoted just above shows.

When we think of definitions we tend to think of the kind found in dictionaries, which contain a catalog of the meanings of words. The word "embryo" can be defined as "fetus" and the words can be substituted for one another in sentences without bringing about any difference in meaning. Prodicus is not doing this. He is distinguishing between things, not words. Pleasure is something different from delight and he attempts to capture the difference. This will be one reason why he is associated with the accurate use of "names." A name is the name of something and to use a name accurately is a matter of using it to refer to the thing it is the name of.

Since delight, enjoyment and good cheer are different kinds of pleasure, when we want to say something that holds for all three kinds, we can say "pleasure" instead of treating each kind separately. In effect, Prodicus laid the ground for taxonomy, in which different species are grouped together under their common genus and what holds for the genus holds for all of its species, while each species has its own characteristics that are not shared by some or by any of the others. This recognition was in turn a basic ingredient for Plato's method of definition by collection and division and Aristotle's method of definition by genus and differentiae.

Whether Prodicus considered this practice a matter of defining as well as distinguishing is unclear. Part of the unclarity comes from the unclarity that surrounds the notion of definition. Since the notion of defining was apparently inaugurated by Gorgias and Prodicus and since we do not know that he had a word (such as "defining") to describe what he was doing, it is best to refrain from saying much on this topic. However, one thing that can be said is that one of the functions of definitions is to help us distinguish and identify things. If we have definitions of delight, enjoyment and good cheer, we can use them to tell whether or not we are feeling delight as opposed to enjoyment or good cheer. It would be anachronistic to expect Prodicus to have formulated this as a requirement that a definition of x states necessary and sufficient conditions for anything to be an x, or to have conceived of definitions the way Socrates, Plato or Aristotle would do, but in these circumstances it is reasonable to say that Prodicus made important basic steps towards the

104 Definition

conceptions of definition and the associated practices of defining things that soon became a dominant feature of Greek philosophy.

Notes

1. This word is usually translated as "order" or "ornament" but here as "credit," which better captures its meaning in this context.
2. Plato, *Meno* 72a.
3. Marcellinus [?], *Life of Thucydides* 36.
4. Hermias, *Scholia on Plato's Phaedrus* 267b, similarly *onomatōn orthotēs*, Plato, *Cratylus* 384c.
5. Plato, *Cratylus* 384c, *Euthydemus* 277e.
6. Plato, *Cratylus* 163d.
7. Plato, *Laches* 197d.
8. Plato, *Protagoras* 340b.
9. These words are adjectives derived from the nouns *hēdonē* (pleasure), *terpsis* (delight) and *khara* (enjoyment).
10. Aristotle, *Topics* 2.6 112b22–3.
11. Alexander, *Commentary on Aristotle's Topics* 181.2–6.
12. Scholium on Plato's *Phaedrus* 267b.

11
ANTILOGIC

The following passages refer to a teaching method closely associated with Protagoras.

> There are two mutually opposed *logoi* on any matter (*pragma*).[1]

> Protagoras made the weaker and stronger *logos* and taught his students to blame and praise the same person.[2]

> This is making the weaker *logos* stronger. And people were rightly annoyed at Protagoras' promise, for it is false and not true, but seems to be likely and it belongs in no art except rhetoric and eristic.[3]

The people referred to in the last passage just quoted seem to have thought that Protagoras claimed to teach people to win any argument, to be successful in any legal case, to get any measure whatsoever passed through the Assembly.[4] This would be a powerful skill indeed, and also one to be dreaded, since the temptation to use it for one's own advantage and to the unfair disadvantage of others or of the whole city would have been hard to resist. But Protagoras surely did not make this claim; it is patently absurd and he could not possibly deliver on it. So what might he have meant by his claim to make a weaker *logos* stronger?

As noted earlier,[5] the word *logos* stands on the borderline between words, things and facts. The meanings of *logos* include speech, statement and argument. *Pragma* (in Fragment 6a) is definitely on the "thing" side, but it is a word that can be applied to a wider variety of entities than physical objects. I have here translated it as "matter," which, like *logos*, leans both ways: we can talk about matters of fact and the subject matter of a science or of a speech, and we can also describe something

DOI: 10.4324/9781003493259-11

as a matter of opinion, a matter for thought, or the matter of a speech (where we are referring to the ideas, evidence and facts being considered).

Adopting this wider notion of *logos* helps us to understand both the "two *logoi*" thesis and the "making the weaker *logos* stronger" thesis. First it is necessary to abandon the common practice of translating *logos* as "argument." This is how the word has most often been translated in connection with Protagoras' claim but is implausible on an ordinary understanding of the word, in which an argument consists of one or more premises and a conclusion alleged to follow from those premises. An argument is what it is; it cannot become weaker or stronger, because that will require changing at least one of the propositions in the argument, and so it will be a different argument. This response covers other types of arguments as well. Further, it is no help to say that making the weaker *logos* stronger means finding a stronger way to argue for the same conclusion because again, this is a matter of finding a different argument.

More generally, presenting your case is a matter of attempting to persuade the audience that what you are proposing is superior to what your opponent or opponents are proposing. In some cases it will be a matter of persuading the audience that what you are saying is true and what the opposition is saying is false. This will be the case where what is at stake is whether or not something happened, for example whether the defendant in a court case did or did not commit a crime. In others, it will be a matter of persuading them that what you are proposing is more likely to be true or advantageous than what the opposition is proposing. This will be the usual case in debates on proposals concerning legislation or policy, where the consequences of adopting or rejecting a proposal are typically uncertain.

Persuading the audience that the opposing side is not worth supporting may include rebutting specific considerations brought by the opposition, perhaps by showing that the claims made by the opponent are inconsistent. But these are not typically the only parts of making your case. In a judicial proceeding, much of your time is spent presenting your side, telling your story and attempting to establish your narrative as dominant – that is to say, stronger than your opponent's narrative. Similarly in the Assembly, much of your speech will be devoted to giving reasons in favor of your own position, not in refuting the claims of the opposition, even though arguing against your opponents is likely to play a part.

On the understanding of *logos* developed just now it is easy to make perfectly good sense of Protagoras' promise or profession to make the weaker *logos* stronger. Since a *logos* can be one side of a case – a narrative, a story, a scenario or an account of how things were in the past, or how things are now, or how things will be in the future – Protagoras' promise amounts to a profession that he will teach his students to make stronger cases, to tell more convincing stories, to give more persuasive accounts, to construct more plausible scenarios. Since he could not guarantee that the case he teaches them to make would be more persuasive than the case made by the opposition (after all, there might be cases where two of his former students are on opposite sides and victory for both would be impossible) his claim, if plausible, will have been that he will teach you to make your own case stronger – to improve your presentation, to make it as persuasive as possible, without *necessarily* being more persuasive than the opposition.

In general, the situations for which Protagoras prepared his students are competitive: there is a winner and a loser. In order to win you have to present a stronger (i.e., more persuasive) case for your side than your opponent. Since you don't in general know what case your opponent will make, you have to make your case as strong as possible. You will need to anticipate your opponent's case and be ready to rebut or refute it. No single technique can be expected to produce victory every time, rather one would need an array of tactics that can be learned, practiced and mastered.

Protagoras could have achieved this result in several ways. Students could have been instructed to construct opposing cases themselves, or in a team with a partner. The cases could have involved real or imaginary situations. He could have had the students observe trials and meetings of the Assembly and afterward analyze the speeches and try to improve them. They might have been made to study sample speeches, perhaps written by Protagoras himself for the purpose. We can also suppose that his instruction involved more than just finding the most persuasive words – it will have included practice in rhetorical style, delivery and word choice among other things, although we have next to nothing to go on for these matters. Still, they would have been important ingredients in making a speech as strong as possible.

In these competitive situations the measure of the success or failure of each side is the response of the audience, the number of votes you get. Victory does not always depend on the factual or logical strength of the case you make, but on what the individual members of the voting body think, which among other things includes how convincing each of them finds the cases that have been made. As we know too well, people's convictions do not always depend on evidence and argument. The Hippocratic treatise *On the Nature of Man*[6] recognizes this fact:

> When the same people debate one another in front of the same audience, victory in the discussion never goes to the same person three times in a row, but now one wins, now another, and now the one who happens to speak most fluently in front of the crowd.[7]

In this way humans (not the objective facts of the situation) are the measure of all things – of all things that are a matter of opinion rather than the simple fact of the matter, things in which the facts are not clear but debatable – that is, in situations for which Protagoras promises to train his students. Thus "a human being is the measure of all things" is true in at least this restricted sense.

After Protagoras' death Plato gave a name to these practices: *antilogikē*, which I shall call "antilogic" for convenience's sake. The word occurs in four places in Plato's dialogues, first in the following passage from the *Phaedrus*, a work largely devoted to the nature of rhetoric.

> [261c] Opponents in the lawcourts (*antidikoi*) speak on opposite sides (*antilegein*)... about what is just and unjust.... A person who does this skillfully (*tekhnēi*) will make the [261d] same thing appear to the same people sometimes just, but when he wants to, unjust.... And when he speaks in the Assembly he will make the same things appear to the city sometimes good and sometimes the opposite.... So antilogic is not restricted to the law courts [261e] and public speaking, but rather, it seems that it must be some single expertise (*tekhnē*) – if in fact it *is* an expertise – that is relevant to everything that is said.
>
> (Plato, *Phaedrus* 261c4–e2)

Plato follows Protagoras in mentioning law courts and the Assembly as venues where antilogic is typically employed, and also in stating that it is relevant to all speaking. He also says that antilogic has to do with arguing both sides of an issue. However, his hostility to antilogic is clear in the assertion that antilogic can be used to make the same people think that the same thing is sometimes just and sometimes unjust,[8] also in using a term for public speaking that can also mean "demagoguery" (*dēmēgoria*), in referring to antilogic as "an expertise (if it really is an expertise)," and in his overstatement of Protagoras' promise to make the weaker *logos* stronger in the passage just below. Elsewhere Plato names Protagoras in connection with antilogic and refers to instruction manuals in which he taught how to argue against experts in any given field and in the same passage attributes this kind of dispute to Sophists in general.

> [232d][Socrates] And what about laws and all kinds of political issues? Don't Sophists promise to make people able to engage in controversies (*amphisbētētikoi*) about them? ... As a matter of fact you can find anything you need to say to contradict (*antilegein*) any expert both in general and within each particular field of expertise (*tekhnē*), laid out published and written down for anybody who wants to learn it.
>
> [Theaetetus] If they didn't promise that, practically no one would bother to discuss with them.... Apparently you're talking about Protagoras' writings on wrestling[9] and [232e] other fields of expertise (*tekhnai*).
>
> [Soc] And on many other things too, my friend. In fact, take expertise in disputation (*antilogikē tekhnē*) as a whole. Doesn't it seem like a capacity that's sufficient for carrying on controversies (*amphisbētēseis*) about absolutely everything? (Plato, *Sophist* 232d-e, Hackett tr.)

Elsewhere in the same dialogue, which is devoted to defining "the Sophist," one of the proposed definitions is

> The money-making branch of expertise (*tekhnē*) in eristic (*eristikē*)[10], antilogic (*antilogikē*), controversy (*amphisbētētikē*), fighting, combat[11], and acquisition.
> (Plato, *Sophist* 226a, Hackett tr.)

Plato's hostility to antilogic is apparent in these passages. For present purposes, it is enough to note that while for Protagoras it was an expertise useful and perhaps needed for success in private and public life, Plato associates it with arguing against anyone on any subject and defeating experts in areas where you have no expertise yourself. But despite Gorgias' boast that this is exactly what rhetoric enables a person to do[12], we may wonder how often in practice a Sophist's pupil would have attempted to persuade people to ignore the advice of experts on technical matters and how much success such an attempt would be likely to enjoy.

Plato associates antilogic with eristic because it engages in disputation and because, he claims, people who make use of antilogic at one time convince people that something is just and at another time that it is unjust – by which I take him to mean that it has no regard for the truth. In that Plato is out to contrast antilogic with philosophy, which he takes to be the honest and serious pursuit of truth, this is a fair criticism of antilogic. On the other hand, in the settings in which antilogic is generally used (promoting one side of a case) the purpose is not the disinterested pursuit of truth but victory as determined by the votes of the jury or Assembly members at the conclusion of a debate. Moreover, the jury and Assembly members in general do not have access to the relevant knowledge: whether or not the accused committed the offense he was charged with, or what will be the outcome if the measure proposed in the Assembly is approved. The philosophical search for truth is irrelevant here. Further, given the contingencies of the kinds of issues for which Protagoras prepared his students, the charge that they convince people that the same thing is just and unjust may misfire. It is not likely that the same person would argue both for and against a proposed measure or would both prosecute and defend the same case. And if we consider where he deals with more than one case, say cases of repaying one's debts, Plato should recognize that sometimes it *is* just to repay one's debts and in other cases it is not.[13] Perhaps Plato is engaging in some sophistry of his own in these charges against antilogic.

The earliest occurrence of the term "antilogic" (in the *Phaedrus* passage quoted above) announces its etymology, a noun derived from the verb *antilegein*, which is in turn derived from the verb *legein*, meaning "to speak" and is connected with *logos*. *Antilegein* means "to speak on opposite sides" and so, to speak against, to contradict, to argue against, to dispute, to refute. *Antilogikē* is a noun[14] whose meaning is "expertise in disputing," "expertise in speaking against," etc. I have given several translations of these words in order to indicate that it is to some extent a matter of choice how to translate them, a matter of deciding which expression in the same semantic range best fits a given context.

Antilogic is commonly taken to have to do with contradiction. Thus the key sentence in the *Phaedrus* passage is often taken as saying that antilogic "consists in causing the same thing to be seen by the same people now as possessing one predicate and now as possessing the opposite or contradictory predicate."[15] I argued above[16] that "argument" is too narrow a translation of *logos* to be a plausible way of viewing Protagoras' "two *logoi*" doctrine. For similar reasons "contradiction" is too narrow a view of the scope of antilogic (a word derived from *logos*), which should be understood as expertise in making a case for one's side in adversarial situations.

Since the goal of antilogic is to enable you to make the strongest possible case for your side and against your opponent's side and if making the strongest possible case requires you to anticipate your opponent's case and rebut it, it has important consequences for philosophy. It is a technique for testing ideas that can be employed in private as well as public settings, as in cooperative as well as competitive situations, sort of like a "friendly" football match. First, it can be used to test other people's ideas. Someone maintains that p and you rebut it and perhaps also make a case for not-p. If you don't convince your interlocutor, she is free to maintain her original view, but if you convince her that she is wrong, then three things may happen: she may abandon her belief that p, or she may produce other reasons to believe p, or she may modify p so as to avoid your objections. If the first of these happens, then the conversation is at an end. If the second or third happens, the conversation may continue until either you or your interlocutor has exhausted your supply of relevant considerations. Further and likewise, antilogic becomes a technique for testing your own ideas. After making the strongest possible case for p and also for not-p, you can see which of the two cases seems to you strongest, modify the original view if you can see a way to do so, test the modified view and eventually end up with something that you find satisfactory.

The Importance of Antilogic

Antilogic was taught by Protagoras and doubtless by other Sophists as well. Its influence can be seen by its prominent appearance in a wide variety of literary genres, beginning with some of the Sophists' performance pieces, such as Prodicus' *Choice of Heracles*,[17] where the figures of Virtue and Vice attempt to persuade the young Heracles to follow their respective ways of life.

The *Antilogies* of Antiphon as described above[18] are excellent examples of antilogic, showing how the same person can make cases both for and against (both for the prosecution and for the defense) and in this way may anticipate what the opponents might say and prepare a ready reply.

Antilogic is also behind Gorgias' performance pieces *Encomium of Helen*[19] and *Defense of Palamedes* even though they present only one side of the situation.

The former work assumes that the audience is familiar with the events – that Helen eloped with Paris, abandoning her husband Menelaus and that this deed brought about the Trojan War – and it does not dispute them. In fact, it avoids mentioning what she did and the catastrophic results that followed. Instead it focuses on the question of responsibility: was Helen responsible for what she did? If she was not responsible, then she does not deserve the blame she has received. It proceeds by listing the possible causes of her actions and showing that she was not responsible no matter which was the real cause, and so, as we are left to understand, she cannot be blamed for the consequences of her deed. The purpose is to forestall any possible argument that Helen was responsible, and the composition of the speech required Gorgias to anticipate what someone might say in order to fasten the blame on her. This is one of the uses to which I have suggested that antilogic can be put. Gorgias' *Defense of Palamedes* too anticipates the content of a prosecution speech and convincingly argues that none of the accounts of the alleged crime the accusers might give are plausible and similarly that none of the scenarios it might present about how the crime took place could have occurred.

The *Twin Arguments*[20] is another example. The author of this text is unknown and there is no particular reason to suppose that it was composed by a Sophist. It might even have been a homework exercise for some of Sophist's students. It first argues that good and bad are different and then that they are the same, and then proceeds to do the same for other seemingly opposed pairs of qualities: *kalon* (beautiful, fine, good, morally good) and *aiskhron* (ugly, disgraceful, shameful), just and unjust, true and false, sane and mad.

Antilogic is prominent in Greek drama too, both in comedy (Aristophanes' *Clouds*, for example) where an essential component was an *agōn* (a contest or debate) relevant to the topic of the play, and in tragedy (Sophocles' *Antigone* is a good case in point). In his *History of the Peloponnesian War,* Thucydides, heavily influenced by the Sophists, devotes much space to speeches of his own composition put into the mouths of politicians, ambassadors and generals in order to reveal the grounds on which political and military decisions were or could have been made and the kind of debates that took place in reaching the decisions, frequently with opposing views presented.[21]

When Protagoras advertised his education as teaching the skill (*tekhnē*) that leads to success in all kinds of conversations, in particular the competitive situations of the Assembly and the lawcourt, he did not exclude other uses of antilogic and quite possibly his teaching included practice in debates on general topics like the one in the following passage. (The last words are significant.)

> After a competitor in the pentathlon had hit Epitimos the Pharsalian with a javelin and killed him unintentionally, Pericles spent an entire day with Protagoras discussing whether the javelin or the person who threw it or the organizers of the event were responsible "according to the most correct account (*logos*)."[22]

Whether or not the conversation actually took place, it illustrates how antilogic can be applied in a friendly discussion far removed from the Assembly and the courts. The question is not simply whether the person who threw the javelin was responsible for Epitimos' death; that is what a judicial trial might have to decide. Two other possibilities are canvassed as well: whether it was the judges of the competition who were responsible (perhaps through negligence), and whether it was the javelin. In fact, the question is not one of legal guilt but of responsibility "according to the most correct account." Such a conversation would almost inevitably be of (what we would consider) a philosophical nature. It would not be concerned simply, or very much, with the particular circumstances of the accident, or with questions of law, but with the more general topics of responsibility and causation, and such a conversation could easily last all day without coming to a definite conclusion. Since the participants were on good terms and respected one another (Pericles' high regard for Protagoras is shown in his decision to entrust to Protagoras the task of drafting the constitution of the Panhellenic colony Thurii.) it is easy to suppose that the conversation, if it took place, began not because the men disagreed but because they were puzzled and that they spent the day jointly exploring this complex issue from many different points of view, putting up reasons why the thrower should be considered strictly responsible and reasons why he should not, and similarly for the judges and the javelin. It is even possible that they discussed the more abstract question of what responsibility "according to the most correct account" *is*, and pursued these issues with no sense of competition or of there being a loser or a winner.

Despite Plato's objections to antilogic this last-mentioned use proved to be vitally important in philosophy. I will conclude this chapter by showing its effects on Socrates. Its influence on Plato and Aristotle will be discussed in Chapters 14 and 15. This discussion will be based on the Socratic method as it appears in Plato's "Socratic" dialogues, which I take to be a type of discussion Socrates actually employed. In it, Socrates discusses important issues with one or more others (known as interlocutors). Socrates claims to know nothing important and does not attempt to convince his interlocutors to adopt his views. Rather, he proceeds by what is known as the Socratic method or *elenchus*, which consists of examining another's opinion on a subject (for example, the nature of the virtue courage) by asking a series of questions, which the interlocutor is free to answer as he likes. These are frequently questions that can be answered "yes" or "no." These questions elicit further views of the interlocutor and the usual result is that the interlocutor is shown to have beliefs that contradict the opinion of his that is under examination. At that point the interlocutor must agree that one or more of his beliefs are false, either the opinion being examined or one of the views that led to the contradiction.

To conduct the Socratic *elenchus* is not easy. It requires you to find beliefs of your opponent that contradict the belief in question. The way Socrates does this sometimes has the ingenuity of Sherlock Holmes, picking up information about his interlocutor's views from a casual conversation, bringing in relevant information about the interlocutor and his family, suggesting that his interlocutor believes something else (and leaving him free to deny it if he disagrees) and so forth, in just the right way to challenge the view under consideration. Surely, we might think, it would be easier to make a case or construct an argument against the view than to proceed in this seemingly haphazard way. But that is not as likely to convince the interlocutor to reconsider his beliefs as the *elenchus* is, because he can simply refuse to accept some of the premises in our argument or some of the considerations in the case we are making, whereas when Socrates is done, he finds that he is in disagreement with himself – and something has to give.

The purpose of including this brief account of the Socratic method is to show how it is related to antilogic. I have proposed that one of the uses to which antilogic was put was to test the strength of one's own case against opposing cases that might be brought against it, searching out its weak points and attempting to make it as strong as possible. Socrates does not present an opposing case; instead, he helps his interlocutors test the strength of their own views and when a view proves fatally weak, he encourages them to modify it or to state another view, which can then be subjected to the same kind of examination. I find this a truly brilliant application (or extension) of antilogic so that from an adversarial, competitive procedure it becomes a cooperative one and one that you can use on yourself as Socrates himself evidently did.[23] In this way, it becomes an outstanding resource for doing genuine philosophy in a disinterested way.

The word "antilogic" is not found in Aristotle's surviving writings, but his conception of dialectic as constructing arguments and rebutting opponents on the basis of "received opinions" is closely related to antilogic's practice of finding arguments and rebuttals. Further, in the *Topics*,[24] his treatise on dialectic, he lists three purposes for which dialectic is useful: training, conversations and the philosophical sciences. Very briefly, training is the kind of thing Protagoras did in teaching antilogic to his students; conversations may include discussions where there is or can be disagreement; they can also include the Socratic kind of conversations. As for its use in "the philosophical sciences" I interpret this to refer to the use of dialectic as part of the procedure involved in determining scientific facts and the principles of sciences[25] since Aristotle declares that "for the philosophical sciences it is useful, because if we are able to raise difficulties on both sides, we shall more easily discern both truth and falsehood on every point."

Like Socrates, Aristotle owed much to antilogic for his own philosophical methods. He approaches many philosophical issues by collecting and setting out the opinions of "the wise and the many" about ideas relevant to his inquiry. He identifies questions and problems a satisfactory theory needs to answer and detects whether and where others' opinions conflict with the evidence and with one another. In cases of disagreement, he tends to prefer the opinions that he considers more authoritative than others. He hopes to establish the truth of all or most of the remaining views and on that basis work out a theory that solves the problems he has identified as requiring solution. This procedure requires a

114 Antilogic

kind of conversation with his predecessors in which Aristotle tests their theories against one another and against his own more elaborated ideas, seeing how well they fare and in many cases drawing on them for suggestions. While this practice is not the same as antilogic, I believe that it can be usefully regarded as an evolution of antilogic along lines sketched out above in connection with the Socratic method.

Notes

1 Protagoras, fragment 6a DK.
2 Eudoxus, fragment 4.
3 Aristotle, *Rhetoric* 1402a24–28.
4 Some translate the claim as "making the weaker argument the stronger one" but the second occurrence of "the" is not required by the Greek text and since, as will be shown in the next paragraph, it makes for a totally implausible claim on Protagoras' part, it should be rejected.
5 P. 86.
6 This text is dated to the fifth century BCE and so is approximately contemporary with Protagoras.
7 *On the Nature of Man* 1.
8 This charge seems to suggest that antilogic is involved with hypocrisy, but it's worth bearing in mind cases where it is morally and legally correct to do just this. For example, it is sometimes correct to use the fact that someone was driving at 75 miles per hour as evidence that he was doing something illegal, but in other cases it can be used as evidence that he was not doing anything illegal.
9 This is a reference to a work called *Kataballontes* which means "throwing down" – that is, knock-out arguments that are sure to defeat an opponent.
10 Eristic is something characterized by *eris*, which means strife, quarrel or hostile dispute. It is used in cases where people argue against one another, typically using bad reasoning or irrelevant considerations.
11 See previous note.
12 Plato, *Gorgias* 456b–7a. However, we need to bear in mind that it is Plato, the author of this dialogue, who puts these words in Gorgias' mouth.
13 Recall the example of the madman's weapon at Plato, *Republic* 331c.
14 More precisely it is an adjective with which we supply the noun *tekhnē*.
15 This is how it is rendered in Kerferd (1981), 61.
16 P. 86.
17 This work is translated in the Appendix of Translated Texts, pp. 180–9.
18 Pp. 51–2.
19 This work is included in the Appendix of Translated Texts, pp. 169–74.
20 This text is translated in the Appendix of Translated Texts, pp. 180–8.
21 Speeches for both sides of a dispute are found as early as the first book of Homer's *Iliad*, but they become more frequent and more prominent from mid-fifth century. Notable in this regard is Aeschylus' *Oresteia*, first performed in 458 BCE, at the beginning of the influence of the Sophists.
22 Plutarch, *Life of Pericles*, Chapter 36.
23 This thought may be behind the assertion that Protagoras was the first to practice the Socratic form of *logos* (Diogenes Laertius 9.52).
24 Aristotle, *Topics* 1.2.
25 See below, p. 152.

12
NOMOS AND *PHUSIS*

Introduction

Most books on the Sophists devote a chapter to the subject of *nomos* and *phusis* as if it were a topic specifically associated with the Sophists. But the authors they cite range from playwrights and poets to historians, orators, essayists, philosophers and other authors, and include very few Sophists. Since this book is about the Sophists the present chapter will restrict itself to the three Sophists known to have contributed to the discussion of this subject. That is not to say that other Sophists did not. It is very likely that some of them did, but the absence of information on their views makes it impossible to say anything definite about them.[1]

Terms of the Debate

The topic of this chapter is standardly stated in its original Greek form because the range of meanings of each word makes it impossible to capture their meanings in any single English word. *Nomos* (pl. *nomoi*) is translated "law," "custom" and "convention," depending on the context, and *phusis* (the origin of our word "physics"), translated "nature," was conceived in a number of ways, two of which are of interest to us: first, nature as what we have in mind when we talk about something's nature, meaning what it really, basically or essentially is, its permanent characteristics, how it would or should normally be; second, nature as in the expression "by nature," where we mean something like "in reality" or "as it really is (perhaps despite appearances to the contrary)."

Phusis is usually used for matters of fact, the way things are and must be, while *nomos* has normative force: it represents the way things should be, what people think is right, in particular, what they think is the right way to live. Here values and morality enter the scene. And since *nomos* is also the word for laws enacted in states – and also repealed – by the decisions of humans, the word has implications of variability from place to place and from time to time.

The two terms were generally thought to be contrastive: what is "by *phusis*" is necessary, universal, inalterable, the same everywhere, and independent of human will (think of the law of gravity); what is "by *nomos*" is contingent, subject to change, different in different places and dependent on human decisions (think of a measure passed by a city council). Looked at like this, they appear to apply to different kinds of phenomena, but they gave rise to interesting questions, such as the following. Is human society due to human nature or is it merely a matter of convention? Is there a universal morality or are morals only a product of local custom? Is human nature selfish, and if so then to what (if any) extent must laws and political institutions be established to rein human nature in? Is this even possible? Am I better off to follow the dictates of *nomos* or those of *phusis*? Do I have a choice?

A wide variety of views were proposed about the relations between *nomos* and *phusis*. According to one, *nomos* and *phusis* are opposed to one another, requiring us to do contrary things. Another viewpoint regarded them as complementary: where *phusis* leaves open a range of possible attitudes and behaviors, *nomos* prescribes which of these we are to adopt. Another approach saw *nomos* as based on *phusis*. The expression "*nomos* of *phusis*" (law of nature) is employed to mean what nature requires as opposed to laws created by humans. Moreover, there were a variety of opinions on how we should negotiate this complex territory. Protagoras promoted the idea that we should adhere to the laws and customs of our community because that is the only way we can live in civilized society; in fact, without *nomos* we would be reduced to a "state of nature" where there is no cooperation and everyone is at the mercy of everyone else. According to another view *nomos* is a sham, simply a conspiracy of the naturally weaker many to defeat the naturally stronger few who have a natural right to rule in their own self-interest. Antiphon writes that it is to our advantage to obey the law when others are looking and to follow *phusis* (that is, to act in our self-interest) when they are not. Others expressed the view that since *phusis* is necessary and inevitable, considerations of *nomos* are simply irrelevant. Protagoras, Hippias and Antiphon fit into this matrix in different ways.

Protagoras

The word *nomos* does not occur in Protagoras' few surviving words and *phusis* only once, where it has no obvious connection with the *nomos-phusis* issue,[2] but as in other matters Protagoras touched on the issue in a way that opened it for the elaborate treatment it received over the following decades. The principal text is his long speech in Plato's *Protagoras* which contains (in the form of a myth) an account of human nature that emphasizes the need of humans to live in communities (320d–3a).[3]

Human nature includes the practical intelligence of craft knowledge, which enables us to feed, clothe and shelter ourselves, and to make other contrivances that are necessary or desirable for life. It also includes *aidōs* and *dikē*, which are, roughly, our concern about what others think about us (*aidōs*) and a sense of fairness towards others (*dikē*). These are qualities required for people to live together in communities, without which we would be solitary and unable to survive because we could not cooperate, share responsibilities or benefit from one another's practical abilities. In their absence, there would inevitably be a war of all against all, which would swiftly lead to annihilation, but their presence enables us to form communities in which to live together in harmony and defend ourselves against the attacks of wild animals and also human enemies – people from other communities. Protagoras did not envision a community of all humanity; his model was the Greek city-states, each of which had its own history, customs, rituals and sense of identity and in many cases a rivalry with neighboring cities which not infrequently led to hostilities.

In this situation it was important for children to be brought up to be citizens of their city, which included learning to follow the social and political practices, and to follow the rituals and traditions specific to their land. This was a matter of education, which began in the cradle and continued until adulthood, with everyone in the community participating in it. Protagoras believed that it takes an entire community to raise a child properly – that is, to be a good citizen of that particular community, which involves the interpersonal virtues of justice, moderation and piety: justice involving one's relations with others, moderation involving one's appetites and ambitions, and piety involving one's relations to the gods, one's parents etc., and, obviously, knowledge of the way things are done in one's community (which includes knowledge of the community's laws) and the bounds of acceptable behavior.

Different Greek cities had different laws, customs, and religious traditions. People were brought up differently in Sparta than in Athens; they saw things differently and in an important sense they lived in different worlds, even though these worlds had much in common, including their language and their worship of the Olympian gods. The differences came to be described as *nomos*: whereas human nature (*phusis*) is the same for each of us, the *nomoi* of one community are different from the *nomoi* of another; what is right or acceptable in one city is not necessarily right or acceptable in another. Acceptance of the *nomoi* of our community stems from our concern for what others (in particular, the people we are in contact with, originally our immediate family, and later the other members of our community) think of us. Since we are born into a particular city, say, Athens, we naturally want to fit in, to become good Athenians, and as *we* see the world, this is the right way to be, perhaps the only correct way. Exposure to people from other cities, who were raised differently, might result in our thinking that these others are wrong or bad, but it might also result in our recognizing that they are just different and that our way of living (which includes, say, worshiping Akadēmos, a divine figure worshiped only in Athens) is only one among many, but still ours, that is, part of our identity. Traveling and living in other cities might even lead us to appreciate other ways of life and accept that what is considered right in Corinth, but not right or even wrong in Athens, is not *simply* wrong.

On this account, nature (i.e., human nature) is the same for all, but each of us is subjected to training which includes inculcation of our community's values. This is no more paradoxical than the fact that people have roughly the same bodies with the same kinds of capacities, including the capacity to learn, but different people learn how to do different things. Some become farm workers and develop special skills that doctors, auto mechanics and teachers (who all have learned the special skills of their own work) do not have.

The belief that the ways of our own city are right (or at least right for our city) if taken in a certain way can lead to the idea of justice, but there is no good evidence that Protagoras took this step. On the other hand, Protagoras' account of human nature and his recognition that not all people agree on what is right and his explanation of this fact was a significant change in outlook. Traditionally it was the gods, Zeus in particular, who decreed what is right and wrong for mortals to do, providing an absolute authority for morality and assurance that transgressions would inevitably be punished.[4] Such a world view could account for disagreement among individuals about what is right and wrong: some people got the message right and some did not. But this easy solution was not so easy to apply to communities whose *nomoi* were different but which worked well enough for normal purposes and where it was not at all clear whether Athens's *nomoi,* Corinth's or Sparta's, or any of them were in accordance with Zeus's commands. Protagoras' myth gives Zeus a fundamental role, since it was he who wished the human race to survive and decreed that all humans should have a share of *aidōs* and *dikē* so as to be able to form stable communities, but he did not establish how those communities should be run or the ways of life and values they would establish. That work was left to humans and, as Protagoras goes on to say, to Sophists in particular, who were specialists in those matters, and best suited to educate the citizens of any city they visited. Thus Protagoras championed the superiority of humans over animals (which lack *aidōs* and *dikē*), accounted for the fact that not all humans are equally good citizens (not all of them have the same amount of *aidōs* and *dikē*, their "shares" are not all equal), did not suppose that there was a single morality and set of customs that was right for all people and all communities, and opened the door for the further study of *nomos* and *phusis*.

Hippias

In his cameo performance in Plato's *Protagoras* Hippias refers to the contrast between *nomos* and *phusis* in the following passage, which appears to favor *phusis*. If I am correct in thinking that the speeches of Prodicus and Hippias as well as Protagoras's account of human nature reflect the interests of those

Sophists and theories they actually held,[5] this passage constitutes evidence that Hippias was known for holding views on the relation between *nomos* and *phusis*.

> Gentlemen who are present, I consider you all to be kinsmen, close friends and fellow citizens by nature (*phusis*), not by convention (*nomos*). For like is by nature akin to like, but *nomos*, the tyrant of the human race, in many ways constrains us contrary to nature. Therefore it would be disgraceful for us, who are the wisest of the Greeks and have assembled together in this headquarters of wisdom and in this greatest and most prosperous house of the city itself, to understand the nature of things but not affirm anything worthy of all this dignity, but disagree with one another as if we were the lowest kind of people.
> (Plato, *Protagoras* 337c–e)

Our problem is that the passage does not make clear what Hippias's views were. It occurs in the scene where the assembled company is trying to persuade Socrates not to abandon his conversation with Protagoras and leave the house in which it was taking place. The reason for Socrates' surprising behavior is that he has been unable to agree with Protagoras as to how to proceed in their discussion, Protagoras prefers to expatiate at length and Socrates insists that when he asks questions he can only understand brief answers, not long speeches. Since Protagoras insists on giving long answers Socrates cannot continue the conversation. When it is his turn to speak Hippias adopts a conciliatory policy: the speeches should be not too long or too short. Socrates yields to this suggestion and agrees to stay. He then proposes a way to continue the conversation that may avoid the long answers given by Protagoras. He suggests that he answer questions posed by Protagoras rather than the other way round, a proposal which Protagoras accepts (338d–e). Hippias' mention of *nomos* and *phusis* at 337d is not the focus of his attempt at persuasion and it is hardly relevant to the solution he proposes. It is simply part of a move to win the favor of the audience, Socrates and Protagoras in particular, by maintaining that as fellow members of the community of the wise they are naturally (by *phusis*) akin and related, and that this relation is more important than the fact that their being citizens of different cities means that they are members of different political communities. He holds that one's citizenship is merely a matter of *nomos*, which constrains people to identify themselves in terms of geographical boundaries which are not natural and are less important than their natural affinities. This is a novel extension of the concept of *phusis*, which when applied to humans was normally taken to include features that all humans share so that there is a single human nature that all humans have. It would follow that for Hippias an individual human can have more than one nature. In the case in point, one's nature as a human being and one's nature as a wise human being. This thought, if pursued, might have led in interesting directions, but as far as we know, no one took it up. In any case, *nomos* and *phusis* have nothing to do with Hippias' proposal to Socrates and Protagoras – which corroborates the interpretation on which they are put into his mouth as a kind of signature line.

The interesting claims that "*nomos* tyrannizes the human race" and that it "often constrains us contrary to *phusis*" are striking but leave unclear just how *nomos* and *phusis* come into conflict and how such conflict is even possible. Antiphon took somewhat the same line and it is possible that Hippias was following Antiphon's position in papyrus Fragment B columns 2–3[6] (or vice versa).

Another statement attributed to Hippias also concerns our subject.

> How can anyone suppose that laws or obeying them are a serious matter, since it often happens that the very people who make them repeal them and substitute others in their place? For example, after declaring war cities often make peace.[7]

If genuine[8] this brief passage raises more questions than it answers. The first sentence appears hostile to the very idea of having laws, but the second sentence (which presupposes that any measure passed by the Assembly is a law) gives a frivolous example, which has the effect of undermining the seriousness of the first sentence. At best it can be seen not as an attack on law but as posing a puzzle.

A parallel case might be found in countries with an absolute ruler, where what is required by one ruler may be prohibited by his successor. Nothing is permanent, so even if we always obey the current ruler, we are just following the orders of the day and we have no basis for understanding the nature of law or what is the right thing to do. This agrees with the charge in the *Protagoras* passage that "*nomos* tyrannizes the human race." If we obey the laws in force in our state at the present moment and obey them unthinkingly simply because they are the laws, and if we do not conceive of a separate standard (such as *phusis*) by which to measure them, then we are in the position described above. So we might see Hippias as criticizing not simply the existence of laws but the unthinking attitude toward them that many people can be expected to have. His solution to this situation would doubtless have been for them to come to him to learn the right way to think about this and other subjects.

Antiphon

Antiphon's views are found in the papyrus fragments of his work *On Truth*[9]. Or at least some of his views are, for only a fraction of the entire work has been preserved, and we have no idea how much is missing or what the lost part of *On Truth* said. As his *Antilogies* show, Antiphon wrote works that present cases for opposite sides of an issue, which makes it entirely possible that the missing part presented equally strong considerations in favor of the opposite side. In what follows I will present the text as we have it, section by section, and discuss each section in turn. None of the fragments gives any indication of its original context.

Fragment B

[Column 2] We know and respect <the *nomoi* of nearby communities>, whereas those of communities far away we neither know nor respect. In this we have become barbarian towards one another, when in fact, by nature we are all endowed with a nature to be both barbarians and Greeks. It is in our power to consider the natural features that are necessary in all humans and provided to all in virtue of their possessing the same abilities. In these none of us is distinguished as there is no distinction between barbarian and Greek. For we all breathe out into the air through our mouth and nostrils, we laugh when we are delighted [Column 3] in our mind, we weep when we are pained, we receive sounds with our hearing, by means of light we see with our vision, and we work with our hands, and walk with our feet …

Antiphon speaks of features that hold for all people (we all breathe through our mouths and nostrils, etc.), which he describes as natural and necessary, and he contrasts their universality with laws and customs, which are different for different peoples. Greeks referred to non-Greeks as barbarians (*barbaroi*) – originally not a necessarily pejorative term, but one which by the mid-fifth century had come to have negative connotations like our word "barbarian."[10] We do not respect the laws and customs of foreigners (*barbaroi*), Antiphon says, and in doing so we have become *barbaroi* (barbarians) towards one another. This statement might have been part of an argument proposing that we treat all peoples and cultures with the same respect we have for members of our own culture, or even more strongly as an encouragement to ignore or abolish cultural differences altogether and join together with everyone as citizens of the world, which would be in accordance with *phusis*. Or it might have been intended as a statement of plain fact, to be taken into account in our personal and political relations with people from elsewhere. In any case, the table-turning assertion that we (humans in general? Greeks or Athenians in particular?) have become barbarized towards one another (either because we are wrong to consider anyone a barbarian, or because by equal right other peoples consider us barbarians) must have been shocking or at least thought-provoking. Whatever its context, this particular application of the familiar contrast between nature, which is universal, and laws and customs, which are valid only locally, resonates with Protagoras' account of human nature. Protagoras thinks our "moral" nature (*aidōs* and *dikē*) is universally shared, Antiphon thinks that the same holds for our physical nature. Both Sophists recognize that different communities have different *nomoi*, but Antiphon has a little more to say: that we tolerate or approve of the *nomoi* of our neighboring communities but are ignorant and tend to be suspicious of those of distant peoples. In other words, we pass judgment on other systems of *nomoi* and assume that the farther away others are the greater the differences there are likely to be between their *nomoi* and ours and that in consequence they deserve less respect.

Fragment A

[Column 1] ... so justice is a matter of not transgressing what the *nomoi* prescribe in whatever city one is a citizen. Thus a person would make most advantage of justice for himself if he treated the *nomoi* as important in the presence of witnesses and treated the decrees of *phusis* as important when alone and with no witnesses present. For the decrees of *nomoi* are extra additions, those of *phusis* are necessary; the decrees of *nomoi* are products of agreement, not natural growth, whereas those of *phusis* are the products of natural growth, not of agreement.

This section of fragment A begins with a positivistic view of the nature of law (*nomos*): a city's laws determine what is just and justice consists of obeying the laws. Laws vary from city to city. They are not natural (if they were they would hold everywhere) but result from agreement. This last is an interesting claim since it applies in particular to democracies such as Athens, the home of Antiphon and the epicenter of sophisticated activity. In contrast to what nature decrees, which it is impossible not to conform to, it is not necessary to obey human laws. How, then, should we decide whether to obey a law or break it? Antiphon points out that it is to our advantage to obey laws when disobedience will be observed and to disobey them (when it is to our advantage to do so) when no one notices. This thought is further developed in the next section.

The last sentence of this section speaks of *nomoi* as extra additions to what *phusis* requires, pointing out that they are products of agreement. This is consistent with Protagoras' position. *Phusis* sets absolute limits (for example, we fall downwards and we cannot fall upwards) but gives no guidelines as to how humans are to behave. That is what *nomoi* do.

[Column 2] If those who made the agreement do not notice a person transgressing the prescriptions of *nomoi*, he is free from both disgrace and punishment, but he is not if they do. But if – which is impossible – anyone violates any of the prescriptions that are innate by *phusis*, the harm is no less even if no one notices and no greater if everyone sees. For he does not suffer harm as a result of opinion but in reality.[11]

There may be some confusion here. It is obvious that we can break human law, but if it is impossible to violate a law of nature, how can there be harm in doing so? Nevertheless, the general point is clear: if you break a (human) law and get away with it you do not suffer any loss either of your reputation or of your life, liberty or property. So on the assumption that we are out for our own advantage, it is sensible to violate laws and customs whenever it is advantageous to do so, always taking care that we won't be found out.

The following section says what kind of things the laws prohibit.

[Column 2, continued] This is the entire reason for considering these matters – that most things that are just according to *nomos* are hostile to *phusis*. For *nomoi* have been established for the eyes as to what [Column 3] they must see and what they must not, and for the ears as to what they must hear and what they must not, and for the tongue as to what it must say and what it must not, and for the hands as to what they must do and what they must not, and for the feet as to where they must go and where they must not, and for the mind as to what it must desire and what it must not. So the things from which the *nomoi* discourage humans are no more in accord with or suited to *phusis* than what they encourage. Living and dying are matters of *phusis*, and living results from what is advantageous, dying from what is not advantageous. [Column 4] But the advantages which are established by the *nomoi* are bonds on *phusis*, and those established by *phusis* are free.

This last claim may be true: natural laws do not require, permit or deter us from doing things within our physical capacities, but human laws do. The law of gravity does not prohibit us from jumping off a bridge, but it governs what happens if we do. However, the first claim, that *nomos* is hostile to *phusis*, is initially puzzling. How can a human law be contrary to nature? No sane person would think of introducing a law that declares the law of gravity null and void or that requires everyone to do things that are simply impossible (such as being in two places at once). On the other hand, it is true that human laws place restrictions on what we can and cannot do, so if one's idea of life without *nomoi* implies that we are free to do anything at all that humans like us can do, the existence of *nomoi* is a check on this freedom. This in effect is the situation that Protagoras conceived human life would be like (and that would make survival impossible) if we were not possessed of *aidōs* and *dikē*.[12]

The next to last sentence links *phusis* with advantage, declaring that living and dying are matters of *phusis*. Indeed living and dying are part of our *phusis* as humans (they are part of what it is to be a human being) although Antiphon seems to be adjusting the meaning of *phusis* here. It is reasonable for him to hold that it is advantageous to stay alive and disadvantageous to us to die, and from this, he might well conclude that things are advantageous that maintain us alive and things that cause death are disadvantageous, from which it would be but a small step (involving perhaps a corresponding shift in the notion of advantage) to hold that things are particularly advantageous if they promote not only our being alive but also our living well, whatever that might include, and disadvantageous things are not only those that cause death but those that hinder our living well. It is not difficult to see that this view if widely adopted, could lead to the war of all against all that Protagoras strove to avoid.

[Column 4, continued] And so (*i*) things that cause grief, at least when thought of correctly, do not benefit *phusis* more than things that give us cheer. Therefore (*ii*) it will not be things that cause pain that are advantageous rather than things that bring pleasure. For (*iii*) things that are truly advantageous must not cause harm but benefit. Accordingly (*iv*) things that are advantageous by *phusis* ...

Here Antiphon associates advantage with pleasure, good cheer and the absence of grief, pain and harm, and appears to move towards hedonism. If so, it would be the first expression of this doctrine on record. However, the claim that "things that cause pain do not help *phusis* any more than things that cause pleasure" does not entail that things that cause pleasure help *phusis* more than things that cause pain. Rather, instead of pursuing pleasure, the view represented here is that we should pursue our advantage, while bearing in mind that "living and dying are matters of *phusis*" (thus, we must all die) and that "living results from what is advantageous, dying from what is not advantageous." Since "things that are truly advantageous must not cause harm but benefit" it follows that if we must endure some pain in order to avoid (or rather, postpone) dying it is advantageous to do so. This makes pleasure and pain subordinate to the notion of advantage, which seems to be a matter of maximizing benefit and minimizing harm.

The reasoning leaves much to be desired. To begin with, it is hard to see how anything can benefit *phusis*, or harm it for that matter. *Phusis* does not appear to be the kind of thing that is subject to benefit or harm. Again, if what he has in mind is human nature and by this, he means the life of individual humans, some sense can be made. Something that benefits *phusis* will amount to its keeping individuals alive or promoting a person's well-being. However, the opposition between *phusis* and *nomos* is very different from the difference between life and death or between living well and living miserably. Finally, the moves from statement (*i*) to statement (*iv*) are questionable on logical grounds. The reasoning seems to be either a single argument for proposition (*iv*):

(*i*) and (*iii*) therefore *(ii)*
(*ii*) therefore (*iv*)

or an argument for (*ii*) followed by an argument for (*iv*):

(*i*) and (*iii*) therefore (*ii*)
(*ii*) therefore (*iv*).

Allowing for some imprecision and the lack of consistent vocabulary (perhaps introduced for stylistic reasons) this argument may have been considered acceptable by the standards of Antiphon's time when the demand for precise expression was not yet high and long before Aristotle invented logic. However, it is important to note that the argument for (*ii*) is invalid or very loose. Invalid because pleasure and pain, so prominent in (*ii*), are absent from both (*i*) and (*iii*), the premises from which (*ii*) is derived. Loose if Antiphon is treating cheer, pleasure and benefit as somehow the same and likewise for grief, pain and harm. In either case, since a gap in the papyrus leaves (*iv*) incomplete, we do not know what Antiphon's conclusion was.

Antiphon next gives examples of how obeying *nomoi* can be disadvantageous.

[Column 4, continued] <But according to *nomos*, those are correct> who defend themselves after suffering [Column 5] and are not first to do wrong, those who treat their parents well even if they have been treated badly by them, and those who allow others to accuse them on oath even if they have not themselves taken an oath. You will find many of the cases I have listed hostile to *phusis*. They allow people to suffer more grief when less is possible and to have less pleasure when more is possible and to receive injury when they can avoid it.

The fragment concludes by demonstrating the inadequacy of *nomoi* to rectify the injustice one has suffered.

[Fragment 5, continued] If some assistance came from the *nomoi* for those who submit to these conditions and some loss to those who do not submit but oppose them, [Column 6] obedience to the *nomoi* would not be unprofitable. But as things are, it is obvious that the justice that stems from *nomos* is insufficient to aid those who submit to it. In the first place, it permits the victim to suffer and the agent to act, and it did not prevent the victim from suffering or the agent from acting at the time of the wrongdoing. Also when the case is brought to trial for punishment, there is no special advantage for the victim over the wrongdoer. For he must persuade the jury that he suffered or be able to win the case by deception. And these same charges are left for the agent to deny.

Fragment C

[Column 1] ... to testify truthfully for one another is customarily considered[13] to be just and no less useful in human affairs. But one who does this will not be just, if in fact it is just not to wrong anyone when one has not been wronged. Anyone who testifies – even if he tells the truth – must somehow be wronging another person, and then he will be wronged himself since he will be hated. In that the one he testifies against is convicted because of his testimony and loses his money or his life because of this person whom he has never himself wronged – this is how he wrongs the man against whom he testifies, in that he wrongs someone who did not wrong him, and he himself is wronged by the man against whom he testified in that he is hated by him [Column 2] for testifying truly. And not only is he wronged by this hatred, but also because for the rest of his life he must be on his guard against the man against whom he testified, since he has an enemy who will do him whatever wrong he can in word and deed. So these are plainly not minor wrongs, neither what he suffers nor what he inflicts.

There is no way both for this to be just and also that one should do no wrong if one has not been wronged. Instead, either one or the other of them must be just, or both of them must be unjust. Further, it is apparent that whichever way it turns out, judging, deciding cases and arbitration are not just, for what benefits some harms others, and in the process, those who are benefited are not wronged, certainly, but those who are harmed are wronged ...

This fragment also appears to be an attack on laws and the legal system, pointing out situations in which the laws benefit wrongdoers or do not guarantee that they will be punished for their wrongdoing, and circumstances in which laws, which are intended to make people do right, paradoxically compel us to do wrong by harming others who have not harmed us. But we can agree with these claims without supposing that things would be better off if there were no laws or legal punishments at all. The same holds for cases in court. We can agree that the accused has a right to attempt to persuade the jury that he is not guilty just as the accuser has a right to attempt to persuade the jury that the accused is guilty, but that does not mean that the jury is equally likely to decide wrongly as rightly, much less that judicial trials should be abolished altogether. Antiphon, who specialized in writing speeches for actual trials, will have known this.

In the end Antiphon's views are not clear, and this is for several reasons. First, he puts several concepts in play (pleasure and pain, benefit and harm, advantage) without (at least in the surviving fragments[14]) making their relations explicit. It is clear that the contrast he finds between *nomos* and *phusis* is not one of direct opposition, but it is difficult to tell just what the relation is. I have followed Gagarin's interpretation,[15] that nature determines what we see with our eyes, but does not determine what we will see; in this way, law and custom impose additional requirements on nature that in no way contradict nature but supplement it. Second, he does not advocate ignoring laws and customs altogether and pursuing life according to nature, for death as well as life is a matter of nature, and yet death is declared not to be advantageous and is presumably not beneficial either. Third, the scope of the terms is not made clear: whose advantage does he have in mind? Each individual? Each city? All humankind? The entire natural world? But these may have different and conflicting advantages. Fourth, the fragments seem to present evidence, but the argument based on the evidence is missing, so we do not know just what he is taking the evidence to show. Fifth, the evidence brought is one-sided and incomplete: true, in a trial defendants are given the opportunity to defend themselves, and may even be acquitted for crimes they have committed. But does Antiphon take this as a good reason to abandon such practices, or to abandon laws altogether? If so, what does he propose to replace them? Sixth and finally, the absence of context means that we do not know that any of this represents Antiphon's actual beliefs. He is frequently labeled as an enemy of *nomos*, but the above considerations, particularly the incomplete character of his presentation, and most importantly his frequent use elsewhere of antilogic make it possible or even, I think, likely that these fragments are only a small part of an exposition of one side of an extended antilogical study of a complex issue, and that the other side was presented with equal force in what has been lost.

Conclusion

The surviving contributions of Sophists to the conversation around *nomos* and *phusis* are meager, but that does not mean that the role of the Sophists was small. So little of their writings have come down to us that there would be no basis for such a conclusion. The importance of the *nomos* and *phusis* issue was so great and the contributors to the debate were so many that it would be surprising if most or all of the Sophists did not take part. However, the absence of further evidence makes it impossible to assess their importance or to discern similarities or differences in doctrine and approach. Still, there is good reason to see sophistic teaching as what made the debate possible in the first place.

The way that the subject of *nomos* and *phusis* was treated is, in fact, the most outstanding proof of the Sophists' importance in the intellectual and political life of the second half of the fifth century, because it is yet one more application of antilogic, Protagoras's practice of arguing on different sides of the same issue, which was a central feature of Antiphon's teaching and almost certainly of other Sophists' teaching as well.

Whereas in a court trial, there are two sides, the prosecutor and the defendant, each arguing as best he can for his own case and against the opponent's, and in political debate there can be more than two sides, with different people raising different issues relative to a proposed measure, the case is different in the discussion around *nomos* and *phusis* because the issues were more complex and the terms in which it was argued were not precise. This is particularly noticeable in Antiphon's fragments, where it is not always clear whether by *phusis* he means "nature" (what we think of when we talk of laws of nature) or human nature – and where his treatment of *nomos* sometimes refers strictly to the laws of a community and sometimes may extend more widely into the area of customary behavior that is neither required nor forbidden by law.

Contributors to the debate staked out and defended a wide variety of positions, including the following: that *phusis* is the right of the stronger (Callicles in Plato's *Gorgias*), that by nature all humans pursue their own self-interest (Glaucon in Plato's *Republic*). That all humans have the same *phusis* was taken by Antiphon[16] to imply that everyone is to some extent akin. Antisthenes claimed that there are higher laws than those of communities, even speaking of the law of *aretē* (virtue, human excellence), Antigone (in Sophocles' tragedy) maintained that there are unwritten laws that supersede laws imposed by humans. Some even regarded such unwritten laws to be decreed by the gods (Xenophon) or by *phusis* (Demosthenes).[17] More generally, some favored *nomos* over *phusis* and others took the opposite position, while still others argued for more nuanced views. Taken as a whole this debate was the most important and long-lasting exploration of central topics in political, social and moral philosophy that had ever occurred. Many of these topics are still highly relevant today, and its pervasiveness even in works such as tragedy and comedy that were destined for a general audience shows how it fascinated the Athenians and doubtless other Greeks as well. It is hard to think of a greater tribute to the importance of Protagoras, the originator of antilogic and the first Sophist.

Notes

1. Guthrie 1969 is still useful for a broader take on *nomos* and *phusis*.
2. Protagoras, fragment 3, discussed above, pp. 18.
3. The entire text is included in the Appendix of Translated Texts, pp. 156–62.
4. Hesiod, *Works and Days* 225–85.
5. See below, pp. 121.
6. See p. 7.
7. Xenophon, *Memorabilia* 4.4.14.
8. Since this is taken from a brief dialogue in Xenophon's *Memoirs of Socrates* it is not at all sure that it accurately represents Hippias' views.
9. Papyrus Oxyrhynchus XI 1364.
10. According to Liddell and Scott's *Greek-English Lexicon*, the change in meaning took place after the Persian War, which ended in 449 BCE.
11. This is one place where "reality" is a better translation of *alētheia* than "truth."
12. See above p. 23.
13. *Nomizetai*, this verb is related to *nomos*.
14. This is an important qualification.
15. Gagarin 2002, 69.
16. Fragment B, above p. 121.
17. The references in this paragraph are taken from Guthrie 1969, Chapter 4.

13
ISOCRATES

Isocrates was born in Athens in 436 BCE, nine years before Plato, and died nine years after him in 338 BCE. In his youth, he associated with Gorgias and other Sophists, and he almost certainly knew Socrates. He came from a prosperous family which lost its wealth during the Peloponnesian War (431–403 BCE) and thereafter earned his living as a speechwriter and as a teacher. Like Antiphon he wrote speeches for others to present in law courts. Later he wrote more politically and educationally oriented works. In or about 392 BCE, he opened a school in Athens where with great success and financial gain he taught the craft of public speaking to young men from Athens and from elsewhere in the Greek world. The primary purpose of his education was to prepare his students to be leaders in their cities, and his subject matter was political speech. Many of his students became successful orators and politicians. These features would seem to qualify him as a non-traveling Sophist (something like Antiphon). However, he positively despised Sophists and wrote an abusive tract called *Against the Sophists* in which he distanced himself from those other teachers of public speaking. In this, he sided with Socrates and Plato. Even more surprising was that he called his school a school of philosophy and that he publicly claimed that what he taught was philosophy, although the content of his teaching had little to do with Socrates' and Plato's concerns.

The way Isocrates described his own work and contrasted it with Sophists on the one hand and with Socrates and Plato on the other reveals much about the competitive intellectual scene in the early fourth century and also about the fluidity of the terms "sophist" and "philosopher" at that time, which saw the decline and death of the age of the Sophists and the invention of philosophy. These are the central topics of this chapter.

DOI: 10.4324/9781003493259-13

Recall that the word *sophistēs* was originally positive, designating wise people and that in the fifth century, even though this older sense continued, the word came to be associated primarily with the people ever since known as Sophists.[1] Most or all of them taught techniques of public speaking but in many cases a variety of other subjects as well. For reasons already discussed[2] the Sophists were both exciting and suspicious, entertaining and useful but possibly dangerous, and they gained the reputation (whether deserved or not) of promising to make their students invincible in argument and debate regardless of the soundness of their arguments or the truth or morality of the claims they supported.

As will be discussed in the following chapter, Plato largely shared this view even though he respected some individual Sophists. In his effort to conceptualize the difference between Socrates and the Sophists, he deployed a series of words that he may have invented, including "rhetoric" (*rhētorikē*) and "sophistic" (*sophistikē*), "philosophy" (*philosophia*) and the use of *philosophos* as a noun "philosopher."[3] He then proceeded to define or demarcate these terms to the benefit of philosophy (as he conceived it) and the detriment of the others.[4]

In founding his school Isocrates marked himself off from other teachers of public speaking, and in the competitive market of the Sophists, it is not surprising that in his earliest work, *Against the Sophists*, Isocrates strove to advertise himself to potential students as teaching something more attractive than the others. He begins by attacking Sophists (who, he says, falsely claim to be "teachers of wisdom and dispensers of happiness" and who promise to teach their students virtue and self-control and "what to do in life") for being "incapable of saying anything pertinent or giving any counsel regarding the present," and as not teaching anything worthwhile.[5] Isocrates claimed to teach his students to aim for wisdom (*sophia*) and to love it, and in consequence, called his students lovers of wisdom (*philosophoi*). For Isocrates, wisdom was concerned with practical matters, and what he taught was oratory, which might make him seem to an outsider to be just another Sophist, but the title and contents of his treatise show that he did not consider himself such.

In the course of the treatise he attacks certain Sophists, who taught political discourse as a series of hard and fast rules to be applied without regard to the unique circumstances of the occasion on which a speech is delivered. According to Isocrates the difference between these Sophists and Isocrates is that Isocrates teaches political discourse the right way whereas the others teach it the wrong way – a relatively fine distinction, but one that shows that for Isocrates "sophist" could be used essentially as a term of abuse.

Isocrates also objects to the earliest Sophists, presumably Tisias and Corax (mid-fifth century),[6] who were reputed to have written were reputed to have composed treatises on the craft of oratory. He admits that these Sophists attempted to teach their students how to speak in court trials but complains that they did not recognize the value of oratory in other settings and derides the unattractive terminology they introduced and techniques they advocated, which he regards as useless.

In his last work, Antidosis, he refers to other antiquated Sophists, whom he faults for idly wasting time concocting hair-splitting arguments on subtle and unanswerable questions:

… some of them maintaining that the sum of things is made up of infinite elements;[7] Empedocles that it is made up of four, with strife and love operating on them; Ion, of not more than three; Alcmaeon, of only two; Parmenides and Melissus, of one; and Gorgias, of none at all.[8]

Elsewhere he calls Anaxagoras and Damon Sophists, says that Solon was the first Athenian to be called a Sophist, and refers to the Seven Wise Men (*sophoi*) as Sophists. Protagoras too is called a Sophist, but like Gorgias he barely gets a mention, and the names of Prodicus, Hippias and Antiphon do not appear at all in Isocrates' writings.

The men he names as Sophists are a strange grouping indeed, especially since they include several figures who are usually regarded not as Sophists but as philosophers. He calls the first group (Empedocles, etc.) Sophists because he regards them as holding obviously false theories and wasting their time putting up ingenious arguments to support them. The same would hold for Anaxagoras, another Presocratic philosopher who, like Empedocles and Democritus, proposed a newfangled physical theory that Isocrates could easily have considered as wild as the others he disparages. Damon is mentioned several times by Plato, who calls him a student of Prodicus, while Herodotus calls Solon a Sophist and other authors refer to the Seven Sages as Sophists as well.

Aristotle divided theoretical philosophy into three sections: mathematics, natural science and metaphysics. Isocrates effectively declared that the last two of these are not philosophy at all and that all "who want to do some good in the world must banish them from their minds."[9]

He did recognize a limited value in studying mathematics and related fields because they are excellent training for the intellect, requiring diligence and close attention. Although he admits that people who study these fields learn useful subjects more easily and quickly, even so, he asserts that they have no use in either public or private matters.[10] Again surprisingly, he gives the same positive recognition to eristic (the word *eristikē* is another Platonic invention), the practice of disputing anything and everything, using bad arguments as well as good, as exemplified by Euthydemus and Dionysodorus.[11] This practice was despised by others but Isocrates evidently understood that exposure to it (but not to the point of excess) could be useful in a variety of ways to a successful public speaker. However, Isocrates held that these subjects should not be pursued for their own sake but as a kind of liberal arts foundation for the study of more important subjects, specifically the subjects that Isocrates taught, which he considered to be philosophy. Clearly, for him, philosophy was not the same thing as it was for Plato.

In fact the first occurrences of the word *philosophia* are found in the writings of Isocrates and Plato. Plato may have been the first person to use the word *philosophia*.[12] He did so initially with reference to Socrates, and later, when his views on the nature of philosophy had changed, referring to his own practice. But nothing in the word *philosophia* limits it to these uses. Its literal meaning, as Plato understands it is "love of wisdom," which can be interpreted as "the search for wisdom" if the wisdom is hard to gain, as it certainly was for both Socrates and Plato. For the Greeks and perhaps still for us, wisdom (*sophia*) is generally accounted a good thing to have and a person who has it is wise (*sophos*). Still, the subject matter of wisdom is left entirely unspecified. In its earliest surviving occurrence (in Homer's *Iliad*) it is not the sage Nestor but an expert carpenter who is called *sophos*. By Plato's time, it was associated with intellectual expertise as well as crafts. Plato refers to Solon as "the wisest (*sophōtatos*) of the seven," referring to the men we know as the Seven Sages and whom the Greeks called "the seven *sophoi*," and Plato's *Apology* is the source of the story that the Delphic oracle proclaimed Socrates to be the wisest (most *sophos*) of humans.[13] In the same work Socrates, who made no pretense of being wise, describes himself as *philosophōn* (searching for wisdom).[14] Later on, after the word *philosophia* had been coined (whether by Isocrates or Plato), Plato conceived it initially as what Socrates did – practicing what is known as the Socratic method. This can be seen in retrospect as an attempt to corral the new word, which carried with it the positive associations of the older word *sophia*, for his own philosophical and polemical purposes, one of which was to contrast what Socrates did with what the Sophists did and also with what Isocrates did, to the detriment of the latter. In the end, Plato had his way since we still use the word "philosophy" primarily for the subject that is the heir to Plato and Socrates. But Plato's victory was not won without resistance, specifically the resistance of Isocrates.

Isocrates distanced himself from the Sophists, but also from Plato, who opened his own school north of the center of Athens, in the neighborhood of the Academy (the open area sacred to the local god Akademos) a few years after Isocrates opened his. Isocrates never refers to Plato by name, although he may have him in his crosshairs when he speaks of sophists who write "laws and republics" which may be direct references to Plato's works *Laws* and *Republic*.[15] (In return, Plato's account of the several *tekhnai* in the *Gorgias*,[16] which implies that rhetoric is inferior to sophistic, which is inferior to philosophy, may have been made with Isocrates in mind.) Isocrates names Socrates only twice but says nothing about his methods of thinking and teaching. He also had a low opinion of people who get too involved with topics discussed by such earlier thinkers as Parmenides and Melissus (whom we, following Plato and Aristotle, regard as philosophers) – topics he regarded as idle and vain.[17]

Isocrates trained people for an active public and primarily political life and he did so by teaching them to be as effective at political speech (*politikos logos*) as their character and abilities allowed. For Isocrates, this study is not *rhētorikē* (a word that, perhaps surprisingly, is not found in any of Isocrates' writings), but *philosophia*, which he defines as follows:

> Since it is not in human nature to attain knowledge that enables us to know what we should do or say, out of the remaining possibilities I consider wise (*sophoi*) those who can by their opinions achieve the best results for the most part, and philosophers (*philosophoi*) are those who study the subjects from which they will most quickly gain this kind of intelligence.[18]

Isocrates is thinking of Socrates or Plato when he declares that it is not in human nature to obtain knowledge that enables us to know for certain what to do or to say. This is a strongly anti-Platonic stance but it is not an unreasonable position to take since Socrates never claimed to have found such knowledge even though he held that it was all-important and searched for it for many years, and Plato did not claim to have obtained knowledge of the Platonic Forms, which according to him was prerequisite for knowing what to do and say.

But Isocrates did not consider expertise in public speaking to be the most important thing that he taught. More important is his view was producing students of good character.[19]

> People can become better and worthier if they conceive an ambition to speak well, to persuade their hearers and seize their advantage.[20]

Isocrates is careful to point out that by "advantage" he means what is conducive to a life based on the love of wisdom (*philosophia*) and the love of honor.

In Aristotle's classification these matters fall under practical, not theoretical thought, an assessment Isocrates would have welcomed after dismissing Aristotle's theoretical subjects as mostly irrelevant and possible impediments to living the best kind of life. For Isocrates, then, it is his students who are philosophers, seeking wisdom of the indicated kinds.

This is how Isocrates positions himself against the useless Sophists of the past and present, including the principal Presocratic philosophers, and the equally useless philosopher Plato, his cross-town rival. It is interesting that his complaint against the "antiquated Sophists" mirrors the complaint we find against philosophy presented in the following extract from Plato's *Gorgias* by Callicles, who also despised philosophers (484c–485e) and regarded Sophists as worthless (520a).

> (484c) Philosophy is no doubt a delightful thing, Socrates, as long as one is exposed to it in moderation at the appropriate time of life. But if one spends more time with it than he should, it's the undoing of mankind. For even if one is naturally well favored but engages in philosophy far beyond that appropriate time of life, he can't help but turn out to be inexperienced (484d) in everything a man who's to be admirable and good and well thought of is supposed to be

experienced in. Such people turn out to be inexperienced in the laws of their city or in the kind of speech one must use in dealing with people on matters of business, whether in public or private, inexperienced also in human pleasures and appetites and, in short, inexperienced in the ways of human beings altogether.... (485a) I believe, however, that it's most appropriate to have a share of both. To partake of as much philosophy as your education requires is an admirable thing, and it's not shameful to practice philosophy while you're a boy, but when you still do it after you've grown older and become a man, the thing gets to be ridiculous, Socrates! (485b) My own reaction to men who philosophize is very much like my reaction to men who speak haltingly and play like children.... (485c) When I see philosophy in a young boy, I approve of it; I think it's appropriate and consider such a person well-bred, whereas I consider one who doesn't engage in philosophy ill-bred, one who'll never count himself deserving of any admirable or noble (485d) thing. But when I see an older man still engaging in philosophy and not giving it up, I think such a man by this time needs a flogging. For, as I was just now saying, it's typical that such a man, even if he's naturally very well favored, becomes unmanly and avoids the centers of his city and the marketplaces – in which, according to the poet, men attain "preeminence" – and, instead, lives the rest of his life in hiding, whispering in a corner with three or (485e) four boys, never uttering anything well-bred or apt.

(Plato, *Gorgias* 484c–485e, Hackett tr.)

Notes

1. See above, p. 8.
2. See p. 6.
3. Plato did not invent this word; it had been earlier used as an adjective.
4. See above, p. 8 and below, pp. 138–9.
5. Quotations from the opening chapter of *Against the Sophists*.
6. He is unusual in calling them Sophists. Unfortunately we have no information about the contents of these treatises.
7. Presumably the Leucippus and Democritus, who put forward the earliest atomic theory, which posited infinite atoms; possibly also Anaxagoras.
8. Isocrates, *Antidosis* 268.
9. Isocrates, *Antidosis* 269.
10. Isocrates, *Antidosis* 266.
11. See Chapter 8.
12. See above, p. 2.
13. Plato, *Apology* 21a.
14. Plato, *Apology* 29d5.
15. Isocrates, *Philip* 12. By contrast Plato speaks of Isocrates in complimentary terms which, however, may be intended ironically (*Phaedrus* 278e– 279a).
16. See p. 137–38.
17. Isocrates, *Antidosis* 269.
18. Isocrates, *Antidosis* 271.
19. Isocrates, *Demonicus* 4, *Panathenaicus* 87. See Schiappa 1991, 173–4.
20. Isocrates, *Antidosis* 277.

14
PLATO'S COMPLICATED RELATIONSHIP WITH THE SOPHISTS

It is generally believed that Plato pictures the Sophists as Socrates' enemies and as a danger to society, but the truth is more complicated and more interesting. Consider Plato's *Protagoras* in which three of the most renowned Sophists are present and take part: not only Protagoras but also Prodicus and Hippias. Protagoras is given the biggest role, but all three are guests in the same house, the house of Callias, the wealthiest person in Athens and a great supporter of Sophists. Each of the three is teaching in a separate area of the household. All three have speaking roles and are shown to have different personalities. There are good reasons to believe that Plato's portrayal of these Sophists is reasonably accurate (allowing for some exaggeration).[1]

His presentation of these Sophists is not hostile, nor do any of the three express hostility towards Socrates. True, there is the moment when Socrates finds himself unable to proceed with the discussion because Protagoras insists on giving long speeches (which Socrates says he cannot follow) and also refuses to give short answers to Socrates' questions, which is the only way Socrates can make the conversation go forward. But it is Socrates, not Protagoras who gets up to leave and in any case what is shown is not hostility, but simply frustration on the part of both men, and thanks to the intervention of Prodicus, Hippias and others a solution is soon found.[2]

Protagoras is presented in a positive light. He is the center of attention, he is given the opportunity to explain the nature of his profession as a Sophist, which he does at length and without interruption. He is shown to hold reasonable views[3] and to defend them with greater success than most of Socrates' other interlocutors have. At one point in the discussion,[4] he identifies a fallacy in Socrates' reasoning (a rare occurrence in Plato's dialogues), and Socrates does not dispute it.

DOI: 10.4324/9781003493259-14

Also at the end of the dialogue, Socrates declares himself to be in the same situation as Protagoras: Protagoras had begun by holding that virtue can be taught and Socrates had disagreed, but now the discussion has amazingly brought each of them around to the opposite position.[5] In his final speech, Protagoras (who was 20 years older than Socrates) declares that "I commend your enthusiasm and the way you find your way through an argument. I really don't think I am a bad man, certainly the last man to harbor ill will. Indeed, I have told many people that I admire you more than anyone I have met, certainly more than anyone in your generation. And I say that I would not be surprised if you gain among men high repute for wisdom."[6]

Of the other two Sophists present, Prodicus is described as having a deep voice, a detail Plato would have no reason to invent. Socrates says that he "really wanted to hear Prodicus, a man who in my opinion is godlike in his universal knowledge."[7] There may be a degree of irony here, but we need to remember the *Apology*, where Socrates is eager to meet people who are reputedly wise in order to learn from them.[8] Later in the *Protagoras*, in the scene described just above, Prodicus attempts to persuade Socrates to remain and continue his conversation with Protagoras by encouraging everyone present to pay more attention to the wiser speaker of the two (without saying whether Socrates or Protagoras was the wiser), to debate the issues, dispense with eristic and aim for the respect of the audience and in that way delight their hearers (337a–c). The way he makes this point exemplifies his well-known technique of drawing distinctions.[9] Later on, after Socrates and Protagoras have resumed their conversation and are discussing the ethical views expressed in a poem of Simonides, Socrates declares that by *khalepon* ("difficult") Simonides means *kakon* ("bad"). When Protagoras challenges him on this Socrates turns to Prodicus, the expert on language, and asks him whether in the dialect of Ceos, the native island of both Prodicus and Simonides, *khalepon* means *kakon*. Prodicus agrees with this outrageous suggestion, which Protagoras refuses to accept and Socrates immediately says that he was joking and that Prodicus was going along with the joke.[10] Again, there is no suggestion of hostility on the part of Prodicus, but rather of an urbane gentleman with a sense of humor who wants to smooth things out for the common good.

Hippias too dissuades Socrates from leaving, praising the intellectual and civilized quality of the people present and complimenting Callias, the host. He brings in the theme of *nomos* and *phusis*, speaking of the present company as kinsmen, intimates and fellow citizens by nature, not by convention, and urging Socrates and Protagoras to act in a manner worthy of the company and their surroundings and to find a compromise that will allow the conversation to continue. Again there is no trace of hostility, but rather something that we might expect of an experienced diplomat like Hippias.

Next consider the *Theaetetus* where Socrates is made to say that when people with philosophical promise come to associate with him and he finds that they are not ready, he sends them to Prodicus.[11] This has been interpreted as a sneer towards Prodicus, but it can equally well be taken as a fine compliment: he believes that Prodicus can get them ready to be taught by Socrates, presumably by mastering Prodicus's method of drawing fine distinctions among closely related things,[12] which would be useful for anyone who wanted to engage in conversations with Socrates, which frequently focused on questions like "what is justice" or "what is courage."

Or take the two Hippias dialogues where Hippias is presented (consistently with his brief appearances in the *Protagoras*) as self-important, eager to talk, but uninterested in and unversed in philosophy. Nevertheless, he is treated with courtesy by Socrates and without any sign on either side that he is a bitter and dangerous enemy.

In the *Gorgias* dialogue, Gorgias is unable to hold his own in conversation with Socrates and is quickly tied in knots,[13] but again there is no hostility on either side. Socrates treats him gently and with respect as was his due as an older man. Gorgias introduces what turns out to be the chief topic of the dialogue (the nature of rhetoric) and then without the least show of anger or discomfort allows his eager and not so urbane student Polus to carry on the conversation.

The only Sophists presented negatively in Plato's dialogues are the brothers Euthydemus and Dionysodorus in the *Euthydemus*, but they are so self-preoccupied that they do not have it in them to be either hostile or friendly to Socrates or anyone else, and Socrates says nothing hostile about them. They are shown as teachers of eristic, the art (if it deserves that name) of using transparently flawed arguments to confute and silence anyone who ventures any opinion on any subject. It is significant that they are described as "newfangled Sophists" (271c), which suggests that their kind of teaching and public presentation was not practiced by the likes of Protagoras, Gorgias, Prodicus or Hippias.

Thus the individual Sophists, including even Thrasymachus[14], are not presented as enemies of Socrates or Plato. Even Euthydemus and Dionysodorus, who are evidently disliked by others present at the conversation in the *Euthydemus*, are not evidently disliked by Socrates, who occasionally appears ironic towards them, but no more so than towards other interlocutors. If Plato's hostility does not come from these sources it seems most likely that it comes from Plato himself. Further, the reasons for Plato's hostility could not have been individual Sophists' behavior towards Socrates, or else that would have been apparent in the Platonic dialogues. It is most likely, then, that it was their practices that he objected to, or what he took the Sophists to represent, or their overall goals as Plato understood them.

We see the first steps in this direction in the *Gorgias*, where Gorgias himself is treated kindly, but his aggressive student Polus receives rougher handling. Gorgias had identified himself as a *rhētōr* (a public speaker and/or a teacher of public speaking) and a teacher of *rhētorikē* (rhetoric/oratory).[15] In the subsequent conversation when Polus asks him to say what *rhētorikē* is Socrates explains that it is not a *tekhnē* (art, craft, skill, expertise) but a *tribē* (knack, practice, routine based on experience; pl. *tribai*). It is a business that is not like a craft but that is characteristic of people who are good at guessing, bold and naturally clever at speaking to people.[16]

Other *tribai* are gourmet cooking, beauticians' work and sophistry. To each of these *tribai* there is a corresponding *tekhnē*: medicine (*iatrikē*) corresponds to gourmet cooking (*opsopoiïkē*), fitness training (*gumnastikē*) corresponds to beauticians' work (*kommōtikē*), legislation (*nomothetikē*) to sophistry (*sophistikē*) and justice (*dikaiosunē*) to rhetoric (*rhētorikē*). Both here and later on in the dialogue, however, he declares that sophistry and rhetoric are the same or at least very similar.[17]

A significant feature of this passage is that it contains the earliest known occurrences of the words he uses as names of arts and knacks, with the exception of *dikaiosunē*, the probable exception of *iatrikē* and the possible exception of *gumnastikē*. Plato invented new words for his philosophical purposes, including many nouns ending in -*ikē*. In fact, the ending -*ikē* of these words has a definite meaning. It shows that the word is an adjective, not a noun. The noun that is implied is *tekhnē*. *Rhētorikē* is not simply "speaking" but the *tekhnē* (that is to say art/skill/practice) of speaking, where the word *tekhnē* implies a system of rules and practices that can be taught.

It is even likely that most of the words ending in -*ikē* that occur in these passages were invented by Plato specifically for the discussion in this dialogue. Important for our purposes is the appearance of *rhētorikē* and *sophistikē* here for the first time. To be precise (since this point is controversial) this passage contains the earliest known occurrences of these words. It is possible that one or more of these words had been used earlier, but the important point is that Plato defined them and gave an account of their relations to one another, and so established the words as referring to specific practices (e.g., rhetoric has to do with certain kinds of public speaking).[18] Also important is the fact that the *Gorgias* also contains what may be the earliest known occurrence of the word *philosophia* meaning philosophy in a technical sense rather than the more general sense of "love of wisdom."

One reason for employing these words was to reify concepts and so make it possible to discuss them, for example, to discuss *sophistikē* without referring to individual Sophists, abstracting from the particular cases to reach the essence of what Sophists do. For another example, the word *rhētōr* was in use in the fifth century, but not the abstract noun *rhētorikē*. More interesting is the case of *philosophia*. The word *philosophos* is found a century earlier than Plato in a fragment of Heraclitus: "Wisdom-loving men must be inquirers into many things indeed,"[19] where "wisdom-loving" is the translation of *philosophoi* (a plural form of *philosophos*); but there the word is an adjective, not a noun, and the *philosophoi* men in question are those men who love (or seek for) wisdom. The noun *philosophia* begins with an equally broad meaning, which occurs even in Plato; the word is not in any surviving text of an earlier author. The *Gorgias* is either the earliest or at least one of the earliest of Plato's works that contains it. The *Hippias Minor*, another early work, associates *philosophia* specifically with Socrates[20] but leaves its precise meaning unclear.

In the *Gorgias* for the first time we find philosophy contrasted with and shown to be superior to another pursuit. In its first occurrences,[21] it is contrasted with what it is to be a successful politician. Politicians change their tune and contradict themselves whenever the mood of the Assembly demands it, whereas philosophy always stays the same, remaining consistent regardless of public opinion. A little later, Callicles, vigorously representing the opposing side, maintains that a little exposure to philosophy is a fine thing for a young person to pursue but only up to a point, while it is disgraceful in an older man since it makes him unable to participate in public affairs and helpless to defend himself in court.[22] Socrates has the last word: unlike rhetoric, sophistry, the beautician's work and gourmet cooking, which aim to please their customers regardless of whether the pleasure they provide is good for them or not, philosophy consistently aims for the good.[23] It follows that philosophy is the key to the crafts of legislation and justice, whereas the corresponding *tribai*, sophistry and oratory – fail in comparison.

This rather schematic argument leaves much to be worked out, but it is clear that Plato is considering sophistry in its own right regardless of its practitioners and that he is doing the same with philosophy.

In the *Gorgias* it is clear that *philosophia* refers to Socrates' conversations, which are intended to eliminate inconsistent beliefs, remove false opinions, and work toward knowledge of the truth. At this point in his career, Plato regarded Socrates as the ideal philosopher and he was concerned with showing that what Socrates did was more important than any other pursuit and that success in it was a prerequisite for success in such admittedly important endeavors as legislation and the administration of justice. In this Plato was extending what he portrayed Socrates doing in the *Apology*[24] where he made the rounds of reputed practitioners of wisdom – politicians, poets and craftsmen – and through his method of questioning discovered that they did not really possess the wisdom they claimed to have. In this way, Socrates decided that he was in fact wiser than these people since they believed that they knew important things when in fact they did not, while he did not harbor any such false conceit, but admitted his ignorance and aimed to replace it with knowledge. In this he was unlike these other people who had no reason to replace their false ideas, since before their conversation with Socrates they did not know that they held contradictory views and after speaking with him, we may imagine, they speedily deleted the conversation from their memory without taking time to reflect on its large-scale implications for their claims to expertise and for their actions. Plato continued this program demonstrating the superiority of *philosophia*.

In other dialogues we find Socrates engaging with claimants to wisdom: a religious expert in the *Euthyphro* and a rhapsode in the *Ion*. Even after Plato begins presenting views of his own, we find him still concerned with proving philosophy superior to other fields of expertise: natural science in the *Phaedo* and *Timaeus*, mathematics, astronomy, music theory and poetry in the *Republic*, medicine in the *Alcibiades I*, divination in the *Timaeus* and again sophistry in the *Phaedrus* and *Sophist*.

As we saw in the case of *sophistikē*, the conceptualization of this challenge requires going beyond individual practitioners of the intellectual endeavors concerned and reifying the endeavors themselves, stripping them of the particularity of their practitioners and the particular circumstances of their application and generalizing appropriately. *Philosophia* too was generalized beyond Socrates's practices and the *philosophos* beyond Socrates the individual. Thus Plato's notions of *philosphia* and the *philosophos* were free to expand and change so that at any moment of Plato's career he could describe *dialektikē* (dialectic), the method associated with *philosophia*, as "the ideal [philosophical] method, whatever it may be."[25]

Some elements of his view of the nature of philosophy and its superiority did not change. Briefly, he found philosophy superior to other disciplines and practices, and to sophistry in particular, for the following reasons: (1) Philosophy recognizes the fallibility of opinion and aims for truth and knowledge, while sophistry is content to concern itself with opinion and persuasion, which amounts to the ignorant persuading the ignorant; (2) Philosophy takes time, it requires lengthy and careful consideration, while sophistry is used in situations where decisions have to be made without certainty and in a limited time; (3) Philosophical discussion is impartial and impersonal, while sophistic takes sides in interactions with individuals, in which considerations of personality and other personal qualities may be relevant to victory; (4) In philosophical discussions, unlike the settings where sophistry is applied, there are no losers; (5) In philosophical conversation like-minded people cooperate and are willing to change their minds, while in the competitive situations where sophistry is used, participants disagree and maintain their positions to the end.

This was Plato's position, but how convincing is it? Opponents might point out that after a lifetime of inquiry Socrates still admitted that knew nothing.[26] Further, Plato's account of the philosopher kings in the *Republic* makes it clear that no one, in his time at least and probably at any time, could possess the knowledge needed to be truly a qualified philosopher king.

In addition to these heavy charges, the Sophists might make a different kind of counter-claim. True, Plato showed that they are not good at philosophy, but they never claimed to be good at philosophy. In fact, they had no conception of philosophy since it had not been identified in their lifetimes (assuming plausible dates for the death of Protagoras, Gorgias, Hippias, Prodicus and Thrasymachus and for the dates of the relevant Platonic dialogues). What they claimed was to teach the skills in public speaking that were seen as important to success in public and private life. (Here I follow Protagoras' account of what he did[27] which I suppose holds more or less well for at least part of the teaching of most or all of the Sophists.)

As stated earlier, the situations for which Protagoras prepared his students involved opposing views and a body of people whose votes would decide the issue. Decisions were made by the jury of the trial or the citizens present at the meeting of the Assembly, on the basis of their opinions as determined only in part by the cases made on either side. The task of the plaintiff and of the defendant in a trial or of the proponents and opponents of proposals before the Assembly was to persuade a majority of the voters to vote in favor of one side or the other. A decision had to be taken even though in those circumstances certain knowledge was rarely attainable, so Plato is being quite unfair when he says that the Sophists taught their students not to obtain knowledge but to master techniques by which an ignorant person can persuade other ignorant people of anything that they like and can persuade them to ignore the judgments of people with expert knowledge.[28] It follows that Socratic conversations are entirely different in nature and purpose from the settings for which the Sophists prepared their students.

The kinds of arguments that the Sophists taught are another target of Plato's objections. Two kinds are especially relevant to our purposes: first, Protagoras' claim that there are two opposing *logoi* on any subject, which is the basis of the practice of antilogic[29] (*antilogikē*) another word first found in Plato. Protagoras's profession to teach people to make the weaker *logos* stronger, which need only have meant that he taught them to improve the case they make for their side in disputes, was early (mis)construed as the promise to make the weaker *logos* the stronger one, in other words, to endow his students with the ability to win any argument no matter how weak or absurd their own side was. In his topical comedy *Clouds*, Aristophanes presents Socrates (!) as a caricature Sophist who teaches young man techniques of argument that enable him to cheat his father's creditors out of their money and justify using physical violence against his own father and mother. The play contains a pitched battle between Just *Logos* and Unjust *Logos* (a deliberate perversion of Protagoras' claim) in which both sides make outrageous assertions that they back up with outrageous arguments and, as we would expect in a comedy, Unjust *Logos* emerges as the winner.

Plato objects to antilogic for yet a different reason: that it can result in "misology" (hatred of arguments), which is experienced by people unskilled in arguments who, listening to arguments pro and con, are first persuaded that one side is true and then that it is false. When this happens a number of times they come to think that reasoning and arguments are useless. The same thing happens, he says, also to people experienced in arguments who are so expert at antilogic that they themselves come to believe that "there is no soundness or reliability in any argument."[30]

However, there is good reason to think that Plato's condemnation of antilogic is unfair. As was discussed above,[31] the Socratic method is closely related to antilogic. As a student of Socrates Plato learned well the variation of antilogic known as the Socratic method and he displays it in many of his works. He came to call his own methods of philosophical inquiry dialectic (*dialektikē*, which is another word ending in *-ikē* invented by Plato). *Dialektikē* is derived from the verb *dialegesthai*, which means "to converse," "to discuss" or "to dialogue" and is etymologically related to "logic" and "antilogic." This suggests that Plato disliked the competitive overtones of "antilogic" implied in the prefix *anti-* and preferred a word suggestive of a more cooperative endeavor.

The close connection between Sophistic teaching and Socratic method makes Plato's hostility to the Sophists and their work puzzling. At this point it almost seems that he is deliberately slandering them without good grounds. But there is another perspective from which Plato's attitude is justified, and that has to do with the overall goals of Socrates and Sophistic education.

Roughly speaking, Socrates and the Sophists (according to Plato's views) agree that their goal and the goal for which they prepare their students and associates is to be the best they can be, which can be called either being successful or possessing *aretē*. Who could object to that? But what they take to be successful or *aretē* are very different. The Sophists prepare their students to be successful in certain settings – competitive settings where success consists in persuading others (particularly the Assembly or a jury) to see things your way. The Sophists have little or nothing to say about what "your way" is or should be, while Socrates aims to make his students better people, people who do the right thing and do so knowing (not just believing or being persuaded) that it is right. Where the Sophists teach tricks of the rhetorical trade, Socrates encourages his students to examine their views and values and to take up rhetoric only after mastering the truth.[32] The Sophists, far from being the alien influence and morally subversive figures they are often made out to be, teach nothing "other than the convictions that the majority express when they are gathered together."[33] How else might they convince the locals? Socrates, by contrast, forces his students to examine their own values (which initially will largely coincide with the values of their city). Since traditional and unreflectively accepted values tend to be inconsistent, it is not surprising that in conversation with Socrates his interlocutors typically find that their views are inconsistent. This opens up a wide range of possibilities that may include beliefs and practices that are far from the traditional views and practices of their city. This might truly be thought subversive. In any case, pursuing it is very different from what the Sophists did. From this point of view, it follows that people who learn techniques of persuasion from the Sophists without sorting out their values and if they do not persuade the Assembly or the jury to do what is right, but only what is agreeable, they are liable to persuade people to do the wrong things. And in the settings for which the Sophists prepare their students, considerations of wrong or right (as opposed to perceived self-interest) may not be taken into account at all, since the goal is to win.

From Socrates' point of view, it is desirable to know that the most important thing to do is to do what is good and to want above all to achieve the good and further determine what is good before persuading people to do what you want. From this point of view, Socrates' criticism of the Sophists is proper. Also, Socrates is always concerned with the soul (*psukhē*) much more than with the body, and this includes his stance on rhetoric.

> Anyone who teaches the art of rhetoric seriously will, first describe the soul with absolute precision and enable us to understand what it is … and demonstrate its nature.[34]

The reason for this is that speech "directs the soul," and so, a rhetorician must know how many kinds of souls there are, be able to tell what kind of soul each person has, and know what kind of speech to use in order to persuade that person about the question at hand and also when to speak and when to be silent.[35]

To this we might well agree with Phaedrus, who says that to accomplish this is no small task. But Socrates himself never attained the knowledge he was after, and if Socrates did not, how likely is it that anyone else can? (Has anyone achieved it yet?) But then if ignorance of this means that we are never prepared to persuade anyone of anything and must continue to discuss these topics with like-minded people, how can we live our private and public lives?

This is a serious question. I suppose that the answer will be along the lines of doing the best we can with the views we have, always being willing to change our minds and adopt better views. Socrates, it must be admitted, is an extreme case – a true philosophical saint who lived the life of the mind and soul to the extent of neglecting as far as he reasonably could his family and his civic responsibilities, the private and public aspects of life that so concerned the Sophists, their students, and almost everyone else including most of us; an ideal philosopher sketching the ideal life that is unencumbered by considerations of responsibilities to others or even to one's body, beyond the bare minimum. A life that is literally contemplative. And one that we cannot actually lead, but that we can use for an ideal, something to approximate as closely as we can.

Plato's negative stance towards sophistry, already manifest in the *Gorgias* and *Phaedrus*, becomes positively abusive in the *Sophist* – with a surprising exception. The announced purpose of this dialogue is to open a discussion of the nature of the Sophist, the statesman and the philosopher[36] that includes an attempt to define the Sophist.[37] The project continues in the dialogue of the *Statesman*, but a dialogue devoted to the philosopher does not exist and apparently was never written. However, the *Sophist* contains some preliminary remarks that will be useful for our purposes.

The *Sophist* turns up no fewer than seven definitions of the Sophist.

1 A hunter who hunts rich, prominent young men in order to earn money by teaching them in private how to persuade people. (222d–3a)
2 A salesman who transports from city to city words and learning having to do with virtue (*aretē*) and sells expertise in virtue wholesale. (224c–d)
3 A salesman who remains in one city and makes his living selling at retail words and learning that have to do with virtue (*aretē*) – words and learning he has acquired from others. (224e)
4 A salesman who remains in one city and makes his living selling at retail his own words and learning that have to do with virtue (*aretē*). (224e)
5 An expert who earns money through his expertise in eristic (*eristikē*), which is a species of disputation (*antilogikē*), controversy, fighting, combat and acquisition. (226a)

6 Someone who cleanses people's souls by cross-examining them, exposing inconsistencies in their beliefs, refuting them and so making it possible for them to learn the truth. (230b–d)
7 An insincere imitator who does not know what he is imitating but pretends to know when he is in front of others and private conversation forces the person he is talking to contradict himself. (267b–8d)
8 The first five definitions are based on familiar negatively charged descriptions of Sophists: they travel from city to city, teach for money, claim to teach virtue and teach persuasive speech and refutation for use in competitive situations. The sixth definition comes as a surprise. It is positive and seems to be a description of Socrates and his method. Here is the relevant text.

[230a] People who think that lack of learning is always involuntary, and that if someone thinks that he is wise he will never be willing to learn anything about what he thinks he's clever at... [230b] So they set out to rid people of their belief in their own wisdom in another way.... They cross-examine someone when he thinks he's saying something when he's saying nothing. Then, since his opinions will vary inconsistently, these people will easily scrutinize them. They collect his opinions together during the discussion, put them side by side, and show that they conflict with one another at the same time on the same subjects in relation to the same things and in the same respects. The people who are being examined see this, get angry at themselves, and become calmer toward others. [230c] They lose their inflated and rigid beliefs about themselves that way, and no loss is pleasanter to bear or has a more lasting effect on them.... The people who cleanse the soul, my young friend, likewise think the soul, too, won't get any [230d] advantage from any learning that's offered to it until someone shames it by refuting it, removes the opinions that interfere with learning, and exhibits it cleansed, believing that it knows only those things that it does know, and nothing more. ... [231b] The refutation of the empty belief in one's own wisdom is the noble kind of sophistry.

[230a5–b8, Hackett tr., slightly modified]

It seems astonishing that Plato would ever say that Socrates practiced any kind of sophistry even if he was unique in practicing a noble kind of sophistry. However, by the time he wrote the *Sophist* Plato's conception of philosophy had changed. In the *Republic*, he speaks of philosopher-kings who administer the state correctly on account of their knowledge of the Platonic Forms, something that Socrates, who admitted that he knew nothing of importance, did not possess. In the *Sophist*, which was written after the *Republic*, philosophy is associated, if not identified, with expertise in dialectic, which here is knowledge of how to divide things by kinds and discriminate by kinds how things can associate and how they cannot.[38] The meaning and importance of this new conception of philosophy are beyond the scope of this book, but it is clear that it has nothing to do with the description of the sixth kind of Sophist quoted above. This is part of the answer: for Plato when he wrote the *Sophist* Socrates was no longer a philosopher. Why, then, call Socrates a Sophist, albeit of a noble kind? Because from his new perspective, Plato recognized what others evidently had thought of Socrates in his lifetime: he was very like the Sophists. True, his lifestyle was not the same: he did not travel from city to city, he did not make people pay to associate with him, he was not ambitious for wealth or fame or political influence, and he did not pretend to teach his associates how to persuade others or to gain political power. But like the Sophists, he dealt in words, discussions, argument and refutation, he employed a developed form of antilogic and we can easily imagine that some of those who discussed matters with him (and were refuted) or some who observed him discussing with others had the same reaction as an unnamed person in the *Euthydemus* dialogue had to Euthydemus and Dionysodorus:

> chattering and making a worthless fuss about matters of no consequence.... of no value whatsoever... men who care nothing about what they say, but just snatch at every word.... Both the activity and the men who engage in it are worthless and ridiculous.[39]

My conclusion, then, is that Plato's dislike of "the Sophist," although not of most of the Sophists he actually knew and mentioned, is the result of his eventual conviction that the life they supported, the "successful" and unreflecting life, was antithetical to the contemplative life of philosophy; worse it was a distraction and worst of all it discouraged people from pursuing philosophy. Even Socrates, Plato's great philosophical hero, who had pointed Plato towards the philosophical life, had not achieved the understanding of the nature of philosophy that Plato achieved over the course of his lifetime.

Notes

1. Pp. 17–18.
2. Plato, *Protagoras* 334d–338e.
3. Pp. 25–26.
4. Plato, *Protagoras* 350c–351a.
5. Plato, *Protagoras* 361a–c.
6. Plato, *Protagoras* 361d7–e5.
7. Plato, *Protagoras* 315e.
8. Plato, *Apology* 21b–e.
9. See above p. 65.
10. Plato, *Protagoras* 341d–343e.
11. Plato, *Theaetetus* 151b.
12. See above, pp. 65.
13. Plato, *Gorgias* 447a–458c.
14. See p. 74 above.
15. Plato, *Gorgias* 449a.
16. Plato, *Gorgias* 463a.

17 Plato, *Gorgias* 465c, 520a–b.
18 See Schiappa (2003) 40–48 for further discussion.
19 Heraclitus, fragment 35DK.
20 Plato, *Lesser Hippias* 363a. See the Appendix of Translated Texts.
21 Plato, *Gorgias* 481d–482a.
22 Plato, *Gorgias* 484c–486a in the Appendix of Translated Texts, pp. 170–1. Isocrates says something similar at p. 130 and 133–4.
23 Plato, *Gorgias* 500a–c.
24 Plato, *Apology* 21b–22e.
25 In the notable words of Richard Robinson 1953, 70–71.
26 Compare Callicles' objections to philosophy at Plato, *Gorgias* 484c–486a (in the Appendix of Translated Texts).
27 Plato, *Protagoras* 319a.
28 Plato, *Gorgias* 459a–c.
29 Discussed above, in Chapter 11.
30 Plato, *Phaedo* 90b.
31 See pages 113.
32 Plato, *Phaedrus* 260e.
33 Plato, *Republic* 493a.
34 Plato, *Phaedrus* 271a.
35 Plato, *Phaedrus* 271b–272a.
36 Plato, *Sophist* 217a.
37 Plato, *Sophist* 218c.
38 Plato, *Sophist* 254d.
39 Plato, *Euthydemus* 304e–305b.

15
ARISTOTLE AND THE SOPHISTS

Aristotle (384–322) may never have met a Sophist of the kind discussed in this book. By the time he first came to Athens (367) the great Sophists were all long dead. Isocrates had written his tract *Against the Sophists* a couple of decades earlier and Plato had invented the words *sophistikē*, *dialektikē* and *philosophia* and had used them to discredit Sophists. Platos' and Isocrates' rival schools were active and actively hostile to Sophists and what they represented. "Sophist" had become a word of reproach. As the following extracts from his work *Sophistical Refutations* show, Aristotle viewed Sophists not as individuals so much as an undifferentiated group of frauds.

> The art of the sophist is a money-making art which trades on apparent wisdom, and so sophists aim at apparent proof…. Sophistry is the appearance of wisdom without the reality.
>
> (*S.E.* 171b28–29, b34)

> By sophistical refutation and reasoning I mean not only the seeming but unreal reasoning or refutation but also one which, though real, only seems to be, but is not really, germane to the subject at hand.
>
> (*S.E.* 169b20–23)

> The sophistic art consists in apparent and not real wisdom, and the sophist is one who makes money from apparent and not real wisdom…. It is essential for those who wish to play the sophist to seek out the kind of argument which we have mentioned… the possession of such a faculty will cause him to appear to be wise, and this is the real purpose which sophists have in view.
>
> (*S.E.* 165a20–23, a28–31)

We may assume that Aristotle absorbed this anti-sophistic stance during his many years at Plato's Academy and even before his association with Plato he may have studied with Isocrates, who was himself hostile to those he identified as Sophists. Aristotle adopted Plato's conception of philosophy and devoted one of his major works to the subject of rhetoric, whose nature and importance he recognized and which he differentiated from sophistry more clearly than Plato had done.

The surviving works of Aristotle mention Protagoras, Gorgias, Prodicus, Antiphon, Thrasymachus, Euthydemus and Polus but do not identify them as Sophists. Rather, Aristotle treats them in the same way he treats his philosophical predecessors, drawing on them as earlier thinkers and practitioners who had ideas and practices that were relevant to topics that he treated, accepting some of their claims and disputing others according to his usual philosophical method, which in part consists in setting out and examining the views of earlier figures, accepting some and critiquing and rejecting others. Several of them (Gorgias in particular) are quoted to illustrate rhetorical features under discussion in the *Rhetoric*, and in the *Sophistical Refutations* Euthydemus is cited as the author of a sophistic argument.

Protagoras alone among the great Sophists receives much attention, being mentioned in five of Aristotle's works, sometimes for his grammatical interests,[1] once for his method of determining the fees his students should pay,[2] once for his rhetorical practice of antilogic,[3] once for his refutation of geometry, which Aristotle considered sophistical[4] and several times in the *Metaphysics*[5] for his doctrine that "a human being is the measure of all things." Aristotle rejects this doctrine because as he understands it, it violates the principle of non-contradiction, which Aristotle regards as the bedrock of all thought, language and reality.

In his discussion of this doctrine Aristotle does not refer to Protagoras as a Sophist and he does not say that it is a sophism. His interpretation of the doctrine is derived entirely from Plato's inventive treatment in the *Theaetetus*[6] and has no independent weight in assessing whether the Platonic interpretation of the doctrine reflects Protagoras' own meaning. Aristotle takes the view seriously because (whether or not Protagoras actually held it) it had at least been mooted and it is relevant to the views he is discussing. In any case, it appears that Aristotle believed that Protagoras had proposed it, and he sees it as posing a threat to the status of the principle of non-contradiction. In such circumstances he does not simply dismiss other views out of hand, but gives reasons for rejecting them, treating their authors as colleagues in his search for truth and as such deserving respect. In this, he shows no less respect for Protagoras than he does for other thinkers with whom he disagrees.

The people he calls Sophists are relatively unknown: Aristippus, Bryson, Dionysius, Lycophron and Polyidus. Of these only Aristippus, Lycophron and Bryson can be discussed even briefly. Aristippus of Cyrene (a Greek city in what is now Libya), who lived from 436 to 356, was a student of Socrates and is recorded as the first of Socrates' students to charge fees for teaching. This might qualify him as a Sophist, but he is better known as a "Socratic," that is, as a philosopher who had been a follower of Socrates. He championed hedonism and founded the Cyrenaic School which flourished initially in Athens and subsequently in Cyrene for some time after his death. Aristotle reports that he ridiculed mathematics on the grounds that unlike the arts and handicrafts, where explanations are given in the form "because it is better, or worse," mathematics pays no regard to good and evil,[7] a comment Aristotle regards as sophistical because it brings in ethical considerations which are irrelevant to the topic under discussion.

Aristotle mentions Lycophron several times. He is quoted as describing law (*nomos*) as "a guarantor of justice to one another,"[8] which may have been a contribution to the conversation on *nomos* and *phusis*, although this is unclear given the absence of further information. (The quotation is given without context.) Aristotle reports that instead of "the man is white" Lycophron said "the man has been whitened" (where "has been whitened" is a single word in Greek) in order to avoid making one thing (the man) two (the man and white), and he likewise rejected "is walking," insisting on using "walks" instead.[9] These remarks might be seen by Aristotle as sophistical. In any case, they have to do with the correct use of language, which since the time of Protagoras had been a concern of many Sophists, and of Socrates and Plato as well. Aristotle himself would puzzle about this and other issues about one and many, finding in the Sophists, as he frequently did, matters relevant to his own more systematic philosophical interests.

Bryson is known to us only for his attempt to square the circle. This was a problem that exercised Greek mathematicians and to which Antiphon had proposed a solution.[10] Like Antiphon's, Bryson's solution, whatever it may have been, cannot have been correct, at least by normal (Euclidean) geometric techniques, but attempts were made, including Bryson's, which Aristotle regards as sophistical. Since so little is known about Bryson it is possible that he was a full-blooded Sophist and the fact that Aristotle refers to him as Bryson the Sophist[11] suggests that is how he was known.

We learn most about Aristotle's conception of Sophistry and Sophists from his work *Sophistical Refutations*, a text that is curiously overlooked in most treatments of the Sophists. Aristotle begins the work by identifying two types of arguments: deductions and refutations. A deduction "rests on certain statements [premises] such that given them, something else [the conclusion] necessarily follows," while a refutation is "a deduction to the contradictory of a given conclusion."[12] This implies that a refutation does not exist in its own right – it is a response to a deduction, specifically, it is an argument that concludes that the deduction's conclusion is not true. If you give an argument whose conclusion is p, then a refutation is an argument whose conclusion is not-p. Aristotle immediately points out that not all deductions and refutations are legitimate, even if they seem to be. For example, they may be invalid, so that the conclusion does not really follow from the premises, or one or more of the premises may be false. In this case, we have what Aristotle calls "apparent" deductions and refutations: they only appear to be genuine deductions and refutations.[13] He goes on to say that some apparent deductions and refutations are sophistical. Sophistry (*sophistikē*) he defines as "the semblance of wisdom without the reality" and a Sophist is "someone who makes money from apparent but unreal wisdom."[14] Aristotle does not say that all merely apparent arguments are sophistical or that everyone who makes a faulty argument is a Sophist – that depends on the intention of the individual.

The money-making aspect of the Sophists' activity which Plato stresses is barely mentioned in the *Sophistical Refutations*, where Aristotle's concern is with arguments, not individuals. His reference to apparent but unreal wisdom recalls the passage in Plato's *Gorgias* where Gorgias boasts that he can teach his students to be more persuasive in speaking in the assembly even than people with expert knowledge about matters falling under that person's expertise, as well as his story about persuading people to undergo cures that his brother, who was a doctor, was unable to persuade them to undergo, and in responding to Socrates' conclusion that "oratory doesn't need to have any knowledge of the state of the subject matters of other kinds of expertise; it only needs to have discovered some device to produce persuasion in order to make itself appear to those who don't have knowledge that it knows more than those who actually do have it." Gorgias is delighted to say "Aren't things made very easy when you come off no worse than the experts even though you haven't learned any other expertise than this one [i.e., rhetoric]?"[15]

According to Aristotle sophistical refutations may depend on homonymy, ambiguity and other features of language. The following argument depends on homonymy: "The same man is both seated and standing and he is both sick and healthy; it is he who stood up who is standing and he who was recovering who is healthy; but it was the seated man who stood up and the sick man who was recovering." As Aristotle explains,

> The sick man does so and so' or 'has so and so done to him' is not single in meaning: sometimes it means the man who is sick now, sometimes the man who was sick formerly. Of course, the man who was recovering was the sick man, who really was sick at the time; but the man who is healthy is not sick at the same time: he is the sick man in the sense not that he is sick now, but that he was sick formerly.

He gives two arguments that depend on ambiguity.

> There must be sight of what one sees; one sees the pillar, therefore the pillar has sight

and

> What you profess to be, that you profess to be; you profess a stone to be, therefore you profess to be a stone.[16]

In Chapter 8, Aristotle identifies two kinds of sophistical deductions and refutations. One kind consists of arguments that appear to be valid but are not (these have already been discussed), while the other kind consists of arguments that are valid but not appropriate. This is the sense in which Bryson's quadrature is called sophistical: "even if the circle is in fact squared, it is not done so in a way suitable to the matter at hand." Just how Bryson's quadrature went and how it failed to be suitable to geometry (the matter hand) are matters of controversy. The information Aristotle provides in *Sophistal Refutations*[17] and elsewhere[18] is insufficiently clear or precise to settle the matter, but it is clear that Bryson's proof employed one or more premises that are not geometrical.

What emerges from Aristotle's treatment of sophistical arguments is that he uses "sophistical" as a label for faulty arguments used in adversarial situations by people who lack the specialized knowledge relevant to the matter at hand, in order to convince an ordinary person (not an expert) that they speak with the authority of an expert, and on that basis win out over their opponents. In general such people will not be teachers of sophistry and they will not always be out to make money from their sophistical arguments. Aristotle elsewhere[19] says that Sophists profess to teach statesmanship (*ta politika*) even though they do not practice that profession themselves. This is a surprising claim since many of the major fifth-century Sophists were actively engaged in political life. (Here he may be taking aim at Isocrates, who had a speech impediment that prevented him from being an effective public speaker.)

I conclude that Aristotle is interested in analyzing the different kinds of faulty arguments and he calls them sophistical following Plato's prejudiced account. He does not have the fifth-century Sophists, particularly in mind in the *Sophistical Refutations*, and possibly he did not have fourth-century Sophists in mind either. If there were many of these latter-day Sophists, we know virtually nothing about them, and it is a reasonable inference that by the time Aristotle was writing, the word "sophist" had largely been demoted to a word of abuse.

Aristotle and Dialectic

Whereas Plato's view of dialectic changed with his views on the nature of philosophy and is difficult to grasp at any time, Aristotle defined dialectic precisely and devoted an entire work, the *Topics*, to it. Aristotle invented logic and developed a basic logical terminology and system of concepts including premise, conclusion, validity and logical consequence. He also identified different forms of reasoning and established numerous types of valid deductive arguments. In fact he gives a detailed treatment of a theory, known as syllogistic, that he claimed accounts for every kind of deductive reasoning. (Here he overstated his accomplishment.) Much of this work is done in the *Prior Analytics* and the results are put to work in the *Posterior Analytics*, which developed the notion of a particular kind of deductive argument that he calls scientific demonstration (*apodeixis*) and which he claimed to be the correct way to conceptualize sciences or intellectual disciplines in general – providing the first ever unified account of the nature of scientific thought. He discusses dialectic in the *Topics*, the work that follows the *Posterior Analytics* in Aristotle's assembled logical treatises which are known collectively as the *Organon*.

Aristotle lists three places where dialectic is useful: "exercise, encounters, and the philosophical sciences."[20] By "exercise" he means debating contests where the usefulness of antilogic is obvious, by "encounters" he has in mind ordinary conversations where the elaborate rules of debate do not apply but where presenting your own views and defending them in the face of disagreement are important, and by "philosophical sciences," he means the science discussed in the *Posterior Analytics*.

Dialectic's use in the "philosophical sciences" is crucially important for Aristotle. He takes geometry as a model for all sciences. Each science has basic principles, for example, definitions of specifically geometrical terms (like line, triangle and right angle) and axioms (such as that things that are equal to the same thing are equal to one another). These are explicitly stated and are taken as basic; everything else is proved deductively from them. We know that all triangles have angles equal to two right angles because this can be proved to follow deductively from the principles. But how do we know the principles? Not by proofs because the principles are the basic (unproved) starting points; if they were provable they would not be principles. How, then? Aristotle devotes only one sentence of the *Topics* to this topic:

> This task belongs properly, or most appropriately, to dialectic; for since dialectic works by examination (*exetastike*) it contains the path to the principles of all disciplines."[21]

This is an unclear and incomplete account of what dialectic does in grasping these basic facts. I believe that the best conjecture as to what he means is that dialectic does not examine the facts that a science studies; that work is for the scientists. Instead dialectic examines the relations among the propositions that express the facts, ascertaining which propositions are logical consequences of which and proving to the satisfaction of oneself and one's fellow scientists that alternative accounts are incorrect, and so making progress towards the discovery of the undemonstrated propositions that are the principles of the science.

The debating contests ("exercises") he has in mind are discussed in book 8 of the *Topics* and probably have some relation to the dialectical training taught in Plato's Academy, where Aristotle had spent many years. The situation envisaged is where you have an opponent who has stated a thesis she wishes to defend. Your goal (as in the Socratic method) is to show that your opponent has other views that are inconsistent with the thesis. This you do by constructing an argument whose premises your opponent believes to be true, but whose conclusion is the negation of the thesis. The way you ascertain whether she believes something is true to ask her. In fact, this is approximately what Socrates does in Plato's "Socratic" dialogues.

The principal difference is that Aristotle has a more precise understanding of logical validity and the nature and forms of arguments. As with the Socratic method, this practice can be used to examine one's own beliefs and so it is a way to pursue philosophical research. The same approach can be used in less formal settings, the "encounters" that Aristotle mentions.

Notes

1 *Rhetoric* 1407b6, *Sophistical Refutations* 173b19, *Poetics* 1456b15.
2 *Nicomachean Ethics* 1164a24.
3 *Rhetoric* 1402a22–28.
4 *Metaphysics* 3.2 998a3.
5 Chiefly *Metaphysics* 11.6 1062b12–19, but also 4.2 1004a6, 4.4 1007b18–25, 4.5 1009a6–25 and 10.2 1053a35–b3.
6 Above, pp. 34.
7 *Metaphysics* 3.2 996a29.
8 *Politics* 1280b10.
9 *Physics* 185b28.
10 See above, p. 54.
11 *History of Animals* 563a7, 615a10.
12 *Sophistical Refutations* 165a1.
13 *Sophistical Refutations* 165a19.
14 *Sophistical Refutations* 165a22.
15 Plato, *Gorgias* 459b–c.
16 Both quotations from *Sophistical Refutations* 165b33–166a10.
17 *Sophistical Refutations* 171b16–172a7.
18 *Posterior Analytics* 75b40.
19 *Nicomachean Ethics* 1180b35, 1181a12.
20 *Topics* 1.2.
21 *Topics* 101b2–4.

APPENDIX
TEXTS RELATING TO THE SOPHISTS

1. Plato, *Protagoras* 314e3–37e6

When we entered [the house of Callias, where Protagoras, Hippias and Prodicus were staying] we found Protagoras walking about in the portico and next to him on one side were Callias the son of Hipponicus and also (315a) his maternal half-brother Paralu, the son of Pericles, and Charmides, the son of Glaucon, while on the other side were Pericles' other son Xanthippus, Philippides the son of Philomelus and Antimoirus of Mende, the most distinguished of Protagoras' students, who is training in the profession in order to become a Sophist. Behind these there followed others, listening carefully to the conversation – for the most part apparently foreigners [non-Athenian Greeks] whom Protagoras gathers from the cities he passes through, bewitching them by his voice like (315b) Orpheus. Others too were following his every word, bewitched, and there were even some natives [Athenians] participating in the dance. I was absolutely delighted to see this dance – how carefully they avoided ever getting in the way of Protagoras, but whenever he and the ones closest to him turned back, these members of the audience parted ranks wonderfully well and in complete order on either side, and moving in a circle each time returned perfectly to the rear of the procession.

And after him (to quote Homer) I spotted Hippias (315c) of Elis seated on a chair in the opposite portico. Around him sitting on benches were Eryximachus the son of Akoumenus, Phaedrus of Myrrinous and Andron the son of Androtion, as well as some foreigners, some of his fellow-citizens and some others. It appeared as if they were asking Hippias some astronomical questions having to do with nature and the heavenly bodies, while he, seated in his chair, proceeded to clarify and give thorough explanations to the questions of each of them.

And then I beheld Tantalus – (315d) for Prodicus of Ceos was in town. He was in a separate room which Hipponicus had previously used as a storeroom, but

Callias had emptied it out and had turned it into a guestroom because of the crowd of his guests. That is where Prodicus was still in bed, covered with sheepskin blankets, in fact, a large number of them as it appeared. Next to him on nearby couches were Pausanias from Cerameis and together with Pausanias a young man who was still a youth, I think, who was both noble (315e) in nature and very beautiful in appearance. I think I heard that his name was Agathon, and I wouldn't be surprised if he turned out to be the young lover of Pausanias. So there was this youth and both Adeimantuses the sons of Cepis and Leucolophides, and some others too were present. What the subject of their discussion was I could not tell from outside even though I would gladly have listened to Prodicus – he seems to me to be terribly wise (316a) and godlike – but his deep voice created a booming sound in the room and made his words indistinct.

We had just come in and right after us came the beautiful Alcibiades (as you say and I (316b) believe you) and Critias the son of Callaischrus. So when we had entered and spent a little time and had observed all this, we went to Protagoras and I said, "Protagoras, I and Hippocrates here have come to see you."

Do you want to converse with me alone or in front of the others?

It makes no difference to us, so you should decide after you have heard why we have come.

So why have your come?

"This is Hippocrates. He is from here, the son of Apollodorus and a member of an important and prosperous family and in my opinion he is a match for anyone his age. I believe (316c) he has set his heart on being a man of account in the city and he thinks that he will best achieve this goal by associating with you. So now consider whether you think you should discuss these matters with us alone or in the presence of others."

"You are right to be concerned on my behalf, Socrates. A foreigner, who travels to important cities and persuades the best of the youth to stop keeping company with other people – both family members and others, old and young – and associate with him claiming that (316d) doing so will improve them, needs to be cautious in doing this. These actions result in a great deal of malice and other forms of ill-will and hostility. But I declare that the art of sophistry (*sophistikê tekhnê*) is ancient, but that the men of old who practiced it in fear of its negative connotations contrived a screen and hid behind it. Some, like Homer, Hesiod and Simonides, called it poetry, others, such as the followers of Orpheus and Musaeus called it rites and prophesy. I have noticed some others called it gymnastics: Iccus of Tarentum and (316e) Herodicus of Selymbria, formerly from Megara, who is still alive and a Sophist inferior to none. Your Agathocles, a great Sophist, made music his screen as did Pythoclides of Ceos and many others. All these I claim used these arts as covers out of fear of malice. But I (317a) disagree with all of them on this matter. I believe that they have not achieved what they wanted – I believe that the leaders in the cities did not fail to notice the purpose of these screens. (The masses notice just about nothing, but simply repeat whatever the leaders proclaim.) Now when someone who is trying to escape can't, but is in plain sight, the attempt is foolish (317b) and necessarily makes people much more hostile. Moreover they think a man like that is capable of anything. So I have taken the completely opposite approach. I agree that I am a Sophist and that I educate people, and I think that this is a better precaution than the other one, to agree rather than deny. I have thought up other devices too and to tell God's truth the result is that I have not suffered at all by (317c) agreeing that I am a Sophist. In fact I have by now been pursuing this art for many years – the total is very large: I am old enough to be the father of any one of you. And so, if you like, it will be a great pleasure to make a speech about all this in the presence of everyone who is in the house.

Since I suspected that he wanted to put on a show for Prodicus and Hippias and was priding himself on the fact that we had arrived (317d) in order to admire him, I said "Why don't we invite both Prodicus and Hippias and the people that are with them to listen to us?"

"Very well." said Protagoras.

"Then shall we arrange a place to sit so that you may hold your conversation sitting down?"

We agreed that it was a good idea, so all of us, delighted as were at the prospect of listening to wise men, gladly took hold of the benches and couches ourselves and arranged them near Hippias, where some benches were already. In the meantime Callias and Alcibiades (317e) had come leading Prodicus (after rousing him from his couch) and his group.

When we were all seated Protagoras said "Now, Socrates, since these people are present too, please remind me of what you were telling me a little while ago about this young man."

2. Plato, *Protagoras* 320c2– 328d4

[Protagoras] "I wouldn't think of begrudging you an explanation, Socrates," he replied. "But would you rather that I explain by telling you a story, as an older man to a younger audience, or by developing an argument?" The consensus was that he should proceed in whichever way he wished. "I think it would be more pleasant," he said, "if I told you a story."

(320d) "There once was a time when the gods existed but mortal races did not. When the time came for their appointed genesis, the gods molded them inside the earth, blending together earth and fire and various compounds of earth and fire. When they were ready to bring them to light the gods put Prometheus and Epimetheus in charge of decking them out and assigning to each its appropriate powers and abilities.

"Epimetheus begged Prometheus for the privilege of assigning the abilities himself. 'When I've completed the distribution,' he said, 'you can inspect it.' Prometheus agreed, and Epimetheus started distributing abilities.

(320e) "To some he assigned strength without quickness; the weaker ones he made quick. Some he armed; others he left unarmed but devised for them (321a) some other means for preserving themselves. He compensated for small size by issuing wings for flight or an underground habitat. Size was itself a safeguard for those he made large. And so on down the line, balancing his distribution, making adjustments and taking precautions against the possible extinction of any of the races.

"After supplying them with defenses against mutual destruction, he devised for them protection against the weather. He clothed them with (321b) thick pelts and tough hides capable of warding off winter storms, effective against heat and serving also as built-in, natural bedding when they went to sleep. He also shod them, some with hooves, others with thick pads of bloodless skin. Then he provided them with various forms of nourishment, plants for some, fruit from trees for others and roots for still others. And there were some to whom he gave the consumption of other animals as their sustenance. To some he gave the capacity for few births; to others, ravaged by the former, he gave the capacity for multiple births and so ensured the survival of their kind.

"But Epimetheus was not very wise, and he absentmindedly used up (321c) all the powers and abilities on the nonreasoning animals; he was left with the human race, completely unequipped. While he was floundering about at a loss, Prometheus arrived to inspect the distribution and saw that while the other animals were well provided with everything, the human race was naked, unshod, unbedded and unarmed, and it was already the day on which all of them, human beings included, were destined to emerge from the earth into the light. It was then that Prometheus, desperate to (321d) find some means of survival for the human race, stole from Hephaestus and Athena wisdom in the practical arts together with fire (without which this kind of wisdom is effectively useless) and gave them outright to the human race. The wisdom it acquired was for staying alive; wisdom for living together in society, political wisdom, it did not acquire, because that was in the keeping of Zeus. Prometheus no longer had free access to the high citadel that is the house of Zeus, and besides this, the guards there were terrifying. But he did sneak into the building that Athena and Hephaestus (321e) shared to practice their arts, and he stole from Hephaestus the art of fire and from Athena her arts, and he gave them to the human race. And it (322a) is from this origin that the resources human beings needed to stay alive came into being. Later, the story goes, Prometheus was charged with theft, all on account of Epimetheus.

"It is because humans had a share of the divine dispensation that they alone among animals worshipped the gods, with whom they had a kind of kinship and erected altars and sacred images. It wasn't long before they were articulating speech and words and had invented houses, clothes, shoes and blankets and were nourished by food from the earth. Thus (322b) equipped, human beings at first lived in scattered isolation; there were no cities. They were being destroyed by wild beasts because they were weaker in every way and although their technology was adequate to obtain food, it was deficient when it came to fighting wild animals. This was because (322c) they did not yet possess the art of politics, of which the art of war is a part. They did indeed try to band together and survive by founding cities. The outcome when they did so was that they wronged each other because they did not possess the art of politics, and so they would scatter and again be destroyed. Zeus was afraid that our whole race might be wiped out, so he sent Hermes to bring *dikê* (a sense of fairness) and *aidōs* (concern about what others think of us) to humans, so that there would be order within cities and bonds of friendship to unite them. Hermes asked Zeus how he should distribute *aidōs* and *dikē* to humans. "Should I distribute them as the other arts were? This is how the others were distributed: one person practicing the art of medicine suffices for many ordinary people; and so forth with the other practitioners. Should (322d) I establish *dikē* and *aidōs* among humans in this way, or distribute them to all?" "To all," said Zeus, "and let all have a share. Cities would never come to be if only a few possessed these, as is the case with the other arts. And establish this law as coming from me: Death to him who cannot partake of *aidōs* and *dikē*, for he is a pestilence to the city."

"And so it is, Socrates, that when the Athenians (and others as well) are debating architectural excellence, or the virtue proper to any other professional specialty, they think that only a few individuals have the right (322e) to advise them, and they do not accept advice from anyone outside these select few. You've made this point yourself and with good reason, I might add. But when the debate involves political excellence, which must proceed (323a) entirely from justice and temperance, they accept advice from anyone and with good reason, for they think that this particular virtue, political or civic virtue, is shared by all, or there wouldn't be any cities. This must be the explanation for it, Socrates. "And so you won't think you've been deceived, consider this as further evidence for the universal belief that all humans have a share of justice and the rest of civic virtue. In the other arts, as you have said, if someone claims to be a good flute-player or whatever, but is not, people laugh at (323b) him or get angry with him, and his family comes round and remonstrates with him as if he were mad. But when it comes to justice or any other social virtue, even if they know someone is unjust, if that person publicly confesses the truth about himself, they will call this truthfulness madness, whereas in the previous case, they would have called it a sense of decency. (323c) They will say that everyone ought to claim to be just, whether they are or not, and that it is madness not to pretend to justice, since one must have some trace of it or not be human.

"This, then, is my first point: it is reasonable to admit everyone as an adviser on this virtue, on the grounds that everyone has some share of it. Next, I will attempt to show that people do not regard this virtue as natural or self-generated, but as something taught and carefully developed in those in whom it is developed. (323d)

"In the case of evils that men universally regard as afflictions due to nature or bad luck, no one ever gets angry with anyone so afflicted or reproves, admonishes, punishes, or tries to correct them. We simply pity them. No one in his right mind would try to do anything like this to someone who is ugly, for example, or scrawny or weak. The reason is, I assume, that they know that these things happen to people as a natural process or by chance, both these ills and their opposites. But in the case of the good things that accrue to men through practice, training and (323e) teaching, if someone does not possess these goods but rather their corresponding evils, he finds himself the object of anger, punishment and reproof. Among these evils are injustice, impiety and in general everything (324a) that is opposed to civic virtue. Offenses in this area are always met with anger and reproof, and the reason is clearly that this virtue is regarded as something acquired through practice and teaching. The key, Socrates, to the true significance of punishment lies in the fact that human beings consider virtue to be something acquired through training. For no one (324b) punishes a wrongdoer in consideration of the simple fact that he has done wrong, unless one is exercising the mindless vindictiveness of a beast. Reasonable punishment is not vengeance for a past wrong – for one cannot undo what has been done – but is undertaken with a view to the future, to deter both the wrong-doer and whoever sees him being punished from (324c) repeating the crime. This attitude towards punishment as deterrence implies that virtue is learned, and this is the attitude of all those who seek requital in public or private. All human beings seek requital from and punish those who they think have wronged them, and the Athenians, your fellow citizens, especially do so. Therefore, by my argument, the Athenians are among those who think that virtue is acquired and taught. So it is with good reason that your fellow citizens accept a blacksmith's or a cobbler's advice in political affairs. And they do think that virtue is acquired (324d) and taught. It appears to me that both these propositions have been sufficiently proved, Socrates.

"Now, on to your remaining difficulty, the problem you raise about good men teaching their sons everything that can be taught and making them wise in these subjects, but not making them better than anyone else in the particular virtue in which they themselves excel. On this subject, Socrates, I will abandon story for argument. Consider this: does there or (324e) does there not exist one thing which all citizens must have for there to be a city? Here and nowhere else lies the solution to your problem. For if such a thing exists, and this one thing is not the art of the carpenter, the blacksmith, or the potter, but justice, and temperance, and piety – what I (325a) may collectively term the virtue of a man, and if this is the thing which everyone should share in and with which every man should act whenever he wants to learn anything or do anything, but should not act without it, and if we should instruct and punish those who do not share in it, man, (325b) woman and child, until their punishment makes them better and should exile from our cities or execute whoever doesn't respond to punishment and instruction; if this is the case, if such is the nature of this thing, and good men give their sons an education in everything but this, then we have to be amazed at how strangely our good men behave. For we have shown that they regard this thing as teachable both in private and public life. Since it is something that can be taught and nurtured, is it possible that they have their sons taught everything in which there is no death penalty for not understanding it, but when their children are faced with (325c) the death penalty or exile if they fail to learn virtue and be nurtured in it – and not only death but confiscation of property and, practically speaking, complete familial catastrophe – do you think they do not have them taught this or give them all the attention possible?"

"We must think that they do, Socrates."

"Starting when they are little children and so continuing as long as they (325d) live, they teach them and correct them. As soon as a child understands what is said to him, the nurse, mother, tutor and the father himself fight for him to be as good as he possibly can, seizing on every action and word to teach him and show him that this is just, that is unjust, this is noble, that is ugly, this is pious, that is impious, he should do this, he should not do that. If he obeys willingly, fine; if not, they straighten him out with threats and blows as if he were a twisted, bent piece of wood. After this (325e) they send him to school and tell his teachers to pay more attention to his good conduct than to his grammar or music lessons. The teachers pay attention to these things, and when the children have learned their letters and are getting to understand writing as well as the spoken language, they are given the works of good poets to read at their desks and have to (326a) learn them by heart, works that contain numerous exhortations, many passages describing in glowing terms good men of old so that the child is inspired to imitate them and become like them. In a similar vein, the music teachers too foster in their young pupils a sense of moral decency and restraint, and when they learn to play the lyre they are taught the (326b) works of still more good poets, the lyric and choral poets. The teachers arrange the scores and drill the rhythms and scales into the children's souls, so that they become gentler, and their speech and movements become more rhythmical and harmonious. For all of human life requires a high degree of rhythm and harmony. On top of all this, they send their children to an athletic trainer so that they may have sound bodies in the service (326c) of their now fit minds and will not be forced to cowardice in war or other activities through physical deficiencies.

"This is what the most able, i.e., the richest, do. Their sons start going (326d) to school at the earliest age and quit at the latest age. And when they quit school, the city in turn compels them to learn the laws and to model their lives on them. They are not to act as they please. An analogy might be drawn from the practice of writing-teachers, who sketch the letters faintly with a pen in workbooks for their beginning students and have them write the letters over the patterns they have drawn. In the same way, the city has drawn up laws invented by the great lawgivers in the past and compels them to govern and be governed by them. She punishes anyone who goes beyond these laws, and the term for this punishment in your city and (326e) others is, because it is a corrective legal action, 'correction.'

"When so much care and attention is paid to virtue, Socrates, both in public and private, are you still puzzled about virtue being teachable? The wonder would be if it were not teachable.

"Why, then, do many sons of good fathers never amount to anything? I want you to understand this too, and in fact it's no great wonder, if what I've just been saying is true about virtue being something in which no one (327a) can be a layman if there is to be a city. For if what I am saying is true – and nothing could be more true: Pick any other pursuit or study and reflect upon it. Suppose, for instance, there could be no city unless we were all flute-players, each to the best of his ability, and everybody was teaching everybody else this art in public and private and reprimanding the poor players and doing all this unstintingly, just as now no one begrudges or (327b) conceals his expertise in what is just and lawful as he does his other professional expertise. For it is to our collective advantage that we each possess justice and virtue, and so we all gladly tell and teach each other what is just and lawful. Well, if we all had the same eagerness and generosity in teaching each other flute-playing, do you think, Socrates, that the sons of good flute-players would be more likely to be good flute-players than the sons of poor flute-players? I don't think so at all. When a son happened to be naturally disposed toward flute-playing, he would progress (327c) and become famous; otherwise, he would remain obscure. In many cases the son of a good player would turn out to be a poor one, and the son of a poor player would turn out to be good. But as flute-players, they would all turn out to be capable when compared with ordinary people who had never studied the flute. Likewise you must regard the most unjust person ever reared in a human society under law as a paragon of justice compared (327d) with people lacking education and law courts and the pervasive pressure to cultivate virtue, savages such as the playwright Pherecrates brought on stage at last year's Lenaean festival. There's no doubt that if you found yourself among such people, as did the misanthropes in that play's chorus, you would be delighted to meet up with the likes of Eurybatus and (327e) Phrynondas and would sorely miss the immorality of the people here. As it is, Socrates, you affect delicate sensibilities, because everyone here is a teacher of virtue, to the best of his ability, and you can't see a single one. You might as well look for a teacher of Greek; you wouldn't find a (328a) single one of those either. Nor would you be any more successful if you asked who could teach the sons of our craftsmen the very arts which they of course learned from their fathers, to the extent that their fathers were competent and their friends in the trade. It would be difficult to produce someone who could continue their education, whereas it would be easy to find a teacher for the totally unskilled. It is the same with virtue and everything else. If there is someone who is the least bit more advanced in virtue than ourselves, he is to be cherished. I consider myself to be such a person, uniquely qualified to assist others (328b) in becoming noble and good and worth the fee that I charge and even more, so much so that even my students agree. This is why I charge (328c) according to the following system: a student pays the full price only if he wishes to; otherwise, he goes into a temple, states under oath how much he thinks my lessons are worth and pays that amount.

"There you have it, Socrates, my mythic story and my argument that virtue is teachable and that the Athenians consider it to be so and that it is no wonder that worthless sons are born of good fathers and good sons of worthless fathers, since even the sons of Polyclitus, of the same age as (328d) Paralus and Xanthippus here, are nothing compared to their father, and the same is true for the sons of other artisans. But it is not fair to accuse these two yet; there is still hope for them, for they are young."

Protagoras ended his virtuoso performance here and stopped speaking. (Hackett tr. slightly modified)

4. Plato, *Gorgias* 454a8– 461b2

(454a) [Socrates] Of what sort of persuasion is oratory (*rhētorikē*) a craft, and what is its persuasion about?" Or don't you think it's (454b) right to repeat that question?

[Gorgias] Yes, I do.

[Soc] Well then, Gorgias, since you think so too, please answer.

[Gorg] The persuasion I mean, Socrates, is the kind that takes place in law courts and in those other large gatherings, as I was saying a moment ago. And it's concerned with those matters that are just and unjust.

[Soc] Yes, Gorgias, I suspected that this was the persuasion you meant, and that these are the matters it's persuasion about. But so you won't be surprised if in a moment I ask you again another question like (454c) this, about what seems to be clear, and yet I go on with my questioning – as I say, I'm asking questions so that we can conduct an orderly discussion. It's not you I'm after; it's to prevent our getting in the habit of second-guessing and snatching each other's statements away ahead of time. It's to allow you to work out your assumption in any way you want to.

[Gorg] Yes, I think that you're quite right to do this, Socrates.

[Soc] Come then, and let's examine this point. Is there something you call "to have learned"?

[Gorg] There is.

[Soc] Very well. And also something you call "to be convinced"?

(454d) [Gorg] Yes, there is.

[Soc] Now, do you think that to have learned, and learning, are the same as to be convinced and conviction, or different?

[Gorg] I certainly suppose that they're different, Socrates.

[Soc] You suppose rightly. This is how you can tell: If someone asked you, "Is there such a thing as true and false conviction, Gorgias?" you'd say yes, I'm sure.

[Gorg] Yes.

[Soc] Well now, is there such a thing as true and false knowledge?

[Gorg] Not at all.

[Soc] So it's clear that they're not the same.

[Gorg] That's true.

(454e) [Soc] But surely both those who have learned and those who are convinced have come to be persuaded?

[Gorg] That's right.

[Soc] Would you like us then to posit two types of persuasion, one providing conviction without knowledge, the other providing knowledge?

[Gorg] Yes, I would.

[Soc] Now which type of persuasion does oratory produce in law courts and other gatherings concerning things that are just and unjust? The one that results in being convinced without knowing or the one that results in knowing?

[Gorg] It's obvious, surely, that it's the one that results in conviction.

[Soc] So evidently oratory produces the persuasion that comes from being convinced, and not the persuasion that comes from teaching, concerning (455a) what's just and unjust.

[Gorg] Yes.

[Soc] And so an orator is not a teacher of law courts and other gatherings about things that are just and unjust, either, but merely a persuader, for I don't suppose that he could teach such a large gathering about matters so important in a short time.

[Gorg] No, he certainly couldn't.

[Soc] Well now, let's see what we're really saying about oratory. (455b) For, mind you, even I myself can't get clear yet about what I'm saying. When the city holds a meeting to appoint doctors or shipbuilders or some other variety of craftsmen, that's surely not the time when the orator will give advice, is it? For obviously it's the most accomplished craftsman who should be appointed in each case. Nor will the orator be the one to give advice at a meeting that concerns the building of walls or the equipping of harbors or dockyards, but the master builders will be the ones. And when there is a deliberation about the appointment of generals or an (455c) arrangement of troops against the enemy or an occupation of territory, it's not the orators but the generals who'll give advice then. What do you say about such cases, Gorgias? Since you yourself claim both to be an orator and to make others orators, we'll do well to find out from you the characteristics of your craft. You must think of me now as eager to serve your interests, too. Perhaps there's actually someone inside who wants to become your pupil. I notice some, in fact a good many, and they may well be embarrassed to question you. So, while you're being questioned by me, (455d) consider yourself being questioned by them as well: "What will we get if we associate with you, Gorgias? What will we be able to advise the city on? Only about what's just and unjust or also about the things Socrates was mentioning just now?" Try to answer them.

[Gorg] Well, Socrates, I'll try to reveal to you clearly everything oratory can accomplish. You yourself led the way nicely, for you do know, don't (455e) you, that these dockyards and walls of the Athenians and the equipping of the harbor came about through the advice of Themistocles and in some cases through that of Pericles, but not through that of the craftsmen?

[Soc] That's what they say about Themistocles, Gorgias. I myself heard Pericles when he advised us on the middle wall.

(456a) [Gorg] And whenever those craftsmen you were just now speaking of are appointed, Socrates, you see that the orators are the ones who give advice and whose views on these matters prevail.

[Soc] Yes, Gorgias, my amazement at that led me long ago to ask what it is that oratory can accomplish. For as I look at it, it seems to me to be something supernatural in scope.

[Gorg] Oh yes, Socrates, if only you knew all of it – that it encompasses and subordinates to (456b) itself just about everything that can be accomplished. And I'll give you ample proof. Many a time I've gone with my brother or with other doctors to call on some sick person who refuses to take his medicine or allow the doctor to perform surgery or cauterization on him. And when the doctor failed to persuade him, I succeeded, by means of no other craft than oratory. And I maintain too that if an orator and a doctor came to any city anywhere you like and had to compete in speaking in the Assembly or some other gathering over which of them should be (456c) appointed doctor, the doctor wouldn't make any showing at all, but the one who had the ability to speak would be appointed, if he so wished. And if he were to compete with any other craftsman whatever, the orator more than anyone else would persuade them that they should appoint him, for there isn't anything that the orator couldn't speak more persuasively about to a gathering than could any other craftsman whatever. That's how great the accomplishment of this craft is, and the sort of accomplishment it is! One should, however, use oratory like any other competitive (456d) skill, Socrates. In other cases, too, one ought not to use a competitive skill against any and everybody, just because he has learned boxing, or boxing and wrestling combined, or fighting in armor, so as to make himself be superior to his friends as well as to his enemies. That's no reason to strike, stab, or kill one's own friends! Imagine someone who after attending wrestling school, getting his body into good shape and becoming a boxer, went on to strike his father and mother or any other family member or friend. By Zeus, that's no reason to hate physical trainers and people who (456e) teach fighting in armor, and to exile them from their cities! For while these people imparted their skills to be used justly against enemies and wrongdoers, and in defense, not aggression, their pupils pervert their (457a) strength and skill and misuse them. So it's not their teachers who are wicked, nor does that make the craft guilty or wicked; those who misuse it, surely, are the wicked ones. And the same is true for oratory as well. The orator has the ability to speak against everyone on every subject, so as in gatherings to be more persuasive, in short, about (457b) anything he likes, but the fact that he has the ability to rob doctors or other craftsmen of their reputations doesn't give him any more of a reason to do it. He should use oratory justly, as he would any competitive skill. And I suppose that if a person who has become an orator goes on with this ability and this craft to commit wrongdoing, we shouldn't hate his teacher and exile him from our cities. For while the teacher (457c) imparted it to be used justly, the pupil is making the opposite use of it. So it's the misuser whom it's just to hate and exile or put to death, not the teacher.

[Soc] Gorgias, I take it that you, like me, have experienced many discussions and that you've observed this sort of thing about them: it's not easy for the participants to define jointly what they're undertaking to (457d) discuss, and so, having learned from and taught each other, to conclude their session. Instead, if they're disputing some point and one maintains that the other isn't right or isn't clear, they get irritated, each thinking the other is speaking out of spite.

They become eager to win instead of investigating the subject under discussion. In fact, in the end some have a most shameful parting of the ways, abuse heaped upon them, having given and gotten to hear such things that make even the by-standers upset with themselves for having thought it worthwhile to come to listen to such (457e) people. What's my point in saying this? It's that I think you're now saying things that aren't very consistent or compatible with what you were first saying about oratory. So, I'm afraid to pursue my examination of you, for fear that you should take me to be speaking with eagerness to win against (458a) you, rather than to have our subject become clear. For my part, I'd be pleased to continue questioning you if you're the same kind of man I am, otherwise I would drop it. And what kind of man am I? One of those who would be pleased to be refuted if I say anything untrue, and who would be pleased to refute anyone who says anything untrue; one who, however, wouldn't be any less pleased to be refuted than to refute. For I count being refuted a greater good, insofar as it is a greater good for oneself to be delivered from the worst thing there is than to deliver someone else from it. I don't suppose there's anything quite so bad for a person as having false belief about the things we're discussing right now. So if you say (458b) you're this kind of man, too, let's continue the discussion; but if you think we should drop it, let's be done with it and break it off.

[Gorg] Oh yes, Socrates, I say that I myself, too, am the sort of person you describe. Still, perhaps we should keep in mind the people who are present here, too. For quite a while ago now, even before you came, I gave them a long presentation, and perhaps we'll stretch things out too long if (458c) we continue the discussion. We should think about them, too, so as not to keep any of them who want to do something else.

[Chaerephon] You yourselves hear the commotion these men are making, Gorgias and Socrates. They want to hear anything you have to say. And as for myself, I hope I'll never be so busy that I'd forego discussions such as this, conducted in the way this one is, because I find it more practical to do something else.

(458d) [Callicles] By the gods, Chaerephon, as a matter of fact I, too, though I've been present at many a discussion before now, don't know if I've ever been so pleased as I am at the moment. So if you're willing to discuss, even if it's all day long, you'll be gratifying me.

[Soc] For my part there's nothing stopping me, Callicles, as long as Gorgias is willing.

[Gorg] It'll be to my shame ever after, Socrates, if I weren't willing, when I myself have made the claim that anyone may ask me anything he (458e) wants. All right, if it suits these people, carry on with the discussion, and ask what you want.

[Soc] Well then, Gorgias, let me tell you what surprises me in the things you've said. It may be that what you said was correct and that I'm not taking your meaning correctly. Do you say that you're able to make an orator out of anyone who wants to study with you?

[Gorg] Yes.

[Soc] So that he'll be persuasive in a gathering about all subjects, not by teaching but by persuading?

(459a) [Gorg] Yes, that's right.

[Soc] You were saying just now, mind you, that the orator will be more persuasive even about health than a doctor is.

[Gorg] Yes I was, more persuasive in a gathering, anyhow.

[Soc] And doesn't "in a gathering" just mean "among those who don't have knowledge"? For, among those who do have it, I don't suppose that he'll be more persuasive than the doctor.

[Gorg] That's true.

[Soc] Now if he'll be more persuasive than a doctor, doesn't he prove to be more persuasive than the one who has knowledge?

[Gorg] Yes, that's right.

(459b) [Soc] Even though he's not a doctor, right?

[Gorg] Yes.

[Soc] And a non-doctor, I take it, isn't knowledgeable in the thing in which a doctor is knowledgeable.

[Gorg] That's obvious.

[Soc] So when an orator is more persuasive than a doctor, a non-knower will be more persuasive than a knower among non-knowers. Isn't this exactly what follows?

[Gorg] Yes it is, at least in this case.

[Soc] The same is true about the orator and oratory relative to the other crafts, too, then. Oratory doesn't need to have any knowledge of the (459c) state of their subject matters; it only needs to have discovered some device to produce persuasion in order to make itself appear to those who don't have knowledge that it knows more than those who actually do have it.

[Gorg] Well, Socrates, aren't things made very easy when you come off no worse than the craftsmen even though you haven't learned any other craft but this one?

[Soc] Whether the orator does or does not come off worse than the others because of this being so, we'll examine in a moment if it has any (459d) bearing on our argument. For now, let's consider this point first. Is it the case that the orator is in the same position with respect to what's just and unjust, what's shameful and admirable, what's good and bad, as he is about what's healthy and about the subjects of the other crafts? Does he lack knowledge, that is, of what these are, of what is good or what is bad, of what is admirable or what is shameful, or just or unjust? Does he employ devices to produce persuasion about them, so that – even though he doesn't know – he seems, among those who don't know either, to know more than (459e) someone who actually does know? Or is it necessary for him to know, and must the prospective student of oratory already be knowledgeable in these things before coming to you? And if he doesn't, will you, the oratory teacher, not teach him any of these things when he comes to you – for that's not your job – and will you make him seem among most people to have knowledge of such things when in fact he doesn't have it, and to seem good when in fact he isn't? Or won't you be able to teach him oratory at all, unless he knows the truth about these things to begin with? How (460a) do matters such as these stand, Gorgias? Yes, by Zeus, do give us your revelation and tell us what oratory can accomplish, just as you just now said you would.

[Gorg] Well, Socrates, I suppose that if he really doesn't have this knowledge, he'll learn these things from me as well.

[Soc] Hold it there. You're right to say so. If you make someone an orator, it's necessary for him to know what's just and what's unjust, either beforehand, or by learning it from you afterwards.

[Gorg] Yes, it is.

(460b) [Soc] Well? A man who has learned carpentry is a carpenter, isn't he?

[Gorg] Yes.

[Soc] And isn't a man who has learned music a musician?

[Gorg] Yes.

[Soc] And a man who has learned medicine a doctor? And isn't this so too, by the same reasoning, with the other crafts? Isn't a man who has learned a particular subject the sort of man his knowledge makes him?

[Gorg] Yes, he is.

[Soc] And, by this line of reasoning, isn't a man who has learned what's just a just man too?

[Gorg] Yes, absolutely.

[Soc] And a just man does just things, I take it?

[Gorg] Yes.

(460c) [Soc] Now isn't an orator necessarily just, and doesn't a just man necessarily want to do just things?

[Gorg] Apparently so.

[Soc] Therefore an orator will never want to do what's unjust.

[Gorg] No, apparently not.

[Soc] Do you remember saying a little earlier that we shouldn't (460d) complain against physical trainers or exile them from our cities if the boxer uses his boxing skill to do what's unjust, and that, similarly, if an orator uses his oratorical skill unjustly we shouldn't complain against his teacher or banish him from the city, but do so to the one who does what's unjust, the one who doesn't use his oratorical skill properly? Was that said or not?

[Gorg] Yes, it was.

(460e) [Soc] But now it appears that this very man, the orator, would never have done what's unjust, doesn't it?

[Gorg] Yes, it does.

[Soc] And at the beginning of our discussion, Gorgias, it was said that oratory would be concerned with speeches, not those about even and odd, but those about what's just and unjust. Right?

[Gorg] Yes.

[Soc] Well, at the time you said that, I took it that oratory would never be an unjust thing, since it always makes its speeches about justice. But when a little later you were saying that the orator could also use (461a) oratory unjustly, I was surprised and thought that your statements weren't consistent, and so I made that speech in which I said that if you, like me, think that being refuted is a profitable thing, it would be worthwhile to continue the discussion, but if you don't, to let it drop. But now, as we subsequently examine the question, you see for yourself too that it's agreed that, quite to the contrary, the orator is incapable of using oratory unjustly and (461b) of being willing to do what's unjust. By the Dog, Gorgias, it'll take more than a short session to go through an adequate examination of how these matters stand! (Hackett tr.)

5. Plato, *Gorgias* 484c5– 486d1

[CALLICLES] Philosophy (*philosophia*) is no doubt something delightful, Socrates, as long as you embrace it with moderation at the right age. But if you devote yourself to it for too long it ruins people. Even if you are very gifted, if you stick to philosophy when you are older, you will inevitably end up inexperienced (484d) in everything a man needs experience who aims to be noble, good and respected. They wind up without experience in the laws of the city, or in the ways of speaking that need to be employed in dealing with people, both in private and in public, or human pleasures and desires and in short they become entirely inexperienced in human nature. So when they engage in some private or political affair (484e) they prove to be ridiculous just as politicians are ridiculous when they come to your discussions and speeches. Euripides' saying applies: "Each person shines and devotes himself and spends the greatest part of the day on whatever he finds himself best at," (485a) but avoids and insults whatever he does badly, but praises the other, supposing that in this way he is praising himself. But I think that the most correct course is to partake of both. It is a fine thing to pursue philosophy to the extent that it is part of your education and not disgraceful to philosophize while you are young, but when someone is already older and continues to philosophize the thing becomes ridiculous, Socrates and I (485b) have the same reaction to people who persist in philosophizing as I do towards people who speak hesitatingly and play games. Whenever I see a child speaking that way and playing, I am delighted and it appears to me to be a mark of freedom and appropriate to the child's age. But when I hear a little boy speaking articulately I think it sad and it hurts my ears and it strikes me as something servile. But when anyone hears (485c) a grown man speaking hesitantly or playing it appears ridiculous, unmanly and deserving of a beating. And this is what I, anyway, feel about people engaging in philosophy. I enjoy seeing philosophy in a young lad and it seems fitting and I think that this person is well brought up, and that one who does not engage in philosophy is raised poorly and will never make himself worthy of any fine or noble (485d) deed. On the other hand when I see an older man continuing to philosophize and not letting it go, Socrates, I think that man needs a beating, since as I was just saying, even if this person is very gifted he will become unmanly, keeping away from the city center and market places where the poet declared that men "gain distinction"; rather he will spend the rest of his life hiding away in a corner (485e) whispering with three or four young men and never utter anything noble, important or competent.

But, Socrates, I am quite well disposed towards you. In fact, I may well be in the same situation as Zethos had regarding Amphion in Euripides' play which I quoted just now. In fact it occurs to me to say to you the same kind of thing that he said to his brother, "Socrates, you are disregarding what you ought to be paying attention to, and even though you have so outstanding a mind (486a) you couldn't correctly put together a speech for counsel in a trial or utter anything likely or persuasive, or make a forceful proposal on behalf of someone else." So, Socrates my friend, (and please don't hold it against me, since what I am about to say is said with goodwill) don't you think it is disgraceful to be in the state I think you are as well as the others who continue to pursue philosophy too far? As it is, if somebody were to grab you or anybody else like you and dragged you off to prison, saying that you had something wrong even though you hadn't, you know that you wouldn't know what (486b) to do for yourself, but you would be totally confused and at a loss for words without anything to say, and when you went to trial, if you had a corrupt and wicked accuser, you would be put to death if he demanded the death penalty. Indeed, Socrates, how is this wise – a craft that takes a well-favored person and makes him worse, unable to defend himself or extricate either himself or anyone else from the greatest dangers, (486c) to be robbed of all his possessions by his enemies and to lose all his civic rights. To put it crudely you can hit a person like that over the head and get off scot-free. Instead, my friend, listen to me. Stop refuting people, practice the fine arts and do so wherever you will get a reputation for good sense and leave these subtleties to others (whether they ought to be called nonsense or gibberish) which will lead to your dwelling in empty houses, competing not with men who refute these trivial matters (486d) but with people who have a life and a reputation and many other good things.

6. Gorgias, *Encomium of Helen*

(1) It brings credit (*kosmos*) to a city to have strong men, as beauty [brings credit] to a body, wisdom to a soul, excellence to an object, and truth to a speech (*logos*); their opposites bring discredit (*akosmia*). A man, woman, speech, deed, city and object that deserves praise by praise should be honored and to what does not deserve praise blame should be placed, since blaming the praiseworthy and praising the blameworthy are equally mistaken and stupid. (2) The same man who correctly says what is right will also refute those people who blame Helen, a woman whose reputation among those who listen to poets has become univocal and unanimous as

has the fame of her name, which has become a memorial to her misfortunes. But I want to give a reckoning in an account that relieves the ill-reputed woman of guilt by revealing her detractors as mistaken and ending their ignorance by making the truth known.

(3) That the woman who is the subject of this account (*logos*) was absolutely supreme among men and women in beauty and birth is not unknown to even a few people. This is clear since her mother was Leda and her real father was a god, Zeus (who is held to be her father because he really was), while a mortal man, Tyndareus, was called her father (but he has been refuted for saying that he was), and the one was the mightiest of men and the other is the ruler of everything.

(4) Born to such parents she had beauty divine and after getting it she kept it and she was not unnoticed. She instilled the strongest passions for love in the greatest number of men and with one body she assembled many bodies of men proud of their greatness. Some had great wealth, others the pride of ancient family birth, others good physical condition due to their own strength, and some had capacities due to acquired wisdom. And they all came driven by competitive love and invincible ambition.

(5) Now who it was that fulfilled his passion by kidnapping Helen, and why and how he did it I will not say. Telling people who know things that they know makes for credibility but does not bring delight. Rather, in my account (*logos*) I will now skip over that earlier time and jump to the beginning of the next account (*logos*), and I will set forth the reasons for which it was likely that Helen's voyage to Troy took place. (6) She did what she did either through the will of Fate and the designs of the gods and decrees of Necessity or because she was taken by force, persuaded by speech (*logoi*), or conquered by Love.

Now if it was because of the first of these, the person who deserves to be accused is the one who makes the accusation: it is impossible to thwart the will of a god by means of human forethought, for it is not in the nature of the mightier to be stopped by the weaker, but rather for the weaker to be led by the stronger and for the stronger to rule and the weaker to obey. But god is stronger than a human in force and wisdom and everything else. Therefore if blame is to be assigned to Fate and a god, Helen is to be freed of her ill fame.

(7) If she was kidnapped by force and lawlessly raped, clearly the kidnapper committed injustice because he raped her, but the kidnapped woman suffered misfortune because she was raped. So the barbarian who undertook the barbarous undertaking is deserving in speech (*logos*), law and deed: in speech deserving of blame, in law deserving to be deprived of his legal rights and indeed deserving to be punished. But the woman who was forced, deprived of her country and orphaned from her dear ones – how would it not be reasonable for her to be pitied instead of reviled? He is the one who did terrible things and she simply suffered them. So it is just to pity her and hate him.

(8) Not even if speech (*logos*) persuaded and deceived her soul, is it hard to make a defense against this charge and free her from blame, as follows. *Logos* is

a powerful master which by means of the smallest and most invisible body accomplishes the most divine deeds. It can put an end to fear, remove grief, instill joy and increase pity. I will prove how this is so. (9) But it is to the opinion of my audience that I must prove it. I both consider and define all poetry to be speech (*logos*) with meter. Those who hear it are overcome with fearful shuddering, tearful pity and mournful yearning and over the good fortunes and ill-farings of other people and their affairs, the soul experiences a feeling of its own, through the words (*logoi*).

Come now, let me shift from one argument (*logos*) to another. (10) It is through words (*logoi*) that inspired incantations bring on pleasure and bring away grief. When blended with the soul's opinion the power of incantation charms, persuades and changes it through witchcraft. Two arts of witchcraft and magic have been discovered that mislead the soul and deceive our opinion.

(11) All who have persuaded or who persuade anyone of anything do so by fashioning false *logos*. For if on all subjects everyone had a memory of the past, (a conception) of the present and foreknowledge of the future, *logos* would not be similarly similar as it is for people who, as things are, cannot easily remember the past, consider the present or divine the future. Thus, in most matters, most people make opinion an adviser to their soul. But opinion is fallible and uncertain and involves those who make use of it infallible and uncertain successes.

(12) What, then, keeps us from supposing that Helen too, against her will, came under the influence of *logoi* just as if she had been taken by the force of mighty men? For it was possible to see how persuasion prevails, which lacks the appearance of necessity but has the same power. For *logos*, which persuaded, compelled the soul, which it persuaded, both to believe what was said and to approve what was done. Therefore, the one who persuaded, since he compelled, is unjust and the one who was persuaded, since she was compelled by *logos*, is wrongly blamed.

(13) As to the fact that persuasion added to *logos* makes whatever impression it likes on the soul, one should attend first to the accounts (*logoi*) of the astronomers, who replace one opinion with another and so make things that are incredible and unclear seem apparent to the eyes of opinion; second, to compulsory competitions which use speeches (*logoi*) in which a single *logos* written with art (*tekhnē*) but not spoken with truth delights and persuades a large crowd; and third, to contests of speeches that pretend to be wise (*philosophoi logoi*)[1], in which it is revealed how easily the swiftness of thought makes our confidence in our opinion change.

(14) The power of *logos* has the same relation (*logos*) to the order of the soul as the order of drugs has to the nature of bodies. For as different drugs expel different humors from the body, and some put an end to sickness and others to life, so some *logoi* cause grief, others joy, some fear, others render their hearers bold and still others drug and bewitch the soul through an evil persuasion. (15) It has been stated that if she was persuaded by *logos* she did not do wrong but suffered misfortune. In my fourth account (*logos*) I will discuss the fourth reason. If it was love that caused

all this, she would have no difficulty escaping responsibility (*aitia*) for her alleged wrongdoing. For the things that we see do not have the nature that we wish, but the nature that they actually have. And it is through sight that the soul is shaped even in the ways it reacts.

(16) When enemy bodies put on enemy armor of bronze and iron against enemies for protection against one and as a barrier against another, if vision observes them it is immediately agitated and it agitates the soul, in consequence, they panic and run away from the impending danger as if it were present. Although habituation to the law is strong, it is evicted by the fear that resulted from vision, which when it entered made them neglect both what is judged honorable by the law and the benefits accruing through victory. (17) As soon as they see frightening things some people immediately lose their present thought at the present moment; that is how fear quenches purpose and drives it out. Also many have fallen into vain labors, dread diseases and incurable madness; that is how vision engraves in our thought images of things seen and leaves behind much that causes fright. And the things that are left behind are like things that are said.

(18) Further, painters delight our vision when they perfectly create a single body and form from many colors and bodies. Also making statues and creating sculptures affords delight to the eyes. In this way they make the vision feel pain and longing. Further, many things instill in many people love and longing for many things and bodies. (19) So if the eye of Helen, delighted by the body of Alexander, transmitted to her soul a readiness and eager desire for love, what is surprising? If love, who is a god, possesses the divine power of gods, how could anyone weaker fend it off and defend against it? And if it is a human illness and a case of the soul's ignorance, it should not be blamed as a fault but should be regarded as a misfortune. For she went as she went, because of the snares of fortune, not the deliberations of her thought and because of the compulsion of love, not the purposeful preparations of craft.

(20) How, then, should it be just to believe the reproaches against Helen, a woman who entirely escapes responsibility, no matter whether she did what she did because she was overpowered by love or persuaded by speech or kidnapped by force or compelled by divine necessity?

(21) By my account (*logos*) I have removed ill fame from a woman. I have stayed faithful to the rule (*nomos*) I stipulated at the beginning of my *logos*. I have attempted to put an end to the injustice of blame and the ignorance of opinion. I wanted to write the *logos* as a praise of Helen and an entertainment for myself.

7. Gorgias, *On What Is Not or On Nature*

(66) He concludes as follows that nothing is: if (something) is, either what-is is or what-is-not (is), or both what-is and what-is-not are. But it is the case neither that what-is is, as he will show, nor that what-is-not is, as he will justify, nor that both what-is and what-is-not are, as he will teach this too. Therefore, it is not the case that anything is.

(67) And in fact, what-is-not is not. For if what-is-not is, it will be and not be at the same time. For in that it is considered as not being, it will not be, but in that it *is* not being, on the other hand, it will be. But it is completely absurd for something to be and not be at the same time. Therefore, it is not the case that what-is-not is. And differently: if what-is-not is, what-is will not be, since they are opposites and if being is an attribute of what-is-not, not-being will be an attribute of what-is. But it is certainly not the case what what-is is not, and so neither will what-is-not be.

(68) Further, neither is it the case that what-is is. For if what-is is, it is either eternal or generated or eternal and generated at the same time. But it is neither eternal nor generated nor both, as we will show. Therefore it is not the case that what-is is. For if what-is is eternal (we must begin at this point), it does not have any beginning. (69) For everything that comes to be has some beginning, but what is eternal, being ungenerated, did not have a beginning. But if it does not have a beginning, it is unlimited, and if it is unlimited it is nowhere. For if it is anywhere, that in which it is different from it, and so what-is will no longer be unlimited since it is enclosed in something. For what encloses is larger than what is enclosed, but nothing is larger than what is unlimited, and so what is unlimited is not anywhere.

(70) Further, it is not enclosed in itself, either. For "that in which" and "that in it" will be the same, and what-is will become two, place and body (for "that in which" in place and "that in it" is the body). But this is absurd, so what-is is not in itself, either. And so, if what-is is eternal, it is unlimited, but if it is unlimited, it is nowhere, and if it is nowhere, it is not. So if what-is is eternal, it is not at all.

(71) Further, what-is cannot be generated either. For if it has come to be, it did so either from a thing that is or from a thing that is not. But it has come to be neither from what-is (for if it is a thing that is, it has not come to be, but already is), nor from what-is-not (for what-is-not cannot generate anything, since what generates anything must of necessity share in existence). Therefore, it is not the case that what-is is generated either.

(72) In the same ways, it is not both eternal and generated at the same time. For these exclude one another, and if what-is is eternal it has not come to be, and if it has come to be it is not eternal. So if what-is is neither eternal nor generated nor both together, what-is would not be.

(73) And differently, if it is, it is either one or many. But it is neither one nor many, as will be shown. Therefore it is not the case that what-is is. For if it is one, it is either a quantity or continuous or a magnitude or a body. But whichever of these it is, it is not one, but being a quantity, it will be divided, and if it is continuous it will be cut. Similarly if conceived as a magnitude it will not be indivisible. And if it is a body, it will be three-dimensional, for it will have length, width and depth. But it is absurd to say that what-is is none of these. Therefore, it is not the case that what-is is one.

(74) Further, it is not many. For if it is not one, it is not many either. For the many is a compound of individual ones, and so since (the thesis that what-is is) one is refuted, (the thesis that what-is is) many is refuted along with it. But it is altogether clear from this that neither what-is nor what-is-not is.

(75) It is easy to conclude that neither is the case that both of them are – what-is and what-is-not. For if what-is-not is and what-is is, then what-is-not will be the same as what-is as regards being. And for this reason, neither of them is. For it is agreed that what-is-not is not, and what-is has been shown to be the same as this. So it too will not be. (76) However, if what-is is the same as what-is-not, it is not possible for both to be. For if both (are), then they are not the same, and if (they are) the same, then (it is) not (the case that) both (are). It follows that nothing is. For if neither what-is is nor what-is-not nor both, and nothing aside from these is conceivable, then nothing is.

(77) Next in order is to teach that even if something is, it is unknowable and inconceivable by humans. For if things that are thought of, says Gorgias, are not things-that-are, what-is is not thought of. And reasonably so. For just as if things that are thought of have the attribute of being white, being thought of would be an attribute of white things, so if things that are thought of have the attribute of not being things-that-are, not to be thought of will necessarily be an attribute of things-that-are. (78) This is why the claim that if things that are thought of are not things-that-are, what-is is not thought of, is sound and preserves the sequence of argument. But things that are thought of (for we must assume this) are not things-that-are, as we will show. Therefore it is not the case that what-is is thought of.

Further, it is completely clear that things that are thought of are not things-that-are. (79) For if things that are thought of are things-that-are, all things that are thought of are – indeed, however, anyone thinks of them. But this is apparently false. For if someone thinks of a person flying or chariots racing in the sea, it is not forthwith the case that a person is flying or chariots racing in the sea. And so, it is not the case that things that are thought of are things-that-are.

(80) In addition, if things that are thought of are things-that-are, things-that-are-not will not be thought of. For opposites have opposite attributes, and what-is-not is opposite to what-is. For this reason, if being thought of is an attribute of what-is, not being thought of will assuredly be an attribute of what-is-not. But this is absurd. For Scylla and Chimaera and many things-that-are-not are thought of. Therefore it is not the case that what-is is thought of.

(81) And just as things that are seen are called visible because they are seen and things that are heard are called audible because they are heard, and we do not reject visible things because they are not heard or dismiss audible things because they are not seen (for each ought to be judged by its own sense, not by another), so also things that are thought of will be, even if they may not be seen by vision or heard by hearing because they are grasped by their own criterion. (82) So if someone thinks that chariots race in the sea, even if he does not see them, he ought to believe that there are chariots racing in the sea. But this is absurd. Therefore it is not the case that what-is is thought of and comprehended.

(83) But even if it should be comprehended, it cannot be expressed to another. For if things-that-are are visible and audible and generally perceptible, and in fact

are external objects, and of these the visible are comprehended by vision and the audible by hearing and not vice versa, how can these be communicated to another? (84) For that by which we communicate is *logos*, but *logos* is not the objects, the things-that-are. Therefore it is not the case that we communicate things-that-are to our neighbors, but [we communicate] *logos*, which is different from the objects. So just as the visible could not become audible and vice versa, thus, since what-is is an external object, it could not become our *logos*. (85) But if were not *logos*, it would not have been revealed to another. In fact, *logos*, he says, is composed of external things, i.e., perceptible things, falling upon us. For from encountering flavor there arises in us the *logos* which is expressed with reference to this quality, and from the incidence of color on the senses arises the *logos* with reference to color. But if so, it is not the *logos* that make manifest the external (object), but the external (object) that comes to be communicative of the *logos*.

(86) Further, it is not possible to say that *logos* is an object in the way visible and audible things are, so that objects which are can be communicated by it, which is an object which is. For, he says, even if *logos* is an object, in any case it differs from all other objects, and visible bodies differ most from *logos*. For the visible is grasped by one organ, *logos* by another. Therefore it is not the case that *logos* makes manifest the great number of objects, just as they do not reveal the nature of one another.

8. Antiphon Fragment B49 DK

Well then, suppose life goes on and he desires to marry and have a wife. That very day, that very night is the beginning of a new lot in life, a new destiny. Marriage is a great trial for a person. If she turns out unsuitable how should he deal with the misfortune? Divorces are difficult – making enemies out of friends who think and breathe the same, who have considered each other worthy people. It is hard to have such a possession, to expect to gain pleasure and yet be wracked with grief.

But let's stop talking about hostile things and speak of the most friendly things of all. What gives more delight to a man than a wife who is his soul-mate? What is sweeter, especially when he is young? But in this very thing where sweetness resides there is sorrow as well, since pleasures are not imported alone but are accompanied by pain and labor. Victors at the Olympic and Pythian games and contests like those, and skills and all pleasures too tend to come as the result of great pains, since honors and prizes – bait that god has given to humans – necessarily require much effort and sweat. If I had another body just like mine, I could not live; I already have to go to so much trouble for my health and to gather my livelihood each day, as well as for the sake of my honor, my self-control, my fame and my reputation. What would happen if I had another body like this one that needed as much attention? Now is it not obvious that even if a man's wife is his soul-mate, she will bring him no fewer pleasures and pains than he does to himself, what with concern for the health of two bodies and gathering livelihood and keeping self-control and concern for his reputation? Suppose there are children. At that point all things are full of cares, and his youthful playfulness has left his thoughts and the expression on his face is no longer the same.

9. Prodicus, *The Choice of Heracles* (Xenophon, *Memorabilia* 2.1.21–34)

(21) Prodicus the wise, in his piece on Heracles which he performed before huge audiences, affirms the same view about *aretē*. It goes something like this, as best I can remember. He says that when he was leaving his childhood and becoming a man – an age when young men at the point of taking charge of their own affairs reveal whether they will take the path of virtue or vice in their life – Heracles went out to a quiet place and was pondering which path to take (22) when two tall women appeared and approached him. One of them was attractive to look at, with a natural nobility, her body adorned with purity, her eyes with modesty, her bearing with self-control, and she was clothed in white. The other had a tendency towards fleshiness and softness, she was beautified so that her complexion seemed to appear to be redder and whiter than it was, her bearing straighter than it was naturally; she had her eyes wide open and her clothing let her beauty shine through. She was always looking at herself and noticing whether anyone else was looking, and she often even looked at her shadow.

(23) When they got near to Heracles, the first one mentioned continued to go in the same way, but the other desired to get to Heracles first and ran to him and said, "Heracles, I see that you are wondering which path to take for your life. If you make me your friend and follow me, I will lead you down the pleasant and easiest path. There is no delight that you will not taste and you will live your life without suffering hardship. (24) In the first place you will not have to worry about wars and troubles, but you will go through life thinking about whatever food and drink you find delicious or what will be most delightful to see or hear or smell or touch, which boyfriend you will most enjoy being with, how you will sleep most comfortably and how you can get all these things with the least effort. (25) If there is ever the least suspicion of a shortage of what it takes to obtain them, don't fear that I will lead you to the point where you have to work and trouble your body and soul to obtain it. You will use what others work for and you will not refrain from any possible source of gain. I give my companions the power to help themselves to everything." (26) When Heracles heard this he asked "My lady, what is your name?" and she replied, "My friends call me Happiness, but my enemies give me the nickname Vice."

(27) At this point the other woman approached him and said "I too have come to you, Heracles. I know your parents and your nature, which I have observed closely in your childhood. This is why I expect that if you take the path towards me you will accomplish extremely fine and noble deeds and I will be still more highly honored and famous for my benefactions. I won't deceive you by starting out with

promises of pleasure, but I will truthfully describe things the way the gods disposed of them. (28) The gods give men nothing that is really good and noble without hard work and diligence, but if you want the gods to be kindly to you you must worship them, if you want to be liked by your friends you must do them well, if you want to be honored by some city you must benefit it, if you think you should be admired for your *aretē* by all of Greece you must try to do good to Greece, if you want the earth to bear fruit in abundance you must cultivate the earth, if you think that you must get rich from cattle, you must take care of them, if you set out to become great through war and want to be able to liberate your friends and subdue your enemies you must learn the arts of war from experts and practice them as they should be employed, and if you want your body to be powerful, you must accustom it to obeying your judgment and you must train it with labor and sweat."

(29) Then Vice interrupted saying, according to Prodicus, "Do you understand how long and hard a path to enjoyment this woman is describing, Heracles? Instead I will lead you on a path to happiness that is short and easy."

(30) And Virtue said, "You wretch! What do you possess that is good? What pleasure do you know since you are unwilling to do anything for the sake of these things – you who don't even wait to have an appetite for pleasures but fill yourself with everything before you want it? You eat before you are hungry and drink before you are thirsty. To eat with pleasure you get cooks, to drink with pleasure you obtain expensive wines and in summer you run around looking for snow, to sleep with pleasure you get not only soft mattresses but bedsteads as well. You desire to sleep not in order to work but because you have nothing to do. You force yourself to have sex before you need it, trying everything and using men as women. This is how you educate your friends, running riot by night and sleeping through the most useful part of the day. (31) Although immortal you have been rejected by the gods and you are dishonored by good people. You never hear the sweetest sound of all, praise of yourself, and you never see the sweetest sight of all, since you have never gazed upon a single good act of your own. Who would trust anything you say? Who would help if you need anything? Who in his right mind would submit to joining your band? They are feeble in body when young and feeble in mind after they grow old. Nurtured in comfort through their youth, they endure their old age miserable and in pain, ashamed at what they have done and oppressed by what they are doing. While running through pleasures in their youth they have stored up hardships for their old age.

(32) But I spend my time with gods and with good humans. No god and no human being does any good action without me. I am honored above all by gods and humans who are akin to me, a beloved co-worker of craftsmen, a faithful guardian of homeowners and a beloved helper of servants, a good participant in the labors of peace and a steady ally of the deeds of war and the best partner in friendship. (33) My friends enjoy food and drink with pleasure and without trouble because they hold off until they desire these things. They sleep more pleasantly than people who go to bed before they are tired, they don't mind waking up, and sleep does not

make them fail to do fulfill their duties, the young enjoy the praise of elders and the old folks glory in the honors of the young, they recall with pleasure their deeds of old and their deeds of the present they delight in doing, since through me they are dear to the gods, beloved by their friends, honored in their countries and when their fated end arrives, they do not lie dishonored by being forgotten, but they flourish celebrated in memory forever. Child of noble parents Heracles, through such hard and laborious effort you may obtain supreme happiness."

(34) This is how Prodicus describes Heracles' education by Virtue, but he adorned his thoughts in words even more magnificent than these words of mine.

10. Plato, *Lesser Hippias* 368b2–e1

[Socrates] Of all the people I know you [Hippias] are absolutely the single person who is the greatest expert in all fields. I once heard you boasting in the marketplace next to the banker's tables about your vast and enviable wisdom. You said that one time you went to the Olympic festival and that you yourself had made everything you were wearing. First off you said that the ring you were wearing was your own work since you were an expert in engraving rings, and a signet seal as well, not to mention an oil-scraper and an oil-bottle that you had made yourself. Next you said that you had cut the leather for the shoes you were wearing and had woven your cloak and little tunic. In fact, what everyone thought to be the most amazing showpiece of your vast wisdom was when you said that the belt of the little tunic that you had woven was just like Persian belts made for luxury clothes. And there was more: you had come with poems – epics, tragedies and dithyrambs – and also many works of all kinds composed in prose, and you had arrived with expertise not only in everything I just mentioned but in other areas as well: rhythms, harmony and spelling and many other things besides, as I seem to remember. But I've forgotten your expertise in memory in which you excel. And I imagine that I have forgotten lots of other things too.

11. Twin Arguments

The author of this text is unknown. The text itself is found at the end of some manuscripts of Sextus Empiricus, who lived in the first or second century CE. It was written in the Doric dialect around 400 BCE (judging from the reference in 1.8 to the "most recent" victory of the Spartans over the Athenians). At this date many Sophists were active. It is included because it is the most extensive example of the practice of antilogic, presenting arguments for opposing theses, for example that good and bad are the same, and that they are not the same, that justice and injustice are the same and that they are not the same. The text has nine sections of which the first five are examples of antilogic. Some have thought that it is a homework exercise written by a not-very-adept student of some Sophist. The philosophical merit of the arguments is slight, but they give a vivid picture of how sophisticated instruction might have proceeded.

1: On Good and Bad

Twin arguments about good and bad are made in Greece by people who pursue wisdom. Some say that the good and the bad are different from one another, while others say that they are the same thing and that something can be good for some and bad for others and sometimes good and sometimes bad for the same person. (2) I am on the side of the latter group. I will consider this from the point of view of human life in which attention must be paid to food, drink and sex. These are bad for the sick but good for someone who is healthy and needs them. (3) And incontinence in these matters is bad for the incontinent but good for people who sell these things and make their living this way. Sickness is bad for the patients but good for the doctors. Death is bad for the dead but good for the undertakers and the gravediggers. (4) Farming that produces abundant crops is good for the farmers but bad for the merchants. For boats to collide and smash is bad for the shipowner but good for the shipbuilders. (5) If an iron tool is rusted, blunt or broken it is bad for others but good for the blacksmith. For a pot to break is bad for others but good for the potters. For shoes to be worn out and torn is bad for others but good for the cobbler. (6) In athletic, musical and martial arts competitions – for example, in a race in an athletic competition – victory is good for the winner but bad for the losers. (7) Likewise too for wrestlers and boxers and all the musicians as well. For example singing and playing the lyre is good for the winner but bad for the losers. (8) In war (and I will first speak of the most recent events) the Spartans' victory over the Athenians and their allies was good for the Spartans but bad for the Athenians and their allies. The Greeks' victory over the Persians was good for the Greeks but bad for the foreigners. (9) The capture of Troy was good for the Achaeans but bad for the Trojans. Likewise for what happened to the Thebans and the Argives. (10) Furthermore, the battle between the Centaurs and Lapiths was good for the Lapiths but bad for the Centaurs. And to be sure the battle and victory that are told of the gods and Giants were good for the gods but bad for the Giants.

(11) But another argument is made, that the good is one thing and the bad another, where just as the word is different so too is the reality. I too distinguish them in this way, since I think that it would be not entirely clear what kind of thing is good and what kind is bad if each of them were the same thing and not something different. This would be surprising. (12) I think that not even someone who holds this view could answer if someone asked him, "Tell me, have you ever done anything good for your parents?" He would reply "Yes – in fact many good things and important ones too." Therefore, you ought to do them many things that are bad, and important ones too, if the good is the same as the bad." (13) Next, have you ever done anything good for your relatives? Then you have made your relatives ill. Next, have you ever done anything bad to your enemies? Then you have done many important good things. (14) Come now and answer me this: Don't you pity the poor for having many important bad things, and also consider them fortunate for faring well and faring well in many ways, if in fact the same thing is bad and good? (15) Nothing keeps

the Great King of Persia from being in the same condition as the poor. For him many great good things are many great bad things, if indeed the same thing is good and bad. Take this as said for everything. (16) I shall go through individual cases, beginning with eating, drinking and sex. These are bad for sick people to engage in and in turn, engaging in them is good for such people if in fact the same thing is good and bad. Also being sick is bad for the sick and also good if the good is the same as the bad. (17) Everything that was said in the previous argument works like this. And I am not saying what the good is, but I am trying to explain that the bad and the good are not the same thing, but each of the two is different.

2: On Virtuous and Shameful[2]

(1) Twin arguments are also made about the virtuous and the shameful. Some say that the virtuous is one thing and the shameful is another, differing in reality just as in name, and others that the same thing is virtuous and shameful. I will try to interpret this in the following way. (2) In the first place, for a boy of a ripe age to gratify a lover is virtuous, but shameful to gratify anyone who is not his lover. (3) For women to bathe is virtuous indoors but shameful in a wrestling school (but it is virtuous for men to bathe in a wrestling school and in a gymnasium). (4) To have intercourse with one's husband in solitude, indoors, is virtuous but to do so outdoors is shameful. (5) And to have intercourse with her own husband is virtuous but to do so with the husband of another is most shameful. And for a man to have intercourse with his own wife is virtuous but to do so with the wife of another is shameful. (6) And dressing up, applying makeup and wearing gold jewelry is shameful for a man but virtuous for a woman. And running away from the enemy is shameful, but running away from one's competitors in a race is virtuous. (7) And to benefit friends is virtuous but to do so to enemies is shameful. (8) And slaughtering friends and fellow citizens is shameful, but doing so to enemies is virtuous. And this holds generally for everything.

(9) Now I will turn to consider what cities and peoples regard as shameful. In the first place for the Spartans it is virtuous for girls to train and to walk about with their arms bare and without wearing tunics, but for the Ionians it is shameful. (10) And it is virtuous for their boys not to learn music and letters, but for the Ionians not to know all these things is shameful. (11) For the Thessalians it is virtuous to cut horses from a herd and to break them in and mules as well and to catch an ox and slaughter it, skin it and butcher it, but in Sicily this is shameful and the work of slaves. (12) The Macedonians think it virtuous for unmarried girls to be in love and have intercourse with a man, but shameful when they are married, but for Greeks these are both shameful to do. (13) For Thracians being tattooed is a decoration for girls, but for everyone else tattoos are a punishment for wrongdoing. The Scythians consider it virtuous for anyone who has killed a man to scalp him and hang his hair on the front of his horse and to gild and silver the skull and then drink out of it and pour libations to the gods from it, but among the Greeks no one would even want

to go into the same house with anyone who had done such things. (14) The Massagetae cut their parents into pieces and eat them, thinking that being buried in their children is the finest possible grave, but in Greece, if anyone did this he would be driven out of Greece and die a dreadful death for having done such shameful and terrible things. (15) The Persians consider it virtuous for men to dress like women and to have intercourse with their daughter, their mother and their sister, while Greeks consider it shameful and illegal. (16) The Lydians consider it virtuous for girls to earn money prostituting themselves and then marry, but no Greek would be willing to marry such a girl. (17) The Egyptians do not think the same things virtuous as others do: here it is virtuous for women to weave and do work, but there the men do that and women do what men do here. For them, it is virtuous to knead clay with their hands and dough with their feet, but for us, it is the opposite.

(18) However, I think that if someone told all people to bring together the things that they think shameful and then to take from these piles the things they regard virtuous, nothing would be left, but alltogether would take them all. Not all people think alike. (19) I will also quote a poem.

For that another law too holds for mortals
You will see if you consider them separately.
For nothing is in every way virtuous or shameful,
but the "right moment" (*kairos*) takes the same things and makes
them shameful and then changes them and makes them virtuous.

(20) To put it generally, all things are virtuous at the right moment and shameful at the wrong moment. What, then, have I achieved? I said I would prove that the same things are shameful and virtuous, and I proved it in all these cases.

(21) But it is also said concerning the shameful and the virtuous that each of them is different. If anyone were to ask people who say that the same thing is shameful and virtuous whether they had ever done anything virtuous, they must agree that it is shameful, if in fact the shameful and the virtuous are the same, (22) and if they know any virtuous man, they know that this same person is shameful too, and if they know that someone is white, this same person is black too, and if it is virtuous to worship the gods, it is also shameful to worship the gods, if in fact, the same thing is shameful and virtuous.

(23) Take this as said for everything. I will now turn to the argument they give. (24) If it is virtuous for a woman to dress up, it is shameful for a woman to dress up, if in fact the same thing is shameful and virtuous, and likewise in other cases. (25) In Sparta it is virtuous for girls to train, in Sparta, it is shameful for girls to train, etc. (26) They say that if some people collected the shameful things from people everywhere on earth and then called them all together and told them each to take whatever things each one considered virtuous, they would all be taken away as being virtuous. I am surprised if the shameful things that were collected will prove to be virtuous and not just what they were. (27) For if they brought horses or cattle or sheep or humans,

they would bring away no other thing, since neither if they brought gold would they bring away bronze, nor if they brought silver would they bring away lead. (28) Do they bring away something virtuous instead of something shameful? Come now, if someone had brought something shameful, would he bring it away as something virtuous? They bring in poets as witnesses, who write for pleasure but not for truth.

3: On Just and Unjust

(1) Twin arguments are also made about the just and the unjust. Some say that the just is one thing and the unjust is another, and others say that the same thing is just and unjust. I will try to support the latter claim. (2) First I will say that it is just to lie and deceive. It is good and just to do this to your enemies but shameful and wicked to do this to your dearest people. But how is it just to do this to your enemies but not to your dearest? Starting with one's parents: if your father or mother needed to eat or drink some medicine and refused to, isn't it just to put it into their soup or their drink without telling them? (3) Therefore it must be just to lie and deceive your parents, and also to steal your friends' things and to treat the people closest to you with violence. (4) Next, if a relative is distressed and overwhelmed with grief and is about to kill himself with a sword or a rope or something else it is just to steal it if you can and to take it away by force if you are late and find him holding it. (5) And how is it not just to enslave your enemies if you can sell their city's entire population into slavery after capturing it? And it is obviously just to break into the public buildings of your city. For if your father has been overpowered by his political enemies and sentenced to death, is it not just to break in, spring your father and save his life? (6) Also to break an oath. If someone who has been captured by the enemy were to promise on oath to betray his city if released, would it be just for him to keep his oath and do it? (7) I, for one, don't think so. Instead, it would be just to save his city, his dear ones and his ancestral temples by breaking his oath. So even oath-breaking is already just. Also robbing temples. (8) I will skip over the temples of individual cities. But those that are the common property of the whole of Greece, at Delphi and Olympia – when the foreigner (Xerxes) was about to capture Greece and its safety depended on money, was it not just to take it and use it for the war? (9) It is just to murder one's dearest, since Orestes and Alcmeon did and the god proclaimed in an oracle that they had acted justly. (10) I will now turn to the arts and poetry. In tragedy and painting, whoever deceives us most in creating things that are like reality is best. (11) I also want to bring in evidence from the earliest poetry. Cleobulina wrote:

> I saw a man stealing and cheating by force.
> In fact, to accomplish things by force – this is most just.

(12) These words are old, but Aeschylus wrote the following lines:

> God does not hold back from deceit that is just.

and

There is a time when god honors an opportunity for lies.

(13) Opposed to this there is another argument, that justice is one thing and injustice another – as the name is different so is the thing. If someone asks people who say that the same thing is unjust and just whether they have ever done something just for their parents, they will agree; and therefore they have done something unjust. For they agree that the same thing is unjust and just. (14) Here's another: if someone knows a just man, he therefore knows that the same man is unjust (and by the same token that a tall man is short too). And if he were to say "Since he has committed many unjust deeds, let him be put to death," let him be put to death also for having done many just deeds. (15) These examples are enough.

Now I will turn to what people say who claim to prove that the same thing is both just and unjust. (16) For that stealing from enemies just proves that this very same thing is unjust too, if the argument of these people is true and likewise for other cases. (17) They also bring in arts in which there is no place for justice and injustice, and the poets write their poetry not for truth but for people's pleasure.

4: On Truth and Falsehood

(1) Twin arguments are also stated concerning the false and the true, of which one declares that true *logos* (speech, statement) and false *logos* are different from one another, and others that they are the same. (2) And I say the following. First, that true and false *logos* are expressed in the same words. Second, when a *logos* is spoken, if events have occurred the way the *logos* is spoken, the *logos* is true, but if they have not occurred, the same *logos* is false. (3) Suppose it accuses someone of sacrilege. If the deed took place, the *logos* is true, but if it did not take place, it is false. The *logos* of the defendant is the same. And the courts judge the same *logos* to be both false and true. (4) Next, if we are seated one next to the other, and we (each) say "I am an initiate of the mysteries," we will all say the same thing, but only I will be true, since in fact I am (the only) one (who is). (5) Now it is obvious that the same *logos* is false whenever falsehood is present to it and true whenever truth is, in the same way, a person is the same individual as a boy and as a youth and as an adult and as an old man.

(6) It is also stated that false *logos* and true *logos* are different from one another, differing in name just as they differ in fact. For if anyone asks those who say that the same *logos* is both false and true whether the *logos* that they are stating is true or false, then if it is false, clearly they (the true *logos* and the false *logos*) are two (and therefore not the same). But if it is true, this same *logos* is also false. And if anyone has ever spoken of or borne witness to things that are true, it follows that these same things are false. And if he knows any man to be true, he also knows the same man to be false. (7) As a result of the argument they say these things because

if the thing occurred the *logos* is true, but if it did not, then it is false. Therefore it is not their name that differs, but the fact of the matter. (8) Moreover, if anyone should ask the jurors what they are judging (since they are not present at the events), (9) these people too agree that the *logos* with which falsehood is mixed is false, and that with which truth is mixed is true. This is the entire difference.

5: (No title)

(1) The mad and the sane say and do the same things and so do the wise and the foolish. (2) First, they use the same words: "earth," "human being," "horse," "fire" and everything else. They also do the same things: they sit and eat and drink and lie down, and do everything else in the same way. (3) Also the same thing is both larger and smaller and more and less and heavier and lighter. For in this way, all things are the same. (4) A talent is heavier than a mina and lighter than two talents. Therefore the same thing is both lighter and heavier. (5) Also, the same person lives and does not live and is the same and not the same: things that are here are not in Libya and things in Libya are not in Cyprus, and the same argument holds for everything else. Thus things both are and are not.

(6) Those who assert these things – that the mad and the sane and the wise and the foolish do and say the same things and assert the other consequences of this argument are wrong. (7) For if anyone asks them if madness is different from sanity and wisdom from foolishness, they say "yes" (8) because they agree that what each kind of person is is clear from what they do. So if they do the same things the wise are mad and everything is mixed up. (9) And we ought to bring up the argument whether it is the sane or the mad who speak at the right time. "But," they say, "they say the same things when someone asks them." But the wise say them at the right time and the mad when they must not. (10) But when they say this they seem to make a small addition, "when they must and when they must not," so that it is no longer the same.

(11) But I think that it is not when something of that (small) size is added that things are changed, but when only the accent is changed, for example, the name Glaúkos and *glauko*s* (the color grey) or the name Xánthos and *xanthós* (the color yellow) or the name Xoúthos and *xouthós* (golden yellow). (12) These differences are due to a change in accent, but others are due to a change in the length of a vowel: *Tŭros* (the city Tyre) and *tūrós* (cheese), *săkos* (shield) and *sākós* (enclosure), and still others to switching the order of letters: *kártos* (strength) and *kratós* (of the head), *ónos* (ass) and *nóos* (mind, intelligence). (13) Since so important a difference occurs when nothing is removed, what happens if we add or remove something? I will show you what happens. (14) If you subtract one from ten there will no longer be ten or even one, and everything else in the same way. (15) As to the claim that the same person both is and is not, I ask "in some respect or in all?" And if he denies that the person is, he is wrong if he says <is not> in all respects. So in one way or another all these things are.

6: On Wisdom and Virtue (*aretē*), whether they can be taught

(1) There is an argument that is neither true nor new – that wisdom and *aretē* cannot be taught or learned. Those who make this argument employ the following proofs. (2) If you give something to someone else you can no longer have it. This is one. (3) Another one is that if it could be taught there would be recognized teachers of it as with music. (4) Third, that wise men born in Greece would have taught their own children and their friends. (5) Fourth, some who have studied with Sophists have gained nothing from it. (6) Fifth, that many who have not associated with Sophists have turned out worthy of esteem.

(7) But I think that this argument is really stupid, since I know that teachers teach letters which the teacher himself in fact knows, and lyre-players teach how to play the lyre. To the second proof, that there are no recognized teachers, what else do Sophists teach but wisdom and virtue (*aretē*)? (8) What about the followers of Anaxagoras and Pythagoras? As to the third, Polyclitus taught his son to make statues. (9) And if someone did not teach it, that is no proof; but if any single person taught it this is evidence that it is possible to teach it. (10) Fourth, if some do not become wise from associating with Sophists – many who have studied have not learned their letters. (11) There is also the matter of nature (*phusis*), which has enabled some who have not studied with Sophists to become capable; naturally clever from birth they readily grasp many things after learning a little from the very people from whom we learn our words, and of these, some learn more and others less, one from his father another from his mother. (12) However, if someone does not believe that we learn our words, but are born knowing them, let him learn from this: if someone were to send his newborn child to Persia and raise him there, he would be deaf to the Greek language and would speak Persian, and if someone brought a newborn child from there to here he would speak Greek. This how we learn our words and we do not know who our teachers are. (13) My argument is now over. You have its beginning, its end and its middle. And I do not claim that it can be taught but these proofs do not satisfy me.

7: [No title]

Some public speakers assert that public offices should be assigned by lot, but their opinion on this is not the best. (1) For if anyone were to ask someone who asserts this, "Why, then don't you assign work to your household slaves by lot so that if your ploughman draws the lot of a gourmet cook he will do the work of a gourmet cook while the gourmet cook will plough and likewise for the others? (3) And why do we not gather together the bronzesmiths and leatherworkers and carpenters and goldsmiths as well and compel them each to do whatever work he is allotted, instead of the one he knows? (4) The same holds in musical contests: the competitors compete in whatever each draws as his lot – perhaps a flute player will play the lyre and a lyre player will play the flute. Also in war, the archers and hoplites will be cavalrymen and the cavalryman will be an archer, so they will all do things that they don't know and can't do. (5) On the other hand, they say that the practice is good and democratic, but I think that this is the opposite of democratic. For in cities there are some that are opposed to the populace, and if the lot falls to them they will destroy the populace. (6) Rather the populace itself should be aware and choose all those who support it and are suitable to command the army and others to guard the laws and so forth.

8: [No title]

(1) I think that it belongs to the same man and the same art to be able both to speak briefly and to know the truth of things, to know how to plead a case correctly in court, to be able to speak in public and to know the arts of speech (*logoi*) and to teach about the nature of all things – both how they are and how they came to be. (2) In the first place, a person who has knowledge of the nature of everything – how will he not be able to teach the city to act correctly about everything? (3) Further, a person who knows the arts of speech will also know how to speak correctly about everything. (4) For anyone who is going to speak correctly must speak about things that he knows. Therefore he will know all things (5) because he knows the arts of all speeches and all speeches are about all the things that are.

(6) But one who is going to speak the facts correctly must know whatever he speaks about, and must correctly teach the city to do things that are good and prevent them from doing things that are bad. (7) Since he knows these things he will also know what is different from them because he will know everything. ….[3] (8) And a person knows how to play the flute if he can play the flute if it is necessary to do so. (9) A person who knows how to plead a case in court must have correct knowledge of what is just, since this is what trials are about. Since he knows this he will also know its opposite and what is different from both of these. (10) He must know all the laws as well. In fact, if he does not know the subject he does not know the laws either. (11) For in music, whoever knows the rules knows music too, and whoever does not know music does not know the rules either. (12) Speech is easy for one who knows the truth of things because he knows everything. (13) Thus he can speak briefly and if necessary he can answer questions about everything. Therefore it is necessary for him to know everything.

9: [No title]

The fairest and most important discovery is memory. It is useful for everything, for wisdom and for life. (2) This is first: if you pay attention the resulting judgment will perceive it more strongly. (3) Practice is second: if you hear something, by hearing the same thing many times and saying it, what you have learned comes to be present in your memory in its entirety. (4) Third, store it with the things you know as in the following example. It is necessary to remember Chrysippus; store this with *khrusos* (gold) and *hippos* (horse). (5) Another example: we store Purilampes with *pur* (fire) and *lampein* (shine). These examples have to do with names. (6) Things we deal with like this: in the case of courage store it with Ares and Achilles and as for bronze-working store it with Hephaestus, for cowardice with Epeios...[4]

Notes

1 These words are usually translated "philosophical arguments," but see above, p. 9.
2 The words translated consistently as "virtuous" and "shameful" (*kalon* and *aischron*) have wider meanings, including "beautiful and ugly" and "appropriate and inappropriate." In some places one or another of these other translations is preferable.
3 The text is corrupt here.
4 The text breaks off here.

BIBLIOGRAPHY

General Overviews (Books)

Guthrie, W.K.C. 1969. "The World of the Sophists." In *A History of Greek Philosophy*, vol. 3, 3–319. *The Fifth-Century Enlightenment.* Cambridge: Cambridge University Press. Republished 1971 in a single volume, *The Sophists*, Cambridge: Cambridge University Press.
Kerferd, G.B. 1981. *The Sophistic Movement*. Cambridge: Cambridge University Press.
Romilly, J. de. 1988. *Les grands sophistes dans l'Athènes de Périklès*. Paris: English translation 1992: *The Great Sophists in Periclean Athens*. Oxford: Oxford University Press.
Bonazzi, M. 2020. *The Sophists. Greece & Rome New Surveys in the Classics*, No. 45. Cambridge: Cambridge University Press.

General Overviews (Articles and Chapters in Books)

Kerferd, G.B. 1997. "The Sophists." In C.C.W. Taylor (ed.), *Routledge History of Philosophy*, vol. 1, 244–270. *From the Beginning to Plato*, Routledge: London:.
Kerferd, G.B. and H. Flashar. 1998. "Die Sophistik." In F. Ueberweg and H. Flashar (eds.), *Grundriss der Geschichte der Philosophie. Die Philosophie der Antike*, vol. 2/1, 1–137. *Sophistik, Sokrates, Sokratik, Mathematik, Medizin*.
Gibert, J. 2002. "The Sophists." In C. Shields (ed.), *The Blackwell Guide to Ancient Philosophy*, 27–50. Oxford: Blackwell Publishing.
Barney, R. 2006. "The Sophistic Movement." In M.L. Gill and P. Pellegrin (eds.), *A Companion to Ancient Philosophy*, 77–97. Oxford: Oxford University Press.
Gagarin, M. and P. Woodruff. 2008. "The Sophists." In P.K. Curd and D.W. Graham (eds.), *The Oxford Handbook of Presocratic Philosophy*, 365–382. Oxford: Oxford University Press.

Encyclopedias

Cancik, H. and Schneider, eds. 1996–2010. *Der Neue Pauly*, 16 vols. and 7 supplementary volumes. Stuttgart: Metzler.

Craig, E., ed. 1998. *Routledge Encyclopedia of Philosophy*. London: Routledge.
Hornblower, S. and A. Spawforth, eds. 2003. *Oxford Classical Dictionary*, 3rd edn. Oxford: Oxford University Press.
Taylor, C.C.W. and M.-K. Lee. 2015. "The Sophists." In Edward N. Zalta (ed.), *The Stanford Encyclopedia of Philosophy* [http://plato.stanford.edu/].
Wissowa, G., W. Kroll, K. Mittelhaus and K. Zeigler, eds. 1894–1972. *Pauly's Realencyclopädie der Classischen Altertumswissenschaft*, 83 vols. and 15 supplementary volumes. Stuttgart: Metzler.

Collections of Source Materials

Diels, H. and W. Kranz. 1952. *Die Fragmente der Vorsokratiker*, 6th ed., 3 vols. Berlin: Weidmann. [abbr. DK]
Graham, D.W. 2010. *The Texts of Early Greek Philosophy: The Complete Fragments and Selected Testimonies of the Major Presocratics*, vol. 2: *The Sophists*. Cambridge: Cambridge University Press.
Laks, A. and G. Most. 2016. *Early Greek Philosophy*, vols. 8–9: *Sophists*. Loeb Classical Library. Cambridge, Mass.: Harvard University Press. [abbr. L-M]

Collections of Essays

Classen, C.J., ed. 1976. *Sophistik*. Wege der Forschung 187. Darmstadt: Wissenschaftliche Buchgesellschaft.
Classen, C.J. 1976 "The Study of Language amongst Socrates' Contemporaries." pp. 215–247 in Classen, C.J., ed. 1976 (see Collections of Essays).
Kerferd, G.B., ed. 1981. *The Sophists and their Legacy: Proceedings of the Fourth International Colloquium of Ancient Philosophy at Bad Homburg 1979. Hermes Einzelschriften* 44. Wiesbaden: Steiner.
Greek Philosophical Society. 1984. *The Sophistic Movement (*Η Αρχαία Σοφιστική*)*.
Montoneri, L. and F. Romano, eds. 1985. *Gorgia e la Sofistica. Atti del Convegno Internazionale (Lentini - Catania, 12-15 dic. 1983.* = *Siculorum Gymnasium* 38, nos. 1–2.
Cassin, B., ed. 1986a. *Positions de la sophistique*. Paris: Vrin.
Cassin, B., ed. 1986b. *Le Plaisir de Parler. Études de sophistique comparée*. Paris: Minuit.

Translations

Untersteiner, M. 1949–1962, reprinted 1967. *I Sofisti. Frammenti e testimonianze*, 4 vols. Rome: La Nuova Italia.
Sprague, R.K., ed. 1972. *The Older Sophists*. Columbia S.C.: University of South Carolina Press.
Dumont, J.-P. 1988. *Les Présocratiques*. Bibliotheque de la Pleiade. Paris: Gallimard.
Dumont. J.-P. 1991. *Les écoles présocratiques*. Paris: Gallimard.
Waterfield, R. 2000. *The First Philosophers: The Presocratics and Sophists*. Oxford: Oxford University Press.
Dillon, J. and Gergel, T. 2003. *The Greek Sophists*. London: Penguin. [abbr: D-G]
Pradeau, J.-F. 2009. *Les Sophistes. Écrits complets*, 2 vols. Paris: Flammarion.

Bibliographies

L'Année Philologique. 1924. [http://www.annee-philologique.com/aph/].
Classen, C.J. 1985. "Bibliographie zur 'Sophistik.'" *Elenchos* 6:76–140.
Paquet, L., Roussel, M., and Lafrance, Y. 1988–1995. *Les Présocratiques: bibliographie analytique*, 3 vols. Montreal: Bellarmin.
McKirahan, R. 2017. *Collections Containing Articles on Presocratic Philosophy*. Online at [http://scholarship.claremont.edu/pomona_fac_pub/93/]
McKirahan, R. 2017. *The Sophists* in *Oxford Bibliographies Online*.

Sophistic Education

Blank, D.L. 1985. "Socratics Versus Sophists on Payment for Teaching." *Classical Antiquity* 4:1–49.
Gagarin, M. 2001. "Did the Sophists Aim to Persuade?" *Rhetorica* 19:275–291.
Corey, D. 2002. "The Case against Teaching Virtue for Pay: Socrates and the Sophists." *History of Political Thought* 23:189–210.

Sophistic and Rhetoric

Gagarin, M. 1990. "Did Plato coin *Rhêtorikê*?" *American Journal of Philology* 111:457–470.
Cole, T. 1991. *The Origins of Rhetoric in Ancient Greece*. Baltimore: Hohns Hopkins Univ. Press.
Gagarin, M. 1994. "Probability and Persuasion: Plato and Early Greek Rhetoric." In I. Worthington (ed.), *Persuasion. Greek Rhetoric in Action*, 46–67.
Schiappa, E. 1995. "Gorgias' Helen Revisited." *Quarterly Journal of Speech* 81:310–324.
Wardy, R. 1996. *The Birth of Rhetoric: Gorgias, Plato, and their Successors*. London.
Ford, A. 2001. "Sophists without Rhetoric: The Arts of Speech in Fifth-Century Athens." In Y.L. Too (ed.), *Education in Greek and Roman Antiquity*, 85–109. Leiden/Boston/Köln.
Gagarin, M. 2001. "Did the Sophists Aim to Persuade?" *Rhetorica* 19:275–291.
Worthington, I. ed. 2007. *A Companion to Greek Rhetoric*. Blackwell's Companions to the Ancienbt World. Oxford: Blackwell.

Sophistry and Philosophy

Nehamas, A. 1990. "Eristic, Antilogic, Sophistic, Dialectic: Plato's Demarcation of Philosophy from Sophistry." *History of Philosophy Quarterly* 7:3–16.

Sophistry and Democracy

Adkins, A.W.H. 1973. "Ἀρετή, τέχνη, Democracy and Sophists: Protagoras 316b-328d." *Journal of Hellenic Studies* 93:3–12.
Robinson, E. 2007. "The Sophists and Democracy beyond Athens." *Rhetorica* 25:109–122.

The Origin of Sophistry

Martin, J. 1976. "Zur Entstehung der Sophistik." *Saeculum* 27:143–164.

Who Were the Sophists?

Kerferd, G.B. 1950. "The First Greek Sophists." *Classical Review* 64:8–10.
Harrison, E.L. 1964. "Was Gorgias a Sophist?" *Phoenix* 18:183–192.
Mortley, R. 1969. "Plato and the Sophistic Heritage of Protagoras." *Eranos* (Uppsala) 67:24–32.
Montiglio, S. 2000. "Wandering Philosophers in Classical Greece." *Journal of Hellenic Studies* 120:86–105.

Aristophanes and the Sophists

Dover, K.J. 1968. *Aristophanes Clouds*. Oxford: Oxford University Press.
Segal, C. 1970. "Protagoras' Orthoepeia in Aristophanes 'Battle of the Prologues' (*Frogs* 1119–97)." *Rheinisches Museum* 113:158–162.
Carey, C. 2000. "Old Comedy and the Sophists." In F.D. Harvey and J.. Wilkins (eds.), *The Rivals of Aristophanes: Studies in Athenian Old Comedy*, 255–264. Swansea: Classical Press of Wales.
Papageorgiou, N. 2004. "Prodicus and the Agon of the *Logoi* in Aristophanes' *Clouds*." *Quaderni Urbinati di Cultura Classica* 78.3:61–69.

Socrates and the Sophists

Taylor, C. 2006. "Socrates the Sophist." In L. Judson and V. Karasmanis (eds.), *Remembering Socrates*, 157–168. New York: Oxford University Press.

Plato and the Sophists

McCoy, M. 2008. *Plato on the Rhetoric of Philosophers and Sophists*. Cambridge: Cambridge University Press.
Tell, H.P. 2011. *Plato's Counterfeit Sophists*. Cambridge MA: Harvard University Press.
Corey, D. 2015. *The Sophists in Plato's Dialogues*. Albany, N.Y.: SUNY Press.

Xenophon and the Sophists

Classen, C. 1984. "Xenophons Darstellung der Sophistik und der Sophisten." *Hermes* 112:154–167.

Aristotle and the Sophists

Classen, C. 1981. "Aristotle's Picture of the Sophists." In G.B. Kerferd (ed.), *The Sophists and Their Legacy*, 7–24. Hermes. Einzelschriften, XLIV. Wiesbaden: Steiner.
Poulakos, J. 1996. "Extending and Correcting the Rhetorical Tradition: Aristotle's Perception of the Sophists." *Philosophy and Rhetoric* 16:35–48.

Individual Sophists

Protagoras

Mueller, C.W. 1967. "Protagoras über die Götter." *Hermes* 95:140–159.
Guthrie, W.K.C. 1969. *A History of Greek Philosophy*, vol. 3: *The Fifth-Century Enlightenment*. Cambridge: Cambridge University Press, 262–269.

194 Bibliography

Mortley, R. 1969. "Plato and the Sophistic Heritage of Protagoras." *Eranos* (Uppsala) 67:24–32.
Mejer, J. 1972. "The Alleged New Fragment of Protagoras." *Hermes* 100:175–178.
Simmons, G. 1972. "Protagoras on Education and Society." *Paedagogica Historica* 12:518–537.
Maguire, J.P. 1973. "Protagoras – or Plato?" *Phronesis* 18:115–138.
Maguire, J.P. 1977. "Protagoras – or Plato? II. The 'Protagoras'." *Phronesis* 22:103–122.
Gigon, O. 1985. "Il libro 'Sugli dei' di Protagora." *Rivista di Storia di Filosofia* 40:419–448.
Woodruff, P. 1985. "Didymus on Protagoras and the Pythagoreans." *Journal of the History of Philosophy* 23:483–497.
Bodéus, R. 1987. "Réflexions sur un court propos de Protagoras." *Les Études Classiques* 55:241–257.
Schiappa, E. 1991. *Protagoras and Logos: A Study in Greek Philosophy and Rhetoric*. Columbia S.C.: University of South Carolina Press.
Huss, B. 1996. "Der Homo-Mensura-Satz des Protagoras. Ein Forschungsbericht." *Gymnasium* 103:229–257.
Decleva Caizzi, F. 1999. "Protagoras and Antiphon: Sophistic Debates on Justice." In A.A. Long (ed.), *The Cambridge Companion to Early Greek Philosophy*, 311–331. Cambridge: Cambridge University Press.
Woodruff, P. 1999. "Rhetoric and Relativism: Protagoras and Gorgias." In A.A. Long (ed.), *The Cambridge Companion to Early Greek Philosophy*, 290–310. Cambridge: Cambridge University Press.
Hourcade, A. 2000. "Protagoras et Démocrite: Le feu divin entre mythe et raison." *Revue de Philosophie Ancienne* 18:87–113.
Brancacci, A. 2002. "Protagora e la *technê sophistikê*. Plato, *Prot*. 316 D-317 C." *Elenchos* 23:21–32.
Schiappa, E. 2003. *Protagoras and Logos: A Study in Greek Philosophy and Rhetoric*, 2nd ed. Columbia: South Carolina.
Corradi, M. 2007. "Protagoras dans son contexte. L'homme mesure et la tradition archaïque de l'*incipit*." *Mètis. Anthropologie des mondes grecs anciens* 5:185–203.
Shortridge, A. 2007. "Law and Nature in Protagoras' Great Speech." *Polis* 24:12–25.
Gagarin, M. 2008. "Protagoras et l'art de la parole." *Philosophie Antique* 8:23–31.
*Brancacci, A. 2012. "La pensée politique de Protagoras." *Revue de Philosophie Ancienne* 30:59–85.
Schlick, A.J. 2012. "Der historische Protagoras in Platons gleichnamigen Dialog." *Museum Helveticum* 69:29–44.
Van Ophuijsen, J.M. et al. eds. 2013. *Protagoras of Abdera: The Man, His Measure*. Philosophia Antiqua 134, Leiden and Boston: Brill.
Bartlett, R.C. 2016. *Sophistry and Political Philosophy: Protagoras' Challenge to Socrates*. Chicago: University of Chicago Press.
Barney, R. 2019. "Protagoras and the Myth of Plato's *Protagoras*." In C. Riedweg (ed.), *Philosophie für die Polis*, Beiträge zur Altertumskunde, vol. 380, 133–158. De Gruyter,.
Huitink, L. and A. Willi. 2021. "Protagoras and the Beginnings of Grammar". *Cambridge Classical Journal* 67 (December 2021):66–92.
Hussey, E. 2021. "Protagoras on political '*technê*'". In T.K. Johansen (ed.), *Productive Knowledge in Ancient Philosophy: The Concept of "technê"*, 15–38. Cambridge: Cambridge University Press.
Silvermintz, D. 2021. *Protagoras*. London: Bloomsbury Academic.

Gorgias

Texts

Guthrie, W.K.C. 1969 *A History of Greek Philosophy: The Fifth-Century Enlightenment*, vol. 3. Cambridge: Cambridge University Press, 269–274.

Buchheim, T. 1989. *Gorgias von Leontinoi: Reden, Fragmente und Testimonien*. Philosophische Bibliothek. Hamburg: Meiner.

MacDowell, D.M. 1982. *Gorgias. Encomium of Helen*. Bristol: Bristol Classical Press.

Ioli, R. 2010. *Gorgia da Leontini Su ciò che non è*. Spoudasmata 130. Zürich and New York: Olms.

Giombini, S. 2012. *Gorgia epidittico*. Passignano sul Trasimeno: Aguaplano.

Logos and Persuasion

Duncan, T. 1938. "Gorgias' Theories of Art." *Classical Journal* 33:402–415.

Calogero, G. 1957. "Gorgias and the Socratic Principle *nemo sua sponte peccat*." *Journal of Hellenic Studies* 77:12–17.

Segal, C. 1962. "Gorgias and the Psychology of the Logos." *Harvard Studies in Classical Philology* 66:99–155.

Innes, D. 1991. "Gorgias, Antiphon and Sophistopolis." *Argumentation* 5:221–231.

Noël, M.-P. 1989. "La persuasion et le sacré chez Gorgias." *Bulletin de l'Association Guillaume Budé*. 139–151.

Noël, M.-P. 1998. "*Kairos* sophistique et mises en forme du *logos* chez Gorgias." *Revue de Philologie, de Littérature et d'histoire anciennes* 72:233–245.

Woodruff, P. 1999. "Rhetoric and Relativism: Protagoras and Gorgias" in A.A. Long (ed.), *The Cambridge Companion to Early Greek Philosophy*, 290–310. Cambridge: Cambridge University Press.

Spatharas, D. 2001. "Patterns of Argumentation in Gorgias." *Mnemosyne* 54:393–408.

Bons, J.A. 2007. "Gorgias the Sophist and Early Rhetoric." In I. Worthington (ed.), *A Companion to Early Greek Rhetoric*. Blackwell Companions to the Ancient World, 37–46. Oxford: Blackwell.

On Not-Being

Kerferd, G.B. 1955. "Gorgias on nature or that which is not." *Phronesis* 1:3–25.

Sicking, C. 1964. "Gorgias und die Philosophen." *Mnemosyne* 17:225–247.

Newiger, H.-J. 1973. *Untersuchungen zu Gorgias' Schrift Über das Nichtseiende*. Berlin: De Gruyter.

Kerferd, G.B. 1981. "The Interpretation of Gorgias' Treatise *Peri tou ontos ê peri phuseôs*." *Deucalion* 36:319–327.

Caston, V. 2002. "Gorgias on Thought and its Objects." In *Presocratic Philosophy: Essays in Honor of A.P.D. Mourelatos*, 202–232. Aldershot: Ashgate..

Curd, P.K. 2006. "Gorgias and the Eleatics." In M. Sassi (ed.), *La costruzione del discorso filosofico nell'età dei Presocratici*, 183–200. Pisa: Editiones della Normale.

Ioli, R. 2009. "Gorgia scettico? Una riflessione sulla presenza del sofista nelle opere del Sesto Empirico." *Rheinisches Museum* 152:331–357.

Güremen, R. 2017. "The Refutation of Gorgias: Notes on a Contradiction." *Peitho: Examina Antiqua* 8 (2017):237–247,
Poster, C. 2017. "Gorgias' *On non-being*: genre, purpose, and testimonia". In R. Reames & E. Schiappa (eds.), *Logos without Rhetoric: The Arts of Language before Plato. Studies in Rhetoric/Communication*, 30–46. Columbia (S. C.): University of South Carolina Press.

Antiphon

Kerferd, G.B. 1956. "The Moral and Political Doctrines of Antiphon the Sophist, a Reconsideration." *Proceedings of the Cambridge Philological Association* 184:26–32.
Morrison, J. 1961. "Antiphon." *Proceedings of the Cambridge Philological Society* 187:49–58.
Morrison, J.S. 1963. "The *Truth* of Antiphon." *Phronesis* 8:35–49.
Guthrie, W.K.C. 1969 *A History of Greek Philosophy*, vol. 3 *The Fifth-Century Enlightenment*. Cambridge: Cambridge University Press, 285–294.
Moulton, C. 1972. "Antiphon the Sophist, *On Truth*." *Transactions and Proceedings of the American Philological Association* 103:329–366.
Saunders, T. 1977–1978. "Antiphon the Sophists on Natural Laws (B44DK)." *Proceedings of the Aristotelian Society* 78:215–236.
Avery, H. 1982. "One Antiphon or Two?" *Hermes* 110:145–158.
Reesor, M. 1987. "The Truth of Antiphon the Sophist." *Apeiron* 20:203–218.
Decleva Caizzi, F. and Bastianni, G. 1989. "Antipho." In *Corpus dei papiri folosofici greci e latini* I,1. Florence.
Ostwald, M. 1990. "*Nomos* and *Phusis* in Antiphon's Περὶ Ἀληθείας." In M. Griffith and D.J. Mastronarde (eds.), *Cabinet of the Muses: Essays on Classical and Comparative Literature in Honor of Thomas G. Rosenmeyer*, 293–306. Atlanta: Scholars Press.
Gagarin, M. 2001. "The Truth of Antiphon's Truth." In A. Preus (ed.), *Before Plato: Essays in Ancient Greek Philosophy VI*, 171–186. Albany NY: State University of New York Press.
Gagarin, M. 2002. *Antiphon the Athenian: Oratory, Knowledge and Justice in the Age of the Sophists*. Austin, Texas: University of Texas Press.
Pendrick, G. 2002. *Antiphon the Sophist: The Fragments*. Cambridge: Cambridge University Press.
Woodruff, P. 2004. "Antiphon, Sophist and Athenian." *Oxford Studies in Ancient Philosophy* 26:323–336.

Hippias

Snell, B. 1944. "Die Nachrichten über die Lehren des Thales und die Anfänge der griechischen Philosophie- und Literaturgeschichte." *Philologus* 96:170–182.
Guthrie, W.K.C. 1969. *A History of Greek Philosophy: The Fifth-Century Enlightenment*, (vol. 3). Cambridge: Cambridge University Press, 280–285.
Classen, C.J. 1965. "Bemerkungen zu zwei griechischen 'Philosophiehistorikern.'" *Philologus* 109:175–181.
Johann, H.-T. 1973. "Hippias von Elis und der Physis-Nomos-Gedanke." *Phronesis* 18:15–25.
Woodruff, P. 1982. *Hippias Major*. Indianapolis: Hackett.
Patzer, A. 1986. *Der Sophist Hippias als Philosophiehistoriker*. Freiburg: Alber.

Balaudé, J.-F. 2006. "Hippias le passeur." In M. Sassi (ed.), *La costruzione del discorso filosofico nell'età dei Presocratici*, 287–304. Pisa: Ed. della Normale.
Brancacci, A. 2013. "La pensée politique d'Hippias." *Méthexis* 26:23–35.

Prodicus

Kerferd, G. 1954. "The 'Relativism' of Prodicus." *Bulletin of the John Rylands Library* 37:249–256.
Guthrie, W.K.C. 1969 *A History of Greek Philosophy: The Fifth-Century Enlightenment*, (vol. 3). Cambridge: Cambridge University Press, 274–280.
Binder, G. and Liesenborghs, L. 1966. "Eine Zuweisung der Sentenz οὐκ ἔστιν ἀντιλέγειν von Prodikos von Keos." *Museum Helveticum* 23:37–43.
Hinrichs, A. 1975. "Two Doxographical Notes: Democritus and Prodicus on Religion." *Harvard Studies in Classical Philology* 79:92–123.
Hinrichs, A. 1975. "The Atheism of Prodicus". *Cronache Ercolanesi* 6:15–21.
Willink, C. 1983. "Prodikos, 'Meteorosophists' and the 'Tantalos' Paradigm." *Classical Quarterly* 33:25–33.
De Romilly, J. 1986. "Les manies de Prodicos et la rigeur de la langue grecque." *Museum Helveticum* 43:1–18.
Kuntz, M. 1993. "The Prodicean 'Choice of Herakles' A Reshaping of Myth." *Classical Journal* 89:163–168.
Sansone, D. 2004. "Heracles at the Y." *Journal of Hellenic Studies* 124:125–142.
Gray, V. 2006. "The Linguistic Philosophies of Prodicus in Xenophon's 'Choice of Heracles'?" *Classical Quarterly* 56:426–435.
Corey, D. 2008. "Prodicus: Diplomat, Sophist and Teacher of Socrates." *History of Political Thought* 29:1–26.
Dorion, L.-A. 2008. "Héraklès entre Prodicos et Xénophon." *Philosophie Antique* 8:85–114.
Wolfsdorf, D. 2008. "Prodicus on the Correctness of Names: The Case of τέρψις, χαρά and εὐφροσύνη." *Journal of Hellenic Studies* 35:1–18.
Bett, R. 2013. "Language, Gods and Virtue. A Discussion of Robert Mayhew, Prodicus the Sophist." *Oxford Studies in Ancient Philosophy* 44:279–311.
Sansone, D. 2015. "Xenophon and Prodicus' Choice of Heracles." *Classical Quarterly* 65:371–377.
Kouloumentas, S. 2018. "Prodicus on the Rise of Civilization: Religion, Agriculture and Culture Heroes." *Philosophie Antique* 18:127–152.

Thrasymachus

Guthrie, W.K.C. 1969. *A History of Greek Philosophy: The Fifth-Century Enlightenment*, vol. 3. Cambridge: Cambridge University Press, 88–97, 294–298.
Maguire, J. 1971. "Thrasymachus – or Plato?" *Phronesis* 16:142–163.
Döring, K. 1993. "Platons Darstellung der politischen Theorien des Thrasymachos und des Protagoras." *Der Altsprachliche Unterricht* 36:13–26.
White, S.A. 1995. "Thrasymachus the Diplomat." *Classical Philology* 90 (1995): 307–327.
Macé, A. 2003. "Un monde sans pitié: Platon à l'école de Thrasymaque de Chalcédoine." *Philosophie Antique* 8:33–60.
Betti, D. 2011. "The Search for the Political Thought of the Historical Thrasymachus." *Polis* (Exeter) 28:33–44.

Euthydemus

Brancacci, A. 2017. "Eristic and Philosophy in *Euthydemus*," *Philosophia* 47: 37–45.

Related Texts

Anonymus Iamblichi

Cole, A.T. 1961. "The Anonymus Iamblichi and his Place in Greek Political Theory." *Harvard Studies in Classical Philology* 65:127–163.

The Sisyphus Fragment

Sutton, D. 1981. "Critias and Atheism." *Classical Quarterly* 31:33–38.
Davies, M. 1989. "Sisyphus and the Invention of Religion ('Critias' TrGH 1 (43) F 19 = B 25 DK)." *Bulletin of the Institute of Classical Studies* 36:16–32.
Kahn, C. 1997. "Greek Religion and Philosophy in the Sisyphus Fragment." *Phronesis* 42:247–262.
Conacher, D.J. 1998. *Euripides and the Sophists*. London: Duckworth.

Twin Arguments. (Dissoi Logoi)

Levi, A. 1940. "On 'Twofold Statements'." *American Journal of Philology* 61:292–306.
Robinson, T.M. 1979. *Contrasting Arguments. An edition of the Dissoi Logoi*. New York: Arno.
Boot, P. 1982. "The Philosophical Position of the Author of the *Dissoi Logoi*." *Philosophical Inquiry* 4: 118–123.
Classen, C.J. 1982. "Contrasting Arguments: An Edition of the Dissoi Logoi by T.M. Robinson." *Phoenix* 86: 83–87.

Antilogic

Sesonske, A. 1968. "To Make the Weaker Argument Defeat the Stronger." *Journal of the History of Philosophy* 6: 217–231.
Tinsdale, C.W. 2010. *Reasons's Dark Champions: Constructive Strategies of Sophistic Argument*. Columbia: South Carolina.

Relativism

Bett, R. 1989. "The Sophists and Relativism." *Phronesis* 34:139–169.
Woodruff, P. 1999. "Rhetoric and Relativism: Protagoras and Gorgias." In Long, A.A. (ed.), *The Cambridge Companion to Early Greek Philosophy*. Cambridge: Cambridge University Press, 290–310.

Logos, Rhetoric and Language

Schiappa, E. 1999. *The Beginnings of Rhetorical Theory in Classical Greece*. New Haven: Yale University Press.

Bringmann, K. 2000. "Rhetorik, Philosophie und Politik um 400 v.Chr. Gorgias, Antiphon und die Dissoi Logoi." *Chiron* 30: 489–503.

Timmerman, D.N. and E. Schiappa. 2010. *Classical Greek Rhetorical Theory and the Disciplining of Discourse*. Cambridge: Cambridge University Press.

Nomos and Phusis

Guthrie, W.K.C. 1969. *A History of Greek Philosophy: The Fifth-Century Enlightenment*, (vol. 3). Cambridge: Cambridge University Press, 55–134.

Ostwald, M. 1990. "*Nomos* and *Phusis* in Antiphon's Περὶ Ἀληθείας." In M. Griffith and D.J. Mastronarde (eds.), *Cabinet of the Muses: Essays on Classical and Comparative Literature in Honor of Thomas G. Rosenmeyer*, 293–306. Atlanta: Scholars Press.

Long, A.A. 2005. "Law and Nature in Greek Thought." In M. Gagarin and Cohen, D.J. (eds.), *The Cambridge Companion to Greek Law*. Cambridge: Cambridge University Press, 412–430.

Views on the Gods

Guthrie, W.K.C. 1969. *A History of Greek Philosophy: The Fifth-Century Enlightenment*, vol. 3. Cambridge: Cambridge University Press, 234–245.

Ethics

Bett, R. 2002. "Is there a Sophistic Ethics?" *Ancient Philosophy* 22:235–261.

INDEX OF SOPHISTS AND PRESOCRATICS AND ACCOMPANYING TEXTS

Alexander of Aphrodisias: *Commentary on Aristotle's Metaphysics* 357.16–21 p.57 n.18; *Commentary on Aristotle's Topics* 181.2–6 p.104 n.11
Antiphon: Fragment B col. 2–3 p.120; B26 p.52; B27 p.52; B28 p.52; B29 p.53; B32 p.53; B49 p.177–78; B50 p.56; B51 p.56; B52 p.56; B53 p.56; B60 p.56; *On Truth* fragment A col. 1 p.122; cols. 2–6 p.122–125; col. 2 p.121; fragment C cols. 1–2 p.125–126
Aristophanes: *Birds* 685–692 p.71
Aristotle: *History of Animals* 563a7 p.153 n.11; 615a10 p.153 n.11; *Metaphysics* 3.2 996a29 p.153 n.7; 998a2–4 p.36 n.27; 998a3 p.153 n.3; 4.2 1004a6 p.153 n.5; *Nicomachean Ethics* 9.1 1164a24 p.153 n.2; 10.9 1180b35 p.153 n.19; 1181a12 p.5 n.7; *Physics* 185a14–17 p.57 n.12; 185b28 p.153 n.9; 193a12–14 p.57 n.15; 193b8–11 p.57 n.16; *Poetics* 1456b15 p.153 n.1; *Politics* 1280b10 p.153 n.8; *Posterior Analytics* 75b40 p.153 n.18; *Rhetoric* 1401a25–29 p.85 n.7; 1402a17 p.95 n.14; 1402a22–28 p.153 n.3; 1402a24–28 p.114 n.1; 1004a14 p.76 n.6; 1407b6 p.153 n.1; 1407b7–8 p.95 n.3; 1409a2 p.76 n.6; 1413a8 p.76 n6; *Sophistical Refutations* 161a1 p.153 n.12; 165a20–23 p.147; 165a28–31 p.147; 165b38–166a10 p.153 n.16; 169b20–23 p.147; 171b16–172a7 p.153 n.17; 171b28–29 p.147; 171b34 p.147; 173b19 p.153 n.1; 173b19–20 p.95 n.5; 177b12ff. p.85 n.7; 183b32 p.76 n.5; *Topics* 100b23–26 p.85 n.12; 101b2–4 p.153n.21; 1.2 pp.178–180, 153 n.20; 112b22–23 p.104n.10

Cicero: *On the Nature of the Gods* 1.118 p.66

Didymus the Blind: Fragment p.35
Diogenes Laertius: *Lives of the Philosophers* 9.52 p.114n.23; 9.53–54 p.94 n.4
Dionysius of Halicarnassus: *On Isaeus* 20 p.76 n.7; *On Literary Composition* 12 p.95 n.19

Epiphanius: *Panarion* 3:507 Hall p.66
Euclid: *Elements* book 1 definition 15 p.37 n.29; book 2 proposition 14 p.57 n.13
Eudoxus: Fragment 4 p.114 n.2

Galen: *On Medical Names* 34.9–38 p.57 n.10
Gorgias: *Encomium of Helen* pp.171–174; *On What is Not or On Nature* pp.174–177

Heraclitus: Fragment B12 p.28; B35 p.9; B40 p.9; B42 p.88; B129 p.9
Hippias: Fragment 6 p.60
Hippocratic Corpus: *On the Nature of Man* p.134 n.10

Index of Sophists and Presocratics and Accompanying Texts   201

Isocrates: *Antidosis* 266 p.134 n.10; 268 p.134 n.8; 269 p.133 n.9; 271 p.133 n.18; 277 p.134 n.20; *Demonicus* 4 p.134 n.19; *Panathenaicus* 87 p.134 n.19; *Philip* 12 p.134 n.15

Minucius Felix: *Octavius* 21 p.66

Philodemus: *On Piety* 1, PHerc 1077 fragment 19.519–541 p.66; *On Piety* 2, PHerc 1428, cols. ii 28–iii 13 p.66; *On Piety* 2, PHerc 1428 fragment 19 p.99

Plato: *Charmides* 163d p.99; *Clitophon* 410b–c p.76 n.2; *Cratylus* 384a–b p.65; 391c p.104; 402a p.28; *Euthydemus* 271c pp.77, 137; 272b p.77, p.85 n.9; 275d2–277c8 pp.78–81; 276d–277b p.83; 277d–278d p.85 n4; 283e–286d p.73 n.18; 286c p.37 n.32; 30; 303c–304a p.85 n.5; 304d4–305b3 p.146 n.38; *Gorgias* 449a p.145; 449c p.26 n.16; 452d–e p.39; 452d p.48 n.11; 452d–453a p.40, 89; 454a8–461b2 pp.162–170; 454e p.40; 455c3 p.16 n.47; 456b p.40, 48 n.11; 456b–457a p.109 n.12; 459a–c p.146 n.27; 459c p.48 n.11; 463a, p.145 n.14; 463b–465c, p.39; 465a p.9 n.31; 465c p.146 n.16; 465d p.39; 481c–482a p.146 n.20; 484c–486a p.146 n.21; 484c5–485a2 pp.133–134; 500a–c p.139n.23; 520a–b p.146n16; 520a pp.14, 39, 133; 520c p.8 n.31; *Greater Hippias* 282c p.73 n.2; 285b–e p.36 n.14; 286a–b p.60; *Laches* 197d 104 n.7; *Lesser Hippias* 363a p.146 n.19; 363a–368a p.59; 363c p.63 n.6; 368b–3 pp.59, 180; *Meno* 71c p.96; 71e1–72a4 pp.96–97; 72a p.104 n.2; 76c p.96; 91e p.36 n.3; 92e p.15 n.16; 95b–c p.16 n.47; *Phaedo* 90b p.146 n.29; *Phaedrus* 260e p.146 n.31; 261c4–e2 p.108; 261c p.76 n.4; 266c 76 n.1; 266d5–267e7 pp.89–91; 267a p.95 n.17; 267c–d p.76 n8; 271a p.146 n.33; 271b–272a p.146 n.34; 272d6–273a1 p.93; 273b–c p.95 n.14; 278e–279a p.134 n.15; *Philebus* 58a p.48 n.11; *Protagoras* 310a8–319a2 p.138–139; 310b–316b p.14 n.5; 314e3–316a5 p.36 n.4; 314e3–317e6 pp.155–156, 63 n.3; 315e p.145 n.7; 318a–b p.15 n.23; 318e p.36 n.5; 319a p.15 n.24, 146 n.26, 320a–322d p.21 n.11; 320c2–328d4 pp.156–162; 323a p.36 n.1; 323d–324c p.23; 323d–328d p.23; 323d–328d p.21; 324a p.22; 329d ff. p.24; 330c–334a p.25; 333d–334c p.64; 334a–c pp.25–26; 334d–338e p.145 n.2; 337a–b p.65; 337a2–c4 pp.99–100; 337a2–b7 p.65; 337c7–e2 p.119; 337e–338b p.61; 339b p.88; 340b p.100; 349e p.15 n.15; 350c–351a p.145 n.4; 358a5–b3 p.100; 361a–c p.145 n.5; 361d7–e5 p.145 n.6; *Republic* 331c p.114 n.13; 336b p. 74; 337d p.76 n.3; 338c p.74; 341b p.74; 343a p.74; 344d p.74; 344d p.74; 450a–b p.74; 493a p.146 n.32; 498c p.74; 519e–520e p.74; 545a p.74; *Sophist* 217a p.146 n.35; 218c p.146 n.36; 222d–223a p.143; 224c–d p.143; 224e p.143; 226a p.143; 226a1 p.109; 230a5–231b8 p.144; 230b–d p.144; 232d1–e1 p.108; 254d p.146 n.37; 267b–268d p.144; *Theaetetus* 151b p.145 n.11; 151e p.27; 152a p.27; 160d p.28; 170a–171c p.95 n.18

Plutarch: *Life of Pericles* 36, p.114 n.22

Proclus: *Commentary on Plato's Timaeus* 1.10.5–6 p.57 n.18

Prodicus: *The Choice of Heracles* pp.178–180

Protagoras: Fragment 1 p.26; Fragment 3a p.18; Fragment 3b p.18; Fragment 4 p.30; Fragment 6a p.114 n.1, Fragment 10 p.18; Fragment 11 p.18

Scholium on Plato, *Phaedrus* 267b p.114 n.1

Sextus Empiricus: *Against the Mathematicians* 9.18 p.66; 9.50–52 p.65

Themistius: *Oration* 30 349b p.66

Tisias vs. Corax p.94

Xenophanes: Fragment 1 p.31; Fragment 8 p.15 n.20; Fragment 11 p.31, 88; Fragment B15 p.31; Fragment B16 p.31; Fragment 18 p.32; Fragment 23 p.31; Fragment 24 p.31; Fragment 25 p.31; Fragment 26 p.31; Fragment 34 p.32

Xenophon: *Memorabilia* 4.4.14 p.128 n.6; *On Hunting* 13.8 p.14 n.4

INDEX OF NAMES

Achilles 19, 20, 60
Aeschylus 114n21
Agamamnon 19, 20
Alcidamas 10, 12, 13
Alcmaeon 131
Alexander of Aphrodisias 55, 57n18, 102–103, 104n11
Anaxagoras 3, 53, 131, 134n7
Anaximander 5
Anaximenes 32
Anonymus Iamblichi 6, 10–12
Antigone 127
Antiphon 6, 7, 10–12, 14, 19, 48n2, 49–53, 55–56, 57n2, 57n6, 57n8, 64, 75, 89, 91, 94, 110, 116, 120–126, 127, 129, 131, 148–149
Antisthenes 12, 127
Anytus 6
Archelaus 75
Aristippus of Cyrene 11–13, 68, 148
Aristophanes 71, 111, 141
Aristotle 1, 7, 11, 13, 34, 36n20, 48n20, 54–56, 57n12, 57n15, 57n16, 60, 62, 68, 70, 75, 77, 76n5, 81, 84, 85, 95n14, 100, 102–103, 104n10, 113, 114n3, 114n24, 131–132, 147–153, 153n1–5, 153n7–9, 153n11–14, 153n16–21

Bryson 11–13, 148–149, 151

Callias 18, 135
Callicles 11–13, 127, 133, 139

Cicero 67
Cleinias 78–79, 81, 84, 80
Corax 4, 13, 16n49, 94, 130
Critias 6, 10, 12, 13, 65
Crito 82

Damon 131
Democritus 17, 131, 134n7
Demosthenes 128
Diagoras of Melos 65
Didymus the Blind 35, 72
Dion viii
Dionysius of Halicarnassus 95n19, 148
Dionysodorus 6, 7, 10–12, 14, 15n25, 77–85, 131, 137, 145

Empedocles 32, 131
Epicurus 65, 67
Euclid 57n14, 59
Eudoxus 12–13, 114n2
Euhemerus 65
Euripides 6, 13
Euthydemus viii 6–7, 10–12, 14, 15n25, 77–85, 131, 137, 145, 148
Evenus 11, 12, 14, 90

Galen 57n11
Glaucon 127
Gorgias viii 6–14, 16n47, 36n16, 48n11, 48n14, 38–51, 59, 62, 64, 75, 76n5, 77, 86–87, 89–91, 94–99, 95n9, 101–310, 109–111, 129, 131, 137, 140, 148, 150

Index of Names

Harpocration 55, 57n9
Hecataeus 5, 9, 28, 29, 32, 88, 138, 146n17
Hermias 100, 102, 103, 104n4
Herodotus 6, 89, 131
Hesiod 9, 19, 20, 32, 60, 72, 73n15, 88, 128n4
Hippias viii, ix, 6, 7, 10–12, 14, 17, 18, 29, 36n14, 36n15, 50–51, 58–62, 63n5, 63n7, 63n9, 64, 77, 83, 89, 90, 116, 118–120, 131, 135, 137, 140
Hippocrates 36n6
Homer 4, 5, 15n11, 32, 59, 60, 63n4, 73n3, 87, 88, 114n21, 132

Iamblichus 15n41
Ion 131
Isocrates viii, 2, 6, 7, 12, 13, 14n7–8, 15n29, 15n37, 48n8, 129–133, 134n15, 134n8–10, 134n17–n21, 147, 148, 151

Leucippus 134n7
Licymnius 12–13, 90
Lycophron 11–12, 14, 148–149

Mamercus 60
Marcellinus 104n3
Marcellinus 104n6
Melissus 43–45, 131–132
Meno 39, 96–97
Miccus 11–12, 14
Musaeus 60

Neoptolemus 60
Nestor 20, 61, 132

Odysseus 19, 20, 73n2
Orpheus 60

Parmenides 44–52, 57n10, 131–132
Pericles 4, 17, 57n8, 112
Perses 20
Perseus 66
Phaedrus 143
Philodemus 67, 68
Plato viii, ix, x, 1–2, 6–9, 13, 14n5–7, 15n15–16, 15n22–24, 15n31, 15n37, 17–18, 22, 27–30, 34, 35, 36n20, 48n8, 58, 61, 65, 73n7, 73n17, 75–77, 81, 83–85, 87, 89, 93, 95n14, 95n17, 95n18, 99–100, 102–103, 104n2, 104n5, 104n7, 104n8, 104n12, 114n12, 114n13,
108–109, 112, 127, 129–133, 134n3, 134n13, 134n14, 135, 137–145, 145n2, 145n4–8, 145n10–11, 145n13, 145n15–17, 146n18–24, 146n26–28, 146n30, 146n32–39, 147–152, 153n15
Plutarch 114n22
Polus 11, 12, 13, 90, 137, 148
Polyidus 11, 12, 14, 148
Proclus 55, 57n19
Prodicus viii, ix, 6, 7, 10, 11, 12, 14, 17, 18, 36n15, 51, 58, 60–62, 64–68, 70–73, 73n7, 77, 83, 89, 90, 94–95, 99–103, 110, 118, 131, 135–137, 140, 148
Protagoras viii, ix, 4–8, 10–14, 17–19, 21–36, 36n6, 38, 39, 49, 50, 55, 57n8, 58, 61–62, 64, 67, 75, 77, 83–84, 86, 90, 95, 99, 101–102, 105–113, 114n1, 114n6, 114n23, 116–123, 127–128, 128n2, 131–137, 140–141, 148–149
pseudo-Demosthenes 11, 12
Pythagoras 3, 9, 59

Seven Sages 3
Simonides 88, 136
Socrates viii, 1, 6, 8, 11, 13, 14n4, 16n46, 19, 21, 24–27, 36n6, 41, 48n10, 61, 62, 64, 71, 73n7, 74, 77–79, 81–84, 85n3, 85n4, 96–99, 101–103, 112–113, 119–120, 129–130, 132–133, 135–145, 148–150, 152
Solon 3, 131–132
Sophocles 6, 127
Stesichorus 60

Thales 60
Theaetetus 27
Themistocles 4
Theodorus 12, 13, 65, 90
Thrasymachus 6, 7, 10–12, 14, 36n16, 51, 74–76, 89–90, 137, 140, 148
Thucydides 5, 6, 89, 111
Tisias 4, 13, 16n, 75, 76n5, 90, 94, 130

Xeniades 11, 12, 14
Xenophanes 5, 9, 30, 31, 32, 33, 73n11, 88
Xenophon 14n4, 15n20, 48n10, 61, 63n10, 63n11, 63n12, 68, 73n12, 128, 128n6, 128n7

Zeno 45

Printed in the United States
by Baker & Taylor Publisher Services